Scott Joplin and the Age of Ragtime

Scott Joplin and the Age of Ragtime

RAY ARGYLE

McFarland & Company, Inc., Publishers
Jefferson, North Carolina, and London

Frontispiece: Scott Joplin—1868–1917. Scott Joplin's contribution to Ragtime as a new musical genre earned him accolades as the King of Ragtime and inspired later composers of jazz, swing, and rock and roll in creating the modern music of global entertainment (Getty Images).

LIBRARY OF CONGRESS CATALOGUING-IN-PUBLICATION DATA

Argyle, Ray.
　　Scott Joplin and the age of ragtime / Ray Argyle.
　　　p.　　cm.
　　Includes bibliographical references and index.

　　ISBN 978-0-7864-4376-5
　　softcover : 50# alkaline paper

　　1. Joplin, Scott, 1868–1917.　2. Composers—United States—Biography.　3. Ragtime music—History and criticism.　I. Title.
ML410.J75A87　　2009
780.92—dc22　　　　　　　　　　　　　　　　　2009010488
[B]

British Library cataloguing data are available

©2009 Ray Argyle. All rights reserved

No part of this book may be reproduced or transmitted in any form or by any means, electronic or mechanical, including photocopying or recording, or by any information storage and retrieval system, without permission in writing from the publisher.

On the cover: *Afternoon Duet with Miró* by Berge Missakian, from the author's collection; (inset) Scott Joplin, Wikipedia; *Maple Leaf Rag*, 1899, by S. Joplin

Manufactured in the United States of America

McFarland & Company, Inc., Publishers
　Box 611, Jefferson, North Carolina 28640
　　www.mcfarlandpub.com

For Deborah

"We make love to Ragtime and we die to it."
— Walter Lippmann, 1914*

*"Our children dance, our people sing,
our soldiers march to Ragtime."*
— H. Kelly Moderwell, 1915†

"Ragtime was a fanfare for the twentieth century."
— Russell Lyons, 1985‡

Drift and Mastery: An Attempt to Diagnose the Current Unrest (p211, M. Kennerley, 1914).
†*The New Republic* (Oct. 16, 1915).
‡*The Lively Audience* (Harper & Row, 1985).

Acknowledgments

A good story is like an iceberg: what you read is only the tip of it. Underneath are hidden chunks of research drawn from interviews, documents, journals, books, newspaper files, and Websites, all yielding history, facts, surmisals and possibilities. So it is with *Scott Joplin and the Age of Ragtime*. In the sources section of this book, I have gone below the surface to elaborate on the story and identify where I have drawn information. The books on whose shoulders much of my story rests are listed in the Bibliography. Of all the early researchers who wrote of Scott Joplin and other Ragtime protagonists, Edward A. Berlin (*King of Ragtime: Scott Joplin and His Era*) and Rudi Blesh and Kathleen Benson (*They All Played Ragtime*) rank as the most formidable. But it is to the people who helped me find my way through the thickets of learning Joplin's story, and writing and getting it published, that I most wish to acknowledge.

I was encouraged early on by Ken McGoogan, the author of *Race to the Polar Sea* and other works of popular history. His wise advice helped me focus on the essential personalities and issues of the Ragtime era.

I received much helpful direction from people who read parts of various drafts. These include Dr. Greg Mackie of the University of British Columbia; Professor Michel Pharand of Ottawa and Kobe University, Japan; Joan Murray, an accomplished curator and author of art history; and Laura A. Foster, the curator of the Frederic Remington Art Museum, Ogdensburg, New York.

For advice on the life of Scott Joplin and other Ragtime musicians, I relied heavily on Jack Hutton, a Ragtime authority and an accomplished pianist I first met when we both worked at the old *Toronto Telegram*, and Ted Tjaden of Toronto, who runs the ragtimepiano.ca Website. Kristin Aguilera of the Museum of Financial History, New York, pointed me to

Acknowledgments

a historic connection between Scott Joplin's "Wall Street Rag" and the financial cycles of boom and bust. I am indebted to the British Museum for providing me with a membership and access to their vast holdings.

Hartley Nathan brought a keen legal eye to those subjects that required an understanding of the law. I also received help from Barry Francis, a dear friend who never lost his ability to ask crucial questions about what I was trying to say; and my late brother, Dr. Edward Argyle, who after a lifetime in the study of science and astronomy retained a remarkable appreciation of the vagaries of popular culture. Elsa Franklin helped by sharing much of her knowledge of publishing. I am indebted to my partner, Deborah Windsor, who unfailingly tolerated my long monologues on life in the Ragtime era and provided constant support.

I am also pleased to acknowledge the financial support of the Ontario Arts Council for the writing of this book.

Contents

Acknowledgments	vii
Prelude	1
Part I — Breaking All the Rules: The 1890s	3
1. A Medley for the Fair: A Time to Start Raggin' It	6
2. My Kind of Town: Hot Nights in the City	16
3. The Making of the Legend: A Boy and a Banjo	26
4. Marching to a Ragtime Tune	38
Part II — The Music Makers Play Main Street: The 1900s	49
5. Writing in Ragtime	51
6. Tin Pan Alley and All That Jazz: Footloose in "Black Bohemia"	65
7. They All Played Ragtime: Scott Joplin and Irving Berlin — A Case of Plagiarism?	79
8. The Girls of Ragtime and the Cult of Celebrity: Murder, Passion and Honor	87
Part III — The Dream That Wouldn't Die: The 1910s	99
9. Dancing in Ragtime	101
10. The Censors and the Erotic Life	112
11. Reporting in Ragtime	124
12. Dreaming of *Treemonisha*	137

Contents

Part IV — After the Rag: The Finale   147

13. Little Mary and the Little Tramp: Ragtime Partners of
  the Silent Screen   149
14. The Rites of Spring: The Martyred Saint of the Ragtime Era   159
15. Ragtime in Revival   169
16. Echoes of the Music: We're All Still Playing Ragtime   179

The Life and Times of Scott Joplin   187
Scott Joplin's Compositions   189
Sources of Quotations   193
Appendix: Ragtime in the Newspapers   201
Bibliography   215
Index   219

Prelude

My aim in writing this book is to bring together the colorful story of America's love affair with Ragtime and its preeminent composer, Scott Joplin, with the remarkable burst of creativity that brought on modern music, culture, and technology at the start of the twentieth century.

On a somber spring day in 1917, only a few of Scott Joplin's closest friends accompanied his wife Lottie Stokes to St. Michael's Cemetery in the Bronx where the composer's body was lowered into a simple grave. He was only forty-nine. He had died of complications of syphilis, a tragic ending to a life marked by notable accomplishment. On that day, there was little realization that Joplin's pioneering role in the development of Ragtime would prove critical to the birth of modern music, but over time his work would clearly influence the evolution of jazz, swing, rock and roll, and rap.

Between the 1890s and the First World War, the syncopated melodies of Ragtime burst forth from the underside of American society, chiefly through the artistry of black musicians. Ragtime was the preferred music in bars and ballrooms from New Orleans to Montreal and from San Francisco to London.

In its classical form as constructed by Scott Joplin, Ragtime represented a sophisticated new style of piano composition. Imitators, recognizing the power of his creations, borrowed the style and applied crude lyrics to simplistic variations that swept through vaudeville houses and music halls on both sides of the Atlantic Ocean. White composers quickly appropriated the traditions of the African American cake walk and soul music to bring Broadway audiences such hit performances as Irving Berlin's perennial favorite, "Alexander's Ragtime Band."

Scott Joplin's memorable compositions include the first great Ragtime hit, *Maple Leaf Rag*, and the all-time most popular pure Ragtime tune, "The Entertainer." Both were written before Joplin was thirty-five, and their endearing popularity has led such present-day Ragtime performers as Mimi Blais to describe Joplin's work as having constructed "the trunk of the tree of modern music."

This book does not presume to offer a critique of Ragtime as a musical genre nor is it intended to supplant the excellent biographies of Scott Joplin by such writers as Edward Berlin, Rudy Blesh, and Terry Waldo. But by examining Joplin's life from the perspective of his influence on twentieth century popular music, it is possible to reach a deeper understanding of the significance of the man and his career.

Listening to Ragtime music, seeing the Broadway play and the movie "Ragtime," and attending events such as the Scott Joplin Ragtime Festival in Sedalia, Missouri—all contributed to my appreciation for this delightful musical genre and the era from which it sprang.

While still in his twenties, Scott Joplin traveled with his Texas Medley Quartette to the Chicago World's Fair and gained his first exposure to metropolitan audiences. So we begin our journey in Chicago: a city bursting with the energy of a new, urban America. We follow Joplin through his troubled first marriage, the premature death of Freddie Alexander, perhaps his greatest love, and on to New York where he immerses himself in the hectic milieu of Tin Pan Alley. Before long, Joplin isolates himself from much of the show business world to concentrate on his great dream to produce a Ragtime opera. With the support of a new mate, Lottie Stokes, he finishes the task but is frustrated through failure to find the backing to produce *Treemonisha*.

Other players and forces were at work in the Ragtime era, and this book does not neglect them. It is due to Ragtime's enduring legacy that we use it as a metaphor for an era when the convergence of culture and technology brought vastly greater access to art, literature, music, and mass media. Actors, dancers, musicians, and writers rebelled against rigid censorship. Modern art made its first brave appearance. The cinema—even in its silent rendition—entranced audiences, although it relied on musical accompaniment, usually Ragtime, for the vital element of sound.

The roots of most of the music we enjoy today go back to the Ragtime era. This book is a tribute to that time, and the vibrancy of a life whose legacy enriches us still.

Part I

Breaking All the Rules: The 1890s

The rhythms of Ragtime began as but minor notes when the world listened through the 1890s for the new sounds of the turn of the century. Player pianos and the Gramophone and the Victrola were being breathlessly cranked up in millions of homes. Musicians composed sprightly new songs to meet the demand for music rolls, recording cylinders, and sheet music. Charles Harris' "After the Ball" became, in 1892, the first tune to sell a million copies. But it was Ragtime that signaled the arrival of a new musical genre—and with it a new era in popular culture.

In the summer of 1893 a young African American composer, singer and pianist, Scott Joplin, took his Texas Medley Quartette to Chicago in search of gigs at the Chicago World's Fair. It was the greatest assemblage of entertainment, science and technology ever gathered together at one location.

The extravagance of the World Fairs gave the burgeoning cities of Europe and America that hosted these spectacles the chance to showcase their proudest achievements. The Paris Exposition of 1889 boasted the new Eiffel Tower, the tallest structure ever built. The Chicago World's Fair earned the moniker of the "White City" for its use of electricity to illuminate its grounds, turning night into day. "The knowledge of the world is being unfolded at one's feet," an enthusiastic journalist reported.

Rejected by the Fair, which refused to give Joplin bookings, his quartet had to settle for one-night stands at gritty saloons that dotted the side streets of the great event. Their repertoire included the earliest arrangements of a boisterous new kind of music and by the end of the decade, Joplin would lay claim to the title of King of Ragtime.

PART I — Breaking All the Rules

Scott Joplin's "The Entertainer" met with immediate success when John Stark published it in 1902. The tune sparked a Ragtime revival when it was chosen as the theme music for the movie *The Sting* in 1974 (The Lilly Library, Indiana University).

As the twentieth century drew near, electricity, the long-distance telephone, and wireless telegraphy connected distant places and people in an instant society. The motion picture projector, the phonograph machine and the player piano launched an age of mass culture. Newly invented typesetting machines and rapid rotary presses gave birth to mass media that spread new ideas about freedom, human rights and the enjoyment of life.

Part I — Breaking All the Rules

For the first time, technology — taken from the Greek *teckhne*, meaning art or craft — put mass audiences within reach of a new generation of artists, writers and musicians who were determined to free themselves of the suffocating rules of rigid convention. These artists were about to change the culture of the world.

The melodies of Scott Joplin and other early Ragtimers, drawn from a mixed heritage of African drums, Caribbean dance rhythms and American black folk tunes, enthralled millions. They listened at home, danced to the new beat of syncopation in ballrooms, and cheered performers in cafés and vaudeville halls from New Orleans to Montreal and from San Francisco to Paris. Today, there is widespread recognition that the music of the Ragtime era survives in the modern manifestations of jazz and the blues, swing, rock and roll, and rap. This is where popular culture all began.

1

A Medley for the Fair
A Time to Start Raggin' It

The saloons where Scott Joplin took his Texas Medley Quartette would have been boisterous places, heavy with smoke and heat and the smells of a day of sweat and drink. The crowds in the bars that catered to patrons of the Chicago World's Fair in the summer of 1893 were likely even more raucous than the patrons of the roadhouses and brothels that were the usual settings for legions of performers who played for tips and free drinks. None of this would have bothered the visitors to the Fair who, we can imagine, would have barreled in through the open door, thirsty for a beer tapped from a keg banked in sawdust and ice to keep it cool. Some, perhaps already showing the effects of too much liquor, might have spoken slurringly of their costly surrender to temptation at the games of chance, the freak shows and the girlie attractions of the Fair.

The Texas Medley Quartette was unusual in that its members varied anywhere from four to eight, with some dropping out and others coming in from night to night. There might be as many as four singers and four others who played various instruments, including the cornet, clarinet, tuba and piano. All were African American and none had yet seen their thirtieth birthday, but only Scott Joplin, their leader, could lay claim to being a son of the Lone Star State.

They had come to Chicago, a brawling city of meat packing plants, foundries and factories and skyscrapers soaring as high as sixteen stories, confident they would find work at the clubs catering to visitors crowding in for the Fair. If it was a typical night, Joplin, a serious young man of just twenty-five, would have looked around the gaslit room with a slight sense of distaste. His glance might have taken in a floor covered with saw-

1. A Medley for the Fair

dust, spittoons filled with saliva, and on the counter, the remnants of the day's free lunch of cold cuts, pickles, stale bread and aging potato salad.

In all likelihood, Joplin's group played out this scenario nightly during their short stay in Chicago. It is certain that a cacophony of sounds — band music, shouts, and the squeals of thrill-seekers riding the never-before-seen Ferris wheel — the invention of one George W. Ferris — would have echoed from the Fairgrounds. This was where, wrote *Harper's* magazine, "Amusement, of cheap and even vulgar sorts, is being substituted for education, because most people prefer being amused to being instructed." For all that, the *Atlantic Monthly* saw the event as "a great moment in civilization."

The Chicago World's Fair, or the World's Columbian Exposition, as it was officially known, was the most spectacular display of entertainment, science and industry that had ever been staged in the United States. For those enchanting summer days of 1893, it made Chicago the proudest city in the nation.

Scott Joplin's innovative music meshed perfectly with the exuberant spirit of the Fair as it celebrated America's coming of age with a grand salute to the four hundredth anniversary of Europe's discovery of the New World. To stage the Fair, six hundred acres of desolate land on the Lake Michigan waterfront, six miles south of the city's business center, had been transformed. In place of garbage dumps and industrial waste was a marvelous "White City" powered by thousands of the new electric lightbulbs that miraculously turned night into day.

Along with the other forty-eight million visitors during the Fair's six-month run, Joplin and his players would have marveled at its fantasy architecture that replicated the great sites of American history. There was hardly a family in the Midwest that did not wish to gaze on these sights. Couples and their children must have darted breathlessly from Philadelphia's Independence Hall to the old Spanish Missions of California and the frontier log cabins of Idaho's mountain pioneers. The grandeur of these sights would have been reflected in the waters of the Grand Basin, a shimmering pool around which the Fair was built. To the delight of fairgoers, a plaster ship steered by Father Time and rowed by scantily clad girls circled a sixty-five-foot female figure, *The Republic*. She held aloft a gilded globe on which was perched an American bald eagle.

It all made a wonderful sight, especially to those with eyes old enough to recall that barely twenty years before, the Great Chicago Fire had leveled their city, claiming three hundred lives and leaving ninety thousand homeless. The rebuilding of Chicago turned it into America's newest big city, boasting a population of more than a million. The new Chicago that Scott Joplin introduced to Ragtime was becoming a temple to the new technologies whose works were plainly visible on its streets and in its factories.

All but the most hidebound welcomed the delights of the new fads, foods and shiny new home conveniences on offer in the shops. They were signs of wealth in which almost all could share. Then there was wealth of another kind, like the walnut-sized diamond on display at the Tiffany exhibit. The man who had built Chicago's new street railway, Charles Yerkes, paid one hundred thousand dollars to take it home to his wife.

The music that Scott Joplin played in Chicago ranged from popular waltzes, march numbers, and songs from the minstrel stage to early experiments in classic piano rag. These sprang from a mixed heritage of African drums, Caribbean dance rhythms and white folk tunes and marches. Ragtime's immediate roots were in the minstrel music, cakewalk tunes and "coon songs" that depicted the simple joys of contented slaves, a fiction that white America clung to long after the Civil War.

Fuelled by the sudden availability of phonograph recordings, the player piano and the mass marketing of sheet music — which most everyone could read — Ragtime swept into respectable dance halls and the parlors of decent white homes from the bordellos and saloons where Negro piano players like Scott Joplin pounded out rhythms that matched their foot-stomping and body-slapping tempos. Their tunes were rendered in the syncopated "ragged" style that was its trademark. The result was music that was great for both listening and dancing, giving the two-step new liveliness and agility.

As much as visitors to the Fair enjoyed its civic boosterism and its blatant claims of American superiority, many preferred listening to musicians like Joplin who performed in the countless saloons and restaurants set up on the outskirts of the Fair. The Creole Show, featuring one of the first all-black troupes to perform for white audiences, is said to have played to packed houses. W.C. Handy, who would be later acclaimed as "Father

1. A Medley for the Fair

of the Blues," performed with Mahoney's Minstrels, and Scott Joplin's friend from St. Louis, Thomas Turpin, also entertained fairgoers.

An all-black exhibit, Dahomey Village, replicated an African settlement complete with drumming, chants and dancing. Plunk Henry, a banjo player so named for the way he attacked his instrument, switched to the piano and began to create rudimentary Ragtime tunes borrowed from his banjo pieces. Rivaling the popularity of a belly dancer called Little Egypt was a piano-playing contest that went on for days. One Chicago newspaper writer dubbed the sounds he heard as "ragged." The term somehow stuck and the emerging music would become known as Ragtime.

The Fair had no space in its official program for freelance black artists like Joplin. But to those who heard his Texas Medley Quartette, its sounds were more beguiling than anything the Fair could offer. Night after night, energy bursting from his lithe body, Joplin would play a catchy new kind of music with a ragged timing that most people had not heard before. Many of his "jig" pieces drew heavily on the tunes of the "cakewalk" dances that had given black slaves an innocent way to parody the promenading of their white masters and their fancy dress balls.

Visitors voted with their feet and abandoned the ornate Music Hall where decorous crowds quickly tired of Wagnerian renditions from a one hundred and fourteen man symphony orchestra. After a spate of public and press criticism its conductor, Theodore Thomas, was summarily fired midway through the Fair. Although his was a "magnificent orchestra with high-class soloists," wrote Robert Graves, a reporter for the Alton (Illinois) *Telegraph*, "Many men think the class of music which Thomas plays torture rather than delight. Thomas is costing so much money that little is left for popular music."

What made Ragtime different from anything heard before was its use of syncopation, a musical technique in which the emphasis in a tune is shifted to its normally unaccented weak beat, usually in 2/4 time. For this reason, Ragtime was never a simple musical form. A high level of sophistication went into its compositions, resulting in complex numbers that demanded much skill in their playing. As Ragtime graduated from the piano to instrumental music and dance tunes, its growing popularity led to a great deal of improvisation, frequently departing from true Ragtime. This was especially true of tunes with lyrics that aimed for mass appeal and played off popular trends.

PART I — Breaking All the Rules

By now, the group was both Texan and quartette in name only. It included four singers, with Joplin filling the role of second tenor, and four instrumentalists, probably playing cornet, clarinet, tuba and piano. There is no record of the exact tunes that Joplin's Texas Medley Quartette played in Chicago. They were undoubtedly a mix of classic cakewalk marches and current novelties like "Daddy Wouldn't Buy Me a Bow Wow," as well as Ragtime innovations. Whatever they were, Joplin would have played them night after night for hours, switching between the piano and the cornet, drawing applause as well as catcalls.

Scott Joplin's personality was shaped by his experience as the son of a former slave, raised with his brothers and sisters by a single mother after their father's desertion. Solidly built, he stood about five feet seven, and enjoyed wearing good suits although he was often careless in his dress, forgetting to put on a tie or shine the scuff from his shoes. Those who knew him sketched a portrait of a young man of shy and introspective disposition, with a somber, sometimes even surly face that was seldom relieved by a smile. But he was said to be unfailingly polite. Some added that he went around as if in a dream, probably composing music in his head. When he spoke, his words were well chosen and carefully said. His handwriting, judging from the one letter of his that has survived—to the Librarian of Congress applying for a copyright—is an almost elegant example of good penmanship.

It is likely that Joplin trained himself to channel a rebellious spirit into writing and playing the lively refrains of Ragtime. Having come up from the ranks of bordellos and saloons, Joplin, like other musicians working the fringes of the Fair, was known as "professor" and he was arguably the most professorial of the lot.

The Chicago World's Fair ran from May 1 to October 30 but by mid–August, Joplin had tired of its nightly grind. Possibly he was having difficulty finding gigs for an eight-person group. Smaller groups and individual performers, white and black, many of them willing to work for tips, would have provided stiff competition. It was time for the Quartette to leave Chicago and get back to the more familiar surroundings of St. Louis and Sedalia. Joplin hit on the idea of working their way from town to town. On August 22 they were in Cedar Rapids, Iowa, where Joplin, serving as advance man and publicity agent, took his singers to the office of the local newspaper, the *Evening Gazette*. There, they gave an

1. A Medley for the Fair

impromptu performance and that night the paper carried a brief item on their visit:

> The Texas Medley Quartette (Colored) en route from Chicago to the Pacific Coast, favored *The Gazette* force with some of its choice melodies this afternoon. The names of the singers are: Please Jackson, first tenor; Scott Joplin, second tenor; R. Denson, baritone; G. Minor, basso. They will remain in the city a few days and will be heard at the hotels and other public places. Their singing is excellent.

The part about touring to the Pacific coast was undoubtedly a bit of public relations hyperbole dreamt up by Joplin. There is no evidence of any such trip. It is known that sometime after breaking off the Quartette's tour, Joplin teamed up with a new friend, a light-skinned fellow musician like himself, Otis Saunders, whom he'd met in Chicago. The two worked their way leisurely back to Joplin's adopted hometown of Sedalia, sitting up all night in the day coaches to which Negroes were segregated as their train rumbled down the Mississippi river valley. They might have sipped liquor and talked of the future.

After a stay in St. Louis where Joplin picked up pocket money by playing piano in the Silver Dollar saloon, a bar run by Tom Turpin's father, Joplin returned to Sedalia. There, he found that new gambling joints, saloons, and brothels had sprung up along the strip of Main Street known as "Battle Row." The Missouri Pacific Railroad had its station a block to the north. By day, the street's hardware, dry goods and feed stores carried on business as usual; but by night, the bars, bordellos and gambling clubs attracted railway and cattlemen, traveling salesmen, and adventurous businessmen with a yen for excitement and companionship. Joplin looked forward to inspecting the new spots. They were the kinds of places to keep him busy night after night, leaving him days of freedom to nurture his ambition to become a serious composer.

The town's fifteen thousand inhabitants liked to call Sedalia "the Queen City of the Prairies" but in the 1890s it was a town still on the frontier of an America rushing toward the twentieth century. Situated midway between St. Louis and Kansas City, it sprang to life just before the Civil War when an astute U.S. army officer, General George Radeen Smith, paid just over two thousand dollars for a hundred and sixty acres that he thought would make a fine town site. What it needed was a railroad station. When he heard the Missouri Pacific was coming through, Smith

PART I — Breaking All the Rules

raised a hundred and sixty thousand dollars from his ranching neighbors and presented it to the railroad. He got his station and Sedalia was born.

Smith was a man with the courage to change his ways. He had come to Missouri with a wife, two daughters and seventy-five slaves, all the result of successful years in Kentucky where he'd studied law and served as a sheriff at the age of twenty-two. True to his Union colors, Smith ended up opposing slavery in a state bitterly divided between Union and Confederate causes. Sedalia became a Union outpost, its soldiers going out to fight off Confederate battalions. After the surrender of the South, the soldiers were kept busy quelling guerilla outlaws — including the notorious Jesse James gang — in the years of near anarchy that plagued Missouri following the war. Within a few years the town was thriving; by 1883 it boasted twenty churches, eight public and five private schools, nine banks, five newspapers and thirty-five saloons.

The new craze for ragtime was fed by dozens of songs, mostly composed by African Americans. Though these composers could make up music only a few of them could write it down. One who could was Thomas Turpin but it took him years to find a publisher for his "Harlem Rag," which finally came out in 1897. The delay cost him the claim to the first published piece of Ragtime music. That honor went to a white man from Kentucky, Ben R. Harney, who published "You're a Good Old Wagon But You've Done Broke Down," in 1895. Its crude, chauvinistic and racist lyrics sang of a woman who had outlived her charms. When Harney performed at Tony Pastor's 14th Street Theater in New York in 1896, he billed himself as "the Creator of Ragtime." He cashed in on his reputation by publishing the *Rag Time Instructor* manual in 1897.

The New York newspapers happily embraced Harney as the creator of Ragtime. A 1901 article in the *New York Sun*, headed Origin of Ragtime, added that "One Ben Harney Said to Have Invented It and Its Name at Louisville." According to the *Sun*:

> About ten years ago a young fellow named Ben Harney went to a party given by colored folks in a suburb of Louisville. While he was there two darkies, who were experts on the banjo, began playing.
>
> While they were playing Harney notices that the rhythm produced by the two banjos was peculiar, but very catchy. So after a while, when called

1. A Medley for the Fair

upon to play something, Harney ran his fingers carelessly over the keys of the piano and tried to imitate the time made by the two banjos.

At first he failed, but before the night had passed he had acquired the time and kept the crowd entertained with snatches from popular songs played in this fashion. One of the darkies who had performed on the banjo became suddenly interested in Harney's playing. Approaching Harney he inquired:

"Marsa Ben, what are yo' playin' dar? That are the funniest kin' oh tune I'se ebber heerd."

"I don't know what it is myself," replied Harney, in an offhand way. "I suppose if I had a dress suit on, like some of these actors at the show, I might give it a new, fashionable name. But as it is I can't think of any name in these rags and you will have to let it go at that."

The darkey sized Harney from head to foot. Harney's clothes were neat and fitted him well. The negro thought the argument a poor one and said:

"What's the difference wha' kin ob rags yo playing' in, Marsa Ben. Yo kin allus git er name fo it. I'se tells yer Marsa Ben, dat Ah ain' very much in labe wid dat tune."

About a week later there was another party in the neighborhood. Harney was present and had to play. The two banjo players were also there and they thumped away together, playing all sorts of tunes. The same darkey who a week previous wanted to know the name Ben was playing abruptly arose, and turning to the guests with a merry laugh, said:

"Ladies an' gen'men. Marsa Ben Harney has got some of de most peculariarist kin' ob music that I ever heerd afo.' Ah I'se begs you kin 'dulgence fo' t' hyer it. I'se don' know de name ob' de tune, but it am de lobliest I'se ebber heerd."

Ben thought the remark very funny and replied: "What do you mean, Jasper? That music I played in those rags last week?"

"Yes," returned Jasper enthusiastically, "dat rag-time music."

Well, after that, rag-time became the real thing in the town, and when Harney came east he introduced it in New York, and it soon was the rage all over the country. And the name rag-time has clung to it ever since.

The story in the *New York Sun*, written in dialect, quite possibly apocryphal and certainly fanciful, was not to be taken seriously but it served to reinforce white superiority in a field that had been traditionally ceded to the African American. If a product of that culture was to thrive, it would certainly be due to white improvisation and improvement.

Regardless, the new music needed fewer than a dozen years around the fin de siècle to migrate from an obscure black subculture into the first uniquely national American musical style. Despite — or perhaps as a result

PART I — Breaking All the Rules

of — moral outrage about Ragtime's presumed vulgarity and overt sexuality, it quickly became the music of choice in honky-tonks from New Orleans to Montreal. In the raucous Tenderloin neighborhood of New York City an observant journalist and songwriter, Monroe H. Rosenfeld, heard piano playing that he thought sounded "like a tin pan" and Tin Pan Alley was suddenly born. It was there that many of the new Ragtime tunes were being written.

Ragtime not only conquered its homeland, it also spread quickly abroad, fostering a legacy that would influence the later arrival of jazz, blues songs and rock and roll. In the years leading up to the Great War of 1914–18 the mania for Ragtime transformed it into a symbol of a new era that was rejecting conventional morality. In Paris, where Ragtime was known simply as "American music," it became a favorite of the cancan dancers at the Moulin Rouge. It was in Paris in 1907 that Claude Debussy, the French Impressionist composer, wrote his rag-inflected "Golliwog's Cakewalk." The great Parisian theatrical impresario, Gabriel Astruc, introduced his audiences to a touring group of black American Ragtimers whose repertoire included cakewalk numbers.

In Canada, the French-speaking population of Quebec, feeling themselves oppressed by their English Canadian masters, took readily to the music of another oppressed people. Jean-Baptiste Lafrenière — regarded by many as the Canadian Strauss for his waltz compositions — switched to writing Ragtime tunes after the Roman Catholic church, practicing a form of religious authoritarianism particular to Quebec, forced the closure of Montreal's popular concert cafés in 1901. Modeled on the concert cafés of Paris and clustered along the St-Laurent Boulevard strip in the downtown east end of Montreal, they offered sexually suggestive music and comedy to crowds who came to eat, drink and indulge in various other forms of sinful behavior.

The closings forced concert places with names like Palais-Royal de Paris and the Eldorado to transform themselves into musical theaters. Lafrenière was the most applauded of all the musicians playing at the new theaters, where the shows were often built around Ragtime tunes. The royalties he collected on his "Taxi Rag" and "Raggity Rag" soon exceeded the wages he had lost when the concert cafés were closed.

English Canada took to Ragtime almost as avidly. In the 1898 Klondike gold rush, miners had carried piano parts over the Chilkoot pass

1. A Medley for the Fair

and into the Yukon where a British bank clerk, Robert Service, wrote his way to fame with verses about how "the jag-time kid was hitting a jag-time tune." A young Jewish pianist in Montreal, Willie Eckstein, teamed up with Harry Thomas to write "novelty rag" tunes of considerable technical difficulty, including "Delirious Rag" and "Perpetual Rag." Joseph Lamb, a young white man from New Jersey, switched from composing waltzes to writing rags while attending St. Joseph's College in Berlin (now Kitchener), Ontario. He and his classmates imbibed at one of the few hotels where students could get a drink, and the "Wolper House Rag," the first of many rags he would write, commemorated those days.

The Ragtime craze also swept through Britain, where rapturous audiences filled the music halls of every city and town. Even the studious critic of the *Times* of London could not ignore the new phenomenon:

> From nowhere but the United States could such music have sprung; it is the music of the hustler; of the feverishly active speculator; of the skyscraper and the grain elevator. America has waited too long for her own music. Her serious musicians must cease to look abroad for their inspiration and turn their faces homeward."

It was a time for raggin' it, and it seemed as if the whole world was getting into the act.

2

My Kind of Town
Hot Nights in the City

The North American city had been slowly coming into form since the Civil War but it was the World's Columbian Exposition that made the city — any city — the hot place to be. And no city was hotter than Chicago on nights when Scott Joplin and other musicians from all over the country, black and white, strained their instruments and their voices to claim the place as their own. They had the same feeling about this town that a later crooner, Frank Sinatra, would put into words in the song, "My Kind of Town (Chicago Is)."

There was no jazz in Chicago in Scott Joplin's time, even though this was where he planted the acorn of Ragtime which would grow into the tree of modern music. And for all Chicago's rightful claim to preeminence in 1893, it wasn't as big as New York, as colorful as New Orleans, as well sited as San Francisco, as cosmopolitan as Montreal, or as lusty and brazen as that Baghdad on the Mississippi, St. Louis.

But Chicago was where the advocates of the City Beautiful movement set the architectural standards that determined the course of city planning for the next thirty years. Some designers complained that the Fair's reliance on European styles set back North American architecture. That didn't stop the United States Senate from adopting a plan in 1901 to redesign the American capital, Washington, in line with the vision of the city's original planner, the French architect Pierre l'Enfant. The plan incorporated many ideas from the Beaux-Arts style first expressed in Chicago, including a monumental core of government buildings, a great public Mall leading to the Washington Monument, and a series of grand public gardens. It also brought together notions of coherent urban planning, utopianism and modernity. It failed, however, to eliminate the odiferous slums that persisted behind the capital's broad avenues, where thousands lived amid crime, disease, filth and poverty.

In cities like Chicago, new technologies of building and transportation brought great changes near the end of the nineteenth century. The use of steel superstructures in place of masonry made multistory buildings a reality, not just an architectural dream. When engineers perfected the elevator, the upper floors became as attractive as the lower ones. A landlord could charge as much rent on the tenth floor as on the ground floor.

While the elevator was lifting cities upward, the electric streetcar and elevated railways pushed them outward. The clang clang of the trolley bell gave people new options about where and how to live, shaking up ingrained habits and changing long-standing cultural patterns. Home-based work, which had put bread on the table for many families, virtually disappeared in the 1890s. Husbands, sons and daughters found they were able to ride public transit to jobs in offices and factories miles away.

The rooflines of compact new neighborhoods in Chicago and other cities became a distinguishing feature of urban skylines. The distinct ethnic character of immigrant settlers, previously confined to the decaying inner core, dominated these districts. It was the beginning of the movement of middle and upper class families to the suburbs. The flight accelerated with the arrival in 1908 of Henry Ford's low-cost Model T. The population dispersal weakened the grip of corrupt big city political machines, and encouraged nascent reform movements dedicated to honest government, improved housing and an end to exploitation of the laboring classes. Battles would be won, but not the war.

As the nineteenth century turned into the twentieth, the flow of African American migration to the northern states began seeping into the inner core of Chicago, as well as cities like St. Louis, Detroit, and Cleveland. The new arrivals moved onto streets once occupied by working class whites. The exchange, with its loss of tax revenue from land owners and businesses, would lead eventually to the unraveling of many American cities after World War II.

By 1900, eight in ten Negroes living in Chicago had been born outside the state. Except for brief periods in 1904 and 1905 when the newcomers made good money working as strikebreakers during packing plant and teamsters' strikes, most got by as day laborers, the men in manufacturing and the women as domestics. Negro doctors, lawyers and teachers were scarce, with the theater, music and the clergy being the only semi-professional fields freely open to African Americans. The 1900 census showed 2,692 musicians at work in Chicago, of whom 207 were black.

Scott Joplin visited Chicago several times throughout his adult life. He would have seen the increasing numbers of African Americans crowding into the city's South Side, a narrow "Black Belt" of thirty blocks of substandard housing that stretched along State Street, a world away from the opulent life of Chicago's Gold Coast of white affluence. Sometimes, they pushed into white areas to the west, especially Hyde Park. A white vigilante club was set up to police real estate sales, windows of homes occupied by blacks were broken, and merchants who sold to the new arrivals faced white boycotts. By 1910, most African Americans in Hyde Park had been driven back to more traditional districts.

Joplin probably returned to Chicago shortly after the 1893 World's Fair but his longest stay was in 1905 when he spent several weeks with his friend Arthur Marshall and his wife above Beau Baum's saloon at 2300 South State Street. Joplin later took an apartment at 2840 Armour Avenue. He would have seen a good deal of his brother Robert, who worked as a part-time musician and singer at various bars and had an apartment nearby at 2635 Armitage Street.

The Marshalls' apartment was across the street from the Pekin Theater, Chicago's most notorious entertainment palace. It claimed to be "the only Negro owned theater in the world" and was run by the gambling lord of the South Side, Robert T. Motts. The Pekin's fare ran to Ragtime, cakewalks and the inevitable "coon songs" that drew white as well as black customers. There were state laws against segregation in hotels, theaters and other public accommodations but they functioned primarily to allow whites to enter black businesses, rather than the reverse.

In Chicago in 1905, Joplin arranged for a new publisher, Will Rossitor, to put out his newest rag, "Eugenia." It was a complex melody and Joplin insisted that the sheet music carry the notation: "Don't play this piece fast. It is never right to play Ragtime fast." While in Chicago he also collaborated with his friend Louis Chauvin on "Heliotrope Bouquet," a piece that attested to the harmonic abilities of Joplin's young friend, whose tragic life was to end too early from a combination of drugs and disease.

2. My Kind of Town

If Joplin ever went to church, it was probably at the behest of his youngest sister, Myrtle — whom he called Johnny — who spent most of her adult life in Chicago. The most famous black church of the time was Olivet Baptist Church, which was growing rapidly with the influx of southern blacks into the city. Founded in 1850, it had a membership of just six hundred in 1903 but by the end of the decade catered to more than five thousand parishioners.

Joplin probably read, at least occasionally, the city's leading black newspaper, *The Chicago Defender*. The paper, founded as a one-man effort in 1905 by Robert S. Abbott, reeked of the worst and the best of the age of yellow journalism — sensational headlines, gaudy graphics, red ink, and militant attacks on racial injustices. Abbott had a peculiar habit of referring to his fellow African Americans (a term probably not heard during his lifetime) not as Negroes or blacks but as "The Race" and black men and women as "Race men" and "Race women."

The *Defender* waged a long but largely ineffective struggle to improve the living conditions of its readers. The paper attacked the policies of white real estate agents who charged higher rents to blacks than whites, and Abbott's editorials deplored the decline of the black neighborhood as the "sporting element" took over many blocks. It was not long before the *Defender*, citing rampant vice, was writing of "men and women half clothed hanging out of a window," "rag-time piano playing ... far into the night," and "shooting and cutting scrapes."

Joplin's last recorded visit to Chicago came in the summer of 1907, when he returned for another stay with Arthur Marshall before moving permanently to New York.

The new culture that arose in the Ragtime era embraced music, journalism, books, new theatrical arts like vaudeville, and new expressions in the visual arts. They all fed off new technologies like Thomas Alva Edison's phonograph and his kinetoscope, a device for watching moving pictures; the cinematograph of France's Lumière brothers that first projected film on a screen; and the electrically powered player piano devised by William Fleming. High-speed rotary presses developed by Fred and Sam Goss began to churn out millions of copies of newspapers, their pages filled with type from the automatic typecasting machine of Otto Mergan-

PART I — Breaking All the Rules

thaler and with pictures taken with William Folmer's new Speed Graphic press camera.*

For the newly emerging mass media, these inventions helped journalists come to grips with the disorder and diversity of large cities, bringing news and opinion to readers more quickly and in greater variety. In New York, the *World's* Nellie Bly wrote of sweat shop factories and exploitation of the poor. Her stories helped change the social culture by focusing attention on the worst ills of turn-of-the-century society. Popular magazines like *McClure's* in the United States, *Maclean's* in Canada and *Tit-Bits*, a sensationally successful digest of books and papers in Britain, were launched to compete with high brow "quality" journals like the American *Harper's* and *Scribner's*. They took advantage of the new process of photoengraving and the rotary press to produce attractive and easy-to-read publications that appealed to the average person. National advertisers quickly discovered the value of magazines as a tool for luring readers into the new consumer society.

After Thomas Edison's incandescent lamp turned night into day, saloons and music halls were among the first to brighten their stages with electric light. It drew thousands from their homes, if only to marvel at the wonder of this new invention. The electric age affected everyone's lives at home and at work, the lightbulb making possible the modern department store, amusement parks, theaters and factory assembly lines. The U.S. Census bureau was able to tabulate the country's 1890 population in record time, using an early form of data processing, the new electrically driven punch cards invented by Herman Hollerith. His company would someday be known by the initials IBM. Bicycle makers, newly prosperous as a result of the pneumatic tire that made it comfortable to ride the roughest cobblestone streets, switched to making the mechanical wonders of the new age, motor cars and airplanes.

Two great oil companies — Standard Oil and Anglo-Persian — tapped into the precious resource that would power the newfangled automobile. Britain's battle cruisers switched to burning oil to drive their turbines, and in Russia, Konstantin Tsiolkovsky developed the principles of rocket flight. In 1895, William Roentgen discovered X-rays in Germany and in 1898,

---

*Folmer started selling cameras to customers of his bicycle manufacturing company in New York and invented the Speed Graphic in 1898. The company became part of Eastman Kodak in 1905. The Speed Graphic would become the mainstay of press photographers for the next half century.

in Paris, Marie Curie revealed her discovery of radium and its strange property of radioactivity.

The cultural impact of the Ragtime era came from the power of the new technological infrastructure that added time, distance and numbers to artistic experience. Technology, according to the American cultural observer, Robert Thompson, was the driving force behind the conversion of popular culture, which had been present in the United States since the Civil War, into a mass culture. "Popular culture was constrained by personal participation," he says. "You participated by attendance at a concert or a play, or you bought sheet music to play on the piano at home."

Popular culture morphed into mass culture when new technology provided the media to bring the experience to people at home. One could watch and listen while a player piano pounded out a Ragtime piece. Seeing a movie was a remote experience. Thompson, a professor of culture at Syracuse University, notes that, while mass culture created a passive audience, it also hugely multiplied its numbers: "The crowds attending a Ringling Brothers circus night after night for a year could not equal the audience an actor would reach with a single motion picture."

It was this ability of technology to replicate individual performance that bothered America's greatest bandmaster, John Philip Sousa. When he sailed with his band on a European tour in 1900, he told the *New York Times* that he "intended to use plenty of Ragtime pieces and Negro melodies." But the "march king" looked with disdain on the passing of entertainment into the hands of ordinary people and their machines. "These talking and playing machines," wrote the technophobic Sousa in his 1906 essay "The Menace of Mechanical Music," would reduce music "to a mathematical system of megaphones, wheels, cogs, disks, cylinders, and all manner of revolving things, which are as like real art as the marble statue of Eve is like her beautiful, living, breathing daughters." Sousa refused for years to allow radio broadcasts of his band's performances. He preferred to keep alive the era of popular culture when people attended live concerts and made their own music and sang to each other. His reaction was typical.

The new music, art and literature were responding to the experiences and the values of a new majority. Joseph Pulitzer put the first comic strip, featuring a ragamuffin boy dubbed the Yellow Kid, in his *New York World* in 1895. It was an art form as visually satisfying to ordinary people as the fine art of any museum, and the kid's nickname gave rise to the term "yellow journalism."

Comic strips in the *World* and other papers might have been the beginning of "dumbing down," but they more likely represented the awakening of people to amusements from their own cultural heritage. In another quarter of a century Gilbert Seldes, the first American intellectual to lend legitimacy to popular culture, would write in *The Seven Lively Arts* that the art forms usually held out as serious culture, such as "vocal concerts, pseudo-classic dancing, the serious intellectual drama, the civic masque, the high-toned moving picture, and grand opera," were really nothing more than "bogus arts" that "persuade people by appealing to their snobbery that they are the real thing." In contrast, he would write, Ragtime music was important for "its intense gaiety, its naiveté, its tireless curiosity about itself."

Ragtime music had something else going for it: it brought frivolity and fun to a generation whose parents had known little but the stern Calvinism of North America's Protestant population. Who could not smile and whose face would not lighten, after a day of exhausting labor in a garment sweatshop or a fiery foundry, on hearing the pulsating tempo of a Ragtime tune? The new music was a welcome relief from such saccharine songs as *A Bird in a Gilded Cage:*

> 'Tis sad when you think of her wasted life
> For youth cannot mate with age;
> And her beauty was sold
> For an old man's gold,
> She's a bird in a gilded cage.

Ragtime music was an invitation to forget such melancholy fates, tap your toes, snap your fingers, and get on your feet and dance. This is what people by the millions did. In dancing to Ragtime music, they turned public dancing from an immoral spectacle into a decent pastime. And they had fun doing it.

Ten million immigrants entered the United States and three million came to Canada in the twenty years before the First World War. In the U.S., many of them disappeared into the polyglot tenderloin making up New York's Lower East Side. E.L. Doctorow, who chronicled their hard-

2. My Kind of Town

ships in his novel *Ragtime*, described them this way: "They went into the streets and were somehow absorbed in the tenements. They were despised by New Yorkers. They were filthy and illiterate. They stank of fish and garlic. They had running sores. They had no honor and worked for next to nothing. They stole. They drank. They raped their own daughters. They killed each other casually."

Farmers, laborers and small merchants also faced hardships. Out of the clash of languages, races, greed and ambition, with millions in North America and Europe still enduring almost unbearable working and living conditions, a new and homogeneous mass society was slowly emerging. Its disparate parts were being connected, one to another, through public education and the mass culture of the press, books, movies, music and art. New ideas for a new century — ideas about science, industry, philosophy, religion, democracy and human rights — were being spread.

Andrew Carnegie, robber baron turned into one of America's greatest benefactors, financed the building of three thousand free public libraries after 1900. They were soon filled with the works of the century's new authors. Music rolls carried the popular new Ragtime tunes to every middle class home owning a player piano, while the first phonograph records were about to be pressed in Tin Pan Alley, the brassy New York neighborhood where songwriters were busy composing America's new popular tunes. Theater and dance were attracting crowds to matinee and evening performances. Five-cent movies drew enthusiastic audiences. Newsboys hawked special editions run off by the new high-speed newspaper presses, sometimes on an almost hourly basis. Painters like Paul Gauguin, Pablo Picasso and Amedeo Modigliano experimented with radical new artistic techniques.

The rapid pace of social change in the Ragtime era — a true turning point — had to be confusing to many who lived through it. The world had neither before witnessed nor faced the consequences of such an outpouring of new technologies. Later generations would grow up accustomed to change. Not so the people of the Ragtime era. How did it affect their lives and how did they respond? How would they regard themselves if they could compare their lives with those of their great-grandchildren?

For all the benefits of modern science and the life-extending feats of modern medicine, they would probably have opted to remain in a more comfortable era. As Mark Train wrote, "We were poor, and didn't know it. We were comfortable and did know it." Were people happier than today? They were probably not as unhappy; their narrower range of options would have given less reason for discontent over unachievable goals. Birth was difficult and death often prolonged and agonizingly painful. In the United States, life expectancy was just fifty for men and fifty-three for women (compared to seventy-five and eighty, respectively, in 2005). But statistics can mislead. Of those who survived childhood and its high infant mortality — reaching almost 15 percent in Great Britain in the 1890s — many developed natural immunities that allowed them to live to a ripe old age, despite the absence of antibiotics.

Ragtime era residents enjoyed one respite their descendants would be denied: a quieter life. Chicago and other large cities fell quiet at dusk; there were few automobiles on the streets, horses were generally in their stables by suppertime, and there was no amplification of music to break the night silence. Nor was there any shortage of smells, either on the streets or in the homes. Uncertain garbage disposal and the presence of backyard privies as well as domestic animals — a horse, a cow or a few goats were common on many properties — contributed familiar odors. The ritual of the weekly bath, a tradition since Victorian times, was yet to be observed in all households.

Magazines extolled the virtues of the "New Woman" as the professions gave up their male exclusivity and accepted, however reluctantly, women into their ranks. Jacketed dresses modeled after men's suits evolved into the popular shirtwaist blouse that became a fashion mainstay of women employed in the new occupations of telephone operator or stenographer. Dresses became shorter; ankles and calves could be revealed. Women bobbed their hair, learned to play tennis and golf, and a few even began smoking in public. And they were having fewer babies.

Professional athletes, especially boxers and football and baseball players, launched the "golden age" of sports. The New York Giants played the Philadelphia Athletics in the first officially sanctioned World Series in 1905. Food habits, reflecting an ingrained set of practices deeply revealing of a people's culture, underwent dramatic change. People ate less bread and potatoes — once the basis of the Western diet — as more meat, fruit and vegetables showed up on the dinner table.

Whenever Scott Joplin or his wife visited their neighborhood grocery store in St. Louis, where they lived from 1901 to 1904, they would

2. My Kind of Town

have found processed foods, including industrially canned fruits and vegetables, filling shelves that once had carried only produce from nearby farms. Iceboxes enabled housewives to buy larger quantities, at lower prices, of fresh meat, eggs, milk and produce. Breakfast became the first meal where people relied mainly on processed foods.

Henry Crowell and the Quaker Oats Company engineered a million dollar advertising campaign that convinced Americans to eat oats, a food once scorned as fodder fit only for horses. In 1894, W.K. Kellogg and his brother decided to run boiled wheat dough through rollers, producing thin sheets of cereal flakes. Grape nuts, shredded wheat and cream of wheat came to market in a cascade of manufactured foods that freed tired housewives from having to make breakfast from scratch. The Coca-Cola Company was sold for twenty-three hundred dollars, cocaine recipe and all, and bottled cola was soon for sale. Close behind were tea bags, the electric toaster, decaf coffee and the U.S. Food and Drug Act.

The ideas the Ragtime generation bestowed on the world — in mass culture, industry and science — were largely put on hold by the Great War, as the conflict of 1914–1918 came to be called. "Because of the Great War," wrote English politician and journalist Roy Hattersley in *The Edwardians*, "progress was suspended and, in the slaughter which followed, the achievements of the century's early years were underrated and overlooked."

Everything changed in the Ragtime era — what people did, how they thought about themselves, and what their dreams were. Scott Joplin dreamt more grandly than most. His dream was to become the first black to compose the music of symphonies and operas. He dreamt of transforming Ragtime from a low beat played in honky-tonk saloons to great orchestral works that would command reverence in the finest performance halls of America and Europe — a dream as big as the times, as bold as Chicago.

3

The Making of the Legend
A Boy and a Banjo

Ragtime came from the black soul of America, at a time when the nation was just beginning to recognize the shame of its past. Scott Joplin had a personal connection to that past — he was one of seven children born to the African American laboring family of Giles Joplin and Florence Givens. They were an honest, clean-living couple who scraped out a meager living, Giles by sharecropping and Florence by taking in laundry and cleaning house for whites. The Joplins, like most Negro families of the time, left little evidence of their passage through the post–Civil War Southwest.

Scott is accounted for in the 1870 census as a two-year-old and his birth is thought to have taken place November 24, 1868, on a farm not far from where the future town of Texarkana would spring up on the Texas-Arkansas border. The Joplins were living on a farm near the town of Marshall, Texas, owned by William Caves, a white man. Scott had an older brother, Monroe, and a second brother a year younger than he, Robert. His mother's parents, Milton and Susan Givens, lived with them. You get the picture: a black sharecropper family eking out a hardscrabble existence on barren Texas scrubland.

One thing saved Scott Joplin: he was surrounded from childhood by music. Giles loved to play the violin while Florence picked at the banjo and sang. The children — and four more were to come along — always joined in. They played the plantation tunes that Giles had learned as a child in North Carolina. Scott never forgot the songs his parents sang and played, songs that helped the slaves endure their long days of picking cotton bolls, hoeing the fields or unloading supplies at the river docks:

3. The Making of the Legend

> I'm gwine to Alabamy, oh
> For to see my mammy, ah
> She went from Ole Virginny, oh
> And I'm her pickaninny, ah
> She lives on the Tombigbee, oh
> I wish I had her wid me, ah

Best of all, Scott was allowed to play his mother's banjo — he'd master it by seven — and to take piano lessons from a white teacher in return for Florence's cleaning the woman's house. This occurred after the Joplins had given up sharecropping and moved into the town of Texarkana. The few dollars Florence earned, added to the meager wages Giles brought home as a laborer, kept the family going. After Giles ran off with another woman, Florence faced the fate of countless black mothers of then and today: struggling to support her family and keep her children from harm's way.

Young Scott's musical skill — or his badgering — impressed his mother to the point where she managed to buy him an old square grand piano. By the time he was eleven, Scott was playing several instruments and improvising his own tunes. One of the most important things in his young life occurred at about this time.

Word had gotten around Texarkana about this remarkable boy. An aging German music teacher, Julius Weiss, offered to take Scott as his pupil. Scott's tutoring went far beyond what most children received in their weekly piano lessons. Weiss introduced the boy to classical compositions and opera, instilling in him an appreciation for music as art as well as entertainment. It was at this point that Joplin began to develop a sophisticated understanding of musical composition that gave him a subtlety and proficiency far beyond his years. It is said that for years afterward, Joplin sent small sums of money to Weiss, just as he did to his father, despite the fact Giles had abandoned his family. These traits of appreciation never left him. Throughout his life, Scott Joplin would often demonstrate the large measure of loyalty that resided in his soul.

Joplin formed his Texas Medley Quartette while still in his teens, probably when he was living in Texarkana. The Quartette was a vocal ensemble that included Scott's brother Will and two neighborhood boys. Another brother, Robert, joined the group, thus establishing that a quartet did not need to be limited to four members.

PART I — Breaking All the Rules

Joplin's group played anywhere it could get work. They performed for dances, church events, club meetings, and weddings. Accommodating the racial prejudice of the time, the Quartette often adopted "black-face minstrelsy," presenting humorous and simplistic vignettes of African American life while blackening their already dark faces with burnt cork.

Obtaining these dates was no little accomplishment for a young black man who otherwise would have been forced to depend on casual saloon jobs for his food, drink and lodging. The only alternative, manual labor on the railroads or sawmills, appears never to have had much appeal for Scott.

When he was around eighteen, Scott moved to Sedalia to live with relatives and attend high school. Possibly he realized he needed a better education if he was to meet his high ambition of a successful career in music. Or perhaps his mother thought that new surroundings would give him an incentive to study. In either event, Joplin attained an unusually good education for a Negro of his era.

In Sedalia, Joplin attended the all-black Lincoln High School. Following his excursion to the Chicago World's Fair, he was urged by several of his friends to sign up for classes at the George R. Smith College in Sedalia. The college was also segregated, but it gave him the chance to study music notation, theory and composition. The college had been built by the daughters of the town's founder and was operated by the Methodist church. Unfortunately, all records of Scott's attendance were lost when it burned to the ground in 1927.

In the twilight world of Sedalia's bars and brothels, Joplin met and charmed many friendly young women of both races. Two of the most popular houses, the Jackson House and the Farm, were known for their white prostitutes. Given the prejudice against interracial sexual contact, Joplin had to be careful in his liaisons with its girls. A friend, Emmett Cook, a drummer and singer with the Quartette, was fined one hundred dollars — suspended on condition he leave town — after being caught with his white paramour, Lottie Wright. She was given the same penalty, but was soon back in town operating her own establishment. It all pointed up the fact that law enforcement was haphazard at best, with local newspapers reporting each month the names of madams who turned up at court to pay their five-dollar fines.

Joplin also played in the Queen City Cornet Band in Sedalia, an

3. The Making of the Legend

outfit made up entirely of black musicians. Two years went by until, when he was twenty-seven, he was able to reassemble the Texas Medley Quartette that he'd taken to Chicago. It was again a double quartet with eight singers and instrumentalists. And it was good enough to gain the attention of the Majestic Booking Agency, which lined up dates for them in several states.

Joplin took the outfit on tour as far east as Syracuse, New York, in 1894. It was there that several businessmen, impressed with his work, financed the publication of two waltzes for which Joplin had written both the words and music. A Syracuse jeweler, A.M. Mantell, took a liking to the young musician and his work and on February 20, 1895, copyrighted Joplin's first published piece, *Please Say You Will*. The Lieter brothers, who ran a piano distributorship, heard Joplin and acquired the rights to "A Picture of Her Face," taking out the copyright on July 3, 1895.

Joplin made little or nothing off these pieces, which drew on the creative talent and skills he had been cultivating since his early teenage years. But he was convinced that some day the world would pay proper attention to his accomplishments. "Boy," he liked to tell fellow musicians, "when I'm dead twenty-five years, people are going to begin to recognize me."

As Ragtime gained popularity and African American entertainers became recognized for something more than "black face" acts, racial divisions were widening in the United States, accentuated by an ongoing depression that deepened after the financial panic of 1893. A collapse in the price of gold and a sudden bursting of the railroad bubble led to massive unemployment. In a single year, a quarter of the railroads in the U.S. fell into the hands of capitalists like J. Pierpont Morgan.

In New Orleans, a French-speaking Creole named Homer Plessy challenged segregated seating on the trains by getting himself arrested for sitting in a white-only coach. He was just one-eighth African. That was sufficient for the Supreme Court to rule in 1896, by a vote of eight to one, that there was nothing unconstitutional about "separate but equal" segregated seating.

As an entertainer, Scott Joplin felt the pinch of the depression when business in the honky-tonks fell off. In a strange way, the financial panic of the mid 1890s and the economic hardship that followed were a boon for Joplin and his kind. The bordellos and low cafés that had previously hired full orchestras to entertain customers cut their costs to the bone. They

PART I — Breaking All the Rules

went with piano players working for tips. Scott continued to pick up sporadic jobs in the joints on Sedalia's "Battle Row" and in other towns of the Midwest.

Joplin benefited from white tolerance for Negro entertainments, but he could not have been unaware that his people were being oppressed as harshly as ever. The few Negroes who lived in Sedalia were restricted to "Lincolnville," the tawdry neighborhood north of the tracks above Main Street. Restaurants, theaters and other places of public business, as well as schools, were tightly segregated. Even many of the saloons were restricted but, exceptionally, Sedalia had a few black police officers. Their authority was limited to arresting others of their race.

Aside from entertainment, baseball and boxing were the only fields in which most Negroes found an opportunity to develop their skills. In Sedalia, it often happened that midway through a game between two black teams, the players would be ordered off the field to make way for all-white teams. An attempt to form a League of Negro Baseball Clubs in 1887 fell apart after just one week of play. Boxing was still illegal in some states; but driven by the lure of gambling and the desperation of penniless young men, especially Negroes, the sport began to flourish.

The greatest fighter of the era, the Texan Jack Johnson, came out of hardscrabble Galveston, the Texas seaport that was ravished by the great hurricane of 1900. Johnson began fighting after his family's home was destroyed in that storm, and he was soon accepted as the Negro heavyweight champion. He could not, however, secure a match with the popular white champion, James J. Jeffries. After Jeffries' retirement, Johnson won the world title by beating Canadian Tommy Burns in a bout in Australia.

Jeffries, having spent five years operating an alfalfa farm, was lured out of retirement to face Johnson in an outdoor fight at Las Vegas on July 4, 1910. It was an epic battle. Johnson knocked out the old champion in the fifteenth round; he'd shown none of the "yellow streak" for which black fighters were supposed to be noted. The unexpected outcome led to race riots across the country in which more than two dozen people died. Fearing more disturbances, the Texas legislature, followed by the U.S. Congress, banned films of the fight. Black poet William Waring Cuney

3. The Making of the Legend

captured the "exuberant African American reaction" in his poem, "My Lord, What a Morning":

> O my Lord
> What a morning,
> O my Lord,
> What a feeling,
> When Jack Johnson
> Turned Jim Jeffries'
> Snow-white face
> to the ceiling.

Johnson's crushing of Jeffries was hard enough to take, but it was the black champion's success with white women — he married several — that white authorities found unable to accept. After his first white wife committed suicide in the nightclub that Johnson owned in Chicago, he was convicted on trumped up charges under the Mann Act, a statute that prohibited interstate transportation of women for immoral purposes. The law had been designed to combat prostitution traffic, but it was often used to harass celebrities whose behavior had offended public taste.

Johnson fled to Europe, while the search for a "white hope" who could reclaim the crown got underway. Johnson lost the championship to one of those white hopes, Kansan Jess Willard, in Havana in April 1915. The circumstances were suspicious. Johnson went down in the twenty-sixth round, but a gloved hand carefully shielded his eyes from the blazing sun.

After losing the title, Johnson returned to the United States in 1920 to serve a year in Leavenworth Prison for his Mann Act conviction. There would not be another black heavyweight champion until Joe Louis defeated James J. Braddock in 1937. Louis' managers would tutor him carefully to avoid Johnson's mistakes. There would be no gratuitous smiling in the ring, no taunting of opponents, no exultation at his knockouts. Most of all, there would be no fraternizing with white women, although later came speculation of affairs between Louis and actresses such as Lana Turner. None of this would bother a later black champion, Mohammed Ali, who would defy both his opponents and the U.S. government — the former in the ring and the latter in his refusal to be conscripted to fight in Vietnam.

The political battles were no less bruising. The nation's brief experience with Reconstruction — the period after the Civil War when victori-

PART I — Breaking All the Rules

ous Union forces policed the South and Negroes were permitted to fill many local offices — had come to an end in the Compromise of 1877 between Democrats and Republicans. By its terms, southern Democrats accepted the disputed election of Republican Rutherford Hayes as president in return for a pledge to withdraw Union troops from the old Confederacy. It effectively ended enforcement of the fifteenth amendment to the constitution, ratified in 1870, that had guaranteed Negroes the right to vote. After eighty-seven African Americans were lynched in 1899, Negro congressmen George H. White of North Carolina tried but failed to get an antilynching law through Congress. His bill would have made the offence a federal crime, taking investigations out of the hands of culpable local sheriffs. It would not be until 2005 that the U.S. Senate would apologize for its inaction. An estimated forty-seven hundred victims of lynchings died between 1882 and 1968.

White's political career came to an end in 1900, making him the last African American to sit in the Congress for another quarter of a century. President William McKinley returned to the White House for a second term that year and promptly committed himself to accepting Southern prejudice: "It will be my constant aim to do nothing, and permit nothing to be done, that will arrest ... this revival of esteem and affection which now animates so many thousands in both the old antagonistic sections." It was the signal for the states to throw up new barriers to Negro voting. Discouraged from joining unions, barred from working in the growing tobacco and textile industries of the South, nearly nine out of ten African Americans were locked into low-paid jobs as servants or farm laborers. For most, only the railroads offered regular jobs as firemen, flagmen, and most commonly of all, as sleeping car porters. Scott Joplin's brother Monroe worked as a porter on Texas trains.

Scott Joplin drew on real events for many of his compositions. A railway publicity stunt that horribly backfired inspired him to write one of his first Ragtime instrumentals, "The Crush Collision March." The Missouri, Kansas and Texas line had arranged to have two of its thirty-five-ton locomotives, each pulling seven boxcars and traveling at a combined speed of one hundred and twenty miles per hour, collide head-on. The spectacle would take place at a spot on the Texas prairie nicknamed after

3. The Making of the Legend

the scheme's promoter, William George Crush. A passenger agent for the railroad, Crush saw a chance for the railway to make a fortune by selling train tickets — five dollars from anywhere in Texas — to view the sorry sight.

At the very instant of collision the boiler of one train exploded, hurling debris over the crowd and killing two spectators. By nightfall of September 15, 1896, Crush had been fired, the wreckage removed, and the encampment that a few hours earlier had been the second largest city in Texas was no more. Crush was rehired the next day and worked the rest of his life for the railroad. It is known that Joplin was back in Texas in 1896 — he was a young man who liked to travel around — but whether he was on hand for the crash is not known.

Joplin published two more pieces in Texas that year, "Combination March" and "Harmony Club Waltz." Up to now, Joplin had not been committed to any specific genre of music, instead appropriating whatever appealed to him, including syncopated rhythms when he found them useful. From this casual use of syncopation he graduated progressively into full-fledged Ragtime. The first and possibly greatest manifestation of Joplin's mastery of the new genre would come shortly after his return to Sedalia.

By 1898 Joplin had published six piano compositions. Once back in Sedalia, he and some of his more enterprising friends, frustrated at being barred from Sedalia's many white-only social clubs, decided it was time for a place of their own. Two were soon organized, the Black 400 club (its name probably a play on the town's tony white social set) and the Maple Leaf Club. The 400 was founded in 1898 by Tony Williams, a black vaudevillian, and he promised "to make the club a high-toned resort and no foolishness will be tolerated."

The rival Maple Leaf Club, organized by two brothers in their mid-twenties, Will and Walker Williams, opened soon afterward in rented premises upstairs from the Blotcher Seed Company. It was there that Joplin would gather with his friends after their stints in the local bars and brothels. The atmosphere Joplin found in the Maple Leaf Club must have stimulated his musical proficiency. Within a few months, he was deep into the composition of his possibly most memorable work of Ragtime, "Maple Leaf Rag."

More than one hundred Ragtime tunes were by now in print, including Joplin's first contribution to the genre, *Original Rags*. They were quickly

PART I — Breaking All the Rules

becoming stock in trade for publishers like John Stark of Sedalia. His main business was selling pianos but he longed to be a big-time publisher of sheet music, the popular new fad on which millions of Americans were spending their nickels and dimes.

After being turned down by several publishers, Joplin took "Maple Leaf Rag" to John Stark. According to one legend — remember that there are no archives of Joplin papers and little documented record of his dealings — he had with him a small boy who danced for Stark as Joplin played the piece in Stark's piano store. Another legend has it that Stark wandered into the Maple Leaf Club one day and heard Joplin playing the tune. It is also said that Stark's daughter Elena, an accomplished piano recitalist, liked "Maple Leaf Rag" and that it was she who urged her father to publish it.

In its first year, 1899, the piece that would become Joplin's greatest hit sold three hundred and sixty copies. Ten years later, a half million copies had been sold. The "Maple Leaf Rag" would earn Joplin between three and four hundred dollars a year for the rest of his life. It meant the difference between penury and comfort, and would immortalize both Joplin and the club after which it was named. He boasted to his protégé, Arthur Marshall, "*The Maple Leaf Rag* will make me the king of Ragtime composers."

"Maple Leaf Rag" followed the complex Ragtime formula of four different tunes, or strains, each of sixteen bars, combining a sophisticated harmony with a lively march rhythm, "essentially a collection and integration of little melodies, played in a manner similar to the way in which black plantation and church songs were sung and black plantation dances were performed." The piece was more notable for its tune than for its lyrics written later by Sydney Brown:

> Oh go 'way, man, I can hypnotize dis nation,
> I can shake de earth's foundation wid de Maple Leaf Rag!
> Oh go 'way, man, just hold yo' breath a minnit,
> For there's not a stunt that's in it, wid de Maple Leaf Rag!

Joplin escaped most of the moral condemnation that was directed at Ragtime because he concentrated on instrumental pieces. He saw himself as educated and cultured, and in those lyrics that he did write he shied away from the vulgar suggestiveness favored by others. Nor did Joplin have time for the blatant racism that an early black Ragtime artist, Ernest

3. The Making of the Legend

Scott Joplin's first and most celebrated composition, "Maple Leaf Rag," came out in 1899 when he lived in Sedalia, Missouri. It established him as a Ragtime star and earned him some $110,000 in royalties during his lifetime (The Lilly Library, Indiana University).

PART I — Breaking All the Rules

Hogan, displayed in his song "All Coons Look Alike to Me." Hogan's lyrics appealed to the prejudices of white audiences:

> All coons look alike to me!
> I've got another beau, you see,
> And he's just as good to me
> As you nigger ever tried to be,
> He spends his money free.
> I know we can't agree,
> So I don't like you no how
> All coons look alike to me.

The self-appointed protectors of public taste, black as well as white, were offended not just by the words but by the fact that Ragtime had broken free of traditional musical styles. Whites looked down on it as not only lacking in sophistication, but also as an unwelcome invitation to embrace the African savagery they thought characteristic of American Negroes. New York's commissioner of docks banned Ragtime from the city's free summer concerts, as did the superintendent of New York's vacation schools. Churchgoing blacks, of whom there were many, joined the attack on Ragtime. Some objected to what they saw as a demeaning of their race, while others thought that disowning the cruder aspects of their culture would make them more respectable in white eyes. Years passed before most white musicians would have anything to do with Ragtime. The American Federation of Musicians at its national meeting in 1901 "swore to play no ragtime and to do all in their power to counteract the pernicious influence ... of the Negro school."

Yet Ragtime had its defenders. A group of doctors who formed the National Society of Musical Therapists had an article published in the *New York Medical Journal* citing Ragtime's ability to arouse depressed people from their melancholy. The *New York Sun* carried this account:

> No matter to what extent music may restore a person to the normal, there can be no question that it may help other influences to incline the person from the normal. There are many compositions, notably among those by Chopin, which are the outcome of more or less melancholy moods, and while they are beautiful and harmless to the healthy, when made a steady diet and source of self-consolation by those suffering from depression from mental or bodily causes, their effect is undoubtedly pernicious, just as a too exclusive a diet of olives would depress the general bodily condition and mental atmosphere or a person so indulging a sickly appetite.

3. The Making of the Legend

On the other hand, Ragtime music, wrote the *Sun*,

> ... being in nowise serious" (is the reverse of depressing). The African jingles of the present day create an emotional atmosphere of restlessness and excitement which is typically American, and is opposed to health only so far as our national restlessness and lack of poise tend to make us a people whose national disease is nervous exhaustion. Roughly speaking, lively music such as Ragtime is likely to rouse depressed persons from their melancholy; sad and pathetic music will soothe the excitable and hypernervous.

Ragtime also was good for children, according to some experts. At a Minneapolis convention of the National Conference of Music Supervisors, the press was told that Ragtime music and the singing of popular songs of the day did not injure the musical mind of the public school child, but rather encouraged individual musical ability. The source of this wisdom was one Ralph L. Baldwin, the musical supervisor of the public schools of Hartford, Conn.:

> I have learned that Ragtime music or the singing of popular songs does not injure the child musically; that is, if not carried to an extreme. Ragtime music is nothing more nor less than a foot tickler, and it is a good change to fall back upon after pursuing music for some time. You know we have to have a change in music once in a while, just as we have to have a vacation or rest from our work, and this lighter vein of music is what brings about this change. It would not be good enough, though, for the public school pupil to just follow the popular songs of the day and do nothing else, for it leads to nothing.

It was Scott Joplin's success with "Maple Leaf Rag" that marked the peak of the first phase of Ragtime's popularity. For all the musical genius reflected in this remarkable composition, it was taken by the public—as well as other musicians—to be a fairly typical "raggin' it" piece, peppy, eminently danceable, but not at the time regarded as anything much out of the ordinary. How wrong they all were. This single piece stamped Scott Joplin as an artist of exceptional power and would become the bedrock on which would rest the legend of this remarkable man.

4

Marching to a Ragtime Tune

> "A Splendid Little War"
> — *English Ambassador John Hay describing the Spanish-American War to Teddy Roosevelt*

Under a sweltering Florida sun, the black soldiers struggled to hold their heads high and stay in step, heavy rifles on their shoulders, while their white officers shouted commands: "Pick 'em up, get in time, straighten that line!" The soldiers appeared lethargic, but who wouldn't at 100 degrees in the shade? Suddenly, there came the music of an army marching band. It had been sent to boost the morale of the troops of the Tenth Cavalry Division of the U.S. Army, gathering in Tampa in the spring of 1898 for the jump-off to Cuba and the decisive battles of the Spanish-American War.

The band was playing "There'll Be a Hot Time in the Old Town Tonight," and the tempo of the soldiers' march quickly picked up to keep time with this irresistible Ragtime tune. It had been first sung by the black entertainer Mama Lou at Babe Connors' Castle Club, the high-priced brothel in St. Louis. It would later become Theodore Roosevelt's campaign theme song. America talked of little else the summer of '98 besides Cuba, TR's Rough Riders, and the nation's mission to dislodge Spain from the New World.

The patriotic musical *Yankee Doodle Dandy* (named after a traditional folk song heard long before James M. Cohen would popularize his lyrics in 1906) opened at the Casino Theater in New York on July 25. It had a ten-week run. While African Americans were winning acceptance as entertainers — the first all-black theatrical production, *A Trip to Coon Town*, had moved to Broadway on April 4 after a tryout tour in Canada — the

4. Marching to a Ragtime Tune

idea that black soldiers could actually fight was repugnant to most Americans.

White songwriters expressed their contempt in racist marching lyrics that ridiculed black fighting capability. These songwriters saw African Americans as fit only for KP (Kitchen Patrol):

> In costumes gorgeous to behold
> A sight one seldom sees
> Fifty coon brass bands will be in line
> And each will play the latest music in Ragtime
> Well-groomed darkies looking fine
> Will shine while marching as the Black K.P.'s

The so-called "Black K.P.'s" of the Tenth Cavalry would rescue Col. Roosevelt at San Juan Hill on July 1, but that was yet to come.

Frederic Remington, the artist and illustrator famous for paintings that depicted the cowboys, Indians, soldiers and settlers who squabbled for the spoils of land, gold and cattle west of the Mississippi, watched the Tenth Cavalry march by from his vantage point on the veranda of the Tampa Bay Hotel. He recognized many of these black troops, having rubbed shoulders with them on his western trips where he had written about them and portrayed them in his paintings. He'd been with them when they'd acquired the nickname of "Buffalo soldiers," bestowed on them by the Indians of the western plains, who saw their curly hair as being similar to that of the buffalo. The four cavalry brigades in which they were concentrated were known as the Immunes, in the false belief that black men were immune to malaria and yellow fever.

Remington was in Tampa for the "rocking chair" stage of the Spanish-American War. Liquor flowed freely while the artist held forth with exaggerated tales of his exploits in the West. Now, he was under hire to *Harper's Weekly*, assigned to write stories of the war and illustrate them with drawings of American soldiers in action against the hated Spanish dictatorship in Cuba.

In his foolhardiness and his creativity — it seemed as if one went with the other — Remington personified the Ragtime era. One foot in the past, he drew on the rich traditions of the West to produce such works as *Smoke Signals* and *If Skulls Could Speak*, pictures showing the plains Indians in lonely vigils under an endless sky. His role as a magazine illustrator and

PART I — Breaking All the Rules

as a correspondent and artist for William Randolph Hearst's newspapers foreshadowed the age of visual media.

Starting in the Ragtime era, the press used the new printing technologies to mix words and images in a single package. This had never been done before. Remington's drawings enabled readers to vicariously endure the terror of battle through art as well as through text. Eventually, photos would replace illustrations, but for now his drawings allowed every patriotic citizen to share in the thrill of victory at the front. It was a new cultural experience.

The two thousand "Buffalo soldiers" marching in Tampa and the twenty-four thousand white troops assigned to the makeshift camps set up along the Florida coast, had nothing good to say about "that dirty little town, except that it was the jumping-off place for Cuba." The only excitement for the soldiers, aside from visits to the many bordellos set up to meet their needs, came from drunken assaults on saloons and theaters in the exotic Ybor City section of Tampa where Cuban immigrants had built up a thriving cigar-making industry.

This was the war that John Hay, the American ambassador to Britain, in a private letter to Remington's friend Colonel Roosevelt, would dub "a splendid little war." It signaled the arrival of the United States as a new imperial power. In a single year, 1898, the United States acquired most of its overseas territory — Hawaii, Guam, Wake Island, Puerto Rico and the Philippines. The Panama Canal Zone followed in 1903. More important than these acquisitions would be the technology and resources that would enable the United States to knit together unparalleled commercial, cultural and military strength on its way to achieving global domination.

Echoes of the Spanish-American War reached Scott Joplin while he was still struggling to find a publisher for his first rags. He had submitted three pieces, "Original Rag," "Sunflower Slow Drag" and his about-to-be famous "Maple Leaf Rag," to a Sedalia publisher, A.W. Perry & Son, but none were accepted. He later managed to sell the rights to "Original Rag" to a Kansas City publisher, Carl Hoffman. But all Joplin received for it was a small one-time payment.

The experience made Joplin receptive to the idea of having a lawyer

4. Marching to a Ragtime Tune

handle his future business dealings. It so happened that a young lawyer, Robert A. Higdon, had just opened up a legal practice in Sedalia. He often dropped in at local dances where Joplin played the piano, and the two became friends. Being on the lookout for clients, it is likely that Higdon suggested he act for Joplin in getting "Maple Leaf Rag" published. It thus fell to him to negotiate Joplin's deal with John Stark.

The deal Higdon struck for Joplin was a simple one, set out on a single typewritten page: a royalty of one cent for every copy sold (at twenty-five cents apiece) and ten free copies for his own use. A copy of the contract has survived, one of the few documents in existence attesting to an event in Joplin's life. The deal was a good deal for both Joplin and Stark, although neither had the foresight to reserve mechanical rights; they never received compensation for reproduction of "Maple Leaf Rag" on player piano rolls or phonograph records.

It took some time for Stark to publish "Maple Leaf Rag." It came off the press sometime between August 10, 1899, the date given on the contract Joplin had signed with Stark, and September 20, the date the U.S. Copyright Office noted its receipt of two copies. Only four hundred copies were printed. For the cover, Stark borrowed an illustration from the American Tobacco Company of two black couples in fancy dress, ready to perform a cakewalk.

It is unclear whether Joplin named the tune for the Maple Leaf Club or whether the club was named after the song. It is known from accounts in Sedalia newspapers that the club came into existence in 1898, but no one knows when Joplin first wrote "Maple Leaf Rag" or first began to play it in public. The club itself didn't last long. Complaints of noise and alleged illegalities led to its closing in 1900.

John Stark was convinced he had published the greatest piece in Ragtime history. He compared "Maple Leaf Rag" to the best of classical music. In his house organ, *House of Classic Rags*, he later wrote: "*Maple Leaf Rag* marks an era in musical composition. It has throttled and silenced those who oppose syncopations. It is played by the cultured of all nations and is welcomed in the drawing rooms and boudoirs of good taste."

Having created a composition that would take its place among the most original and memorable American music ever written, Joplin now set his sights on moving to a higher level. He burned with the desire to create theatrical spectacles. His first effort, in the fall of 1899, was a production called *The Ragtime Dance*, featuring a singing narrator and a group of dancers.

Joplin formed a production company and rented Wood's Opera House in Sedalia. The musical's plot revolved around a white man's impressions of a black social affair:

> I attended a ball last Thursday night
> Given by the dark town swells.
> Ev'ry coon came out in full dress alright
> And the girls were society belles.

Joplin's use of the insulting racist term coon was standard for the time, the appellation being commonly used by both whites and blacks as a synonym for an African American.

Joplin took advantage of opportunity wherever he could find it. In 1900, he took on a commission to write a waltz for a newly formed white social club, the Augustain Club. His "Augustan Club Waltz" (complete with misspelling) was published by John Stark and was well received by local whites. More remarkably, Joplin was favorably covered by local white newspapers. The *Sedalia Sentinel* respectfully referred to him as "the celebrated Scott Joplin ... the world's greatest composer of syncopated music." The *Democrat* remarked that "Sedalia can proudly say that she has one of the most wonderful musicians in the world in the person of Scott Joplin, who is considered a wonder in the art of music by the leading musicians of this and foreign countries."

He was also gaining a broader national attention. A reporter for a New York music journal, after interviewing Joplin in Sedalia, wrote:

> Scott Joplin considers it too hard work for him to sit at the piano and compose. He gets his inspirations while walking along the street or in his bed at night, and when a melody comes to him, he immediately puts it down on music paper, which he always carries with him. He is unassuming and never has much to say, and seldom speaks of his music.

Through it all, Joplin remained a young man of simple tastes. The white pianist Samuel Brunson Campbell, who as a teenage runaway had been befriended by Joplin, recalled that "he liked a little beer and gambled some. But he never let such things interfere with his music ... a very black negro, about five feet seven inches tall; a good dresser, usually neat, but sometimes a little careless with his clothes; gentlemanly and pleasant, with a liking for companionship."

4. Marching to a Ragtime Tune

The publication of "Maple Leaf Rag," Campbell would later remember, "blew the lid off the musical world and set it into the greatest musical craze that the world has ever known." A slight exaggeration perhaps, but a measure of the enthusiasm Joplin could arouse in those around him.

For Scott Joplin, the Spanish-American War would have seemed very far away indeed.

In full military dress, sketchbook in hand, Frederic Remington rode his horse cautiously up the dirt road leading to San Juan Ridge on the blisteringly hot afternoon of July 1, 1898. From ditches and behind hillside bluffs towering above him, Remington would later write, invading American soldiers were pressing their attack against Spanish battalions defending the heights protecting Santiago, the most important port on the south coast of Cuba.

"Look out, sharp-shooter!" came the warning call from a half-dozen soldiers huddled under a nearby tree.

"Wheet!" sounded the shot from a Mauser rifle, fired by a Spanish sharpshooter trying to pick off the mix of cowboys and Ivy League college men who made up the First U.S. Volunteer Cavalry, better known as Teddy Roosevelt's Rough Riders.

"It was right next to my ear, and two more," Remington would write. He recounted how he quickly slipped from his saddle, throwing his two hundred and forty pound frame to the ground before scrambling on his hands and knees through the tall guinea grass. It was then his sketchbook fell from his grasp. He had no intention of trying to retrieve it. "From the vantage of a little bank under a big tree, I had my first glimpse of San Juan Hill, and the bullets whistled about."

The day's battle would give Remington the subject for his most famous picture about the fighting in Cuba, the *Charge of the Rough Riders*. It would not be painted until after the war but it would become an icon of the American triumph. Remington didn't actually witness Colonel Roosevelt's cresting of the heights that day; nevertheless he was able to report for *Harper's* readers that "Only a handful of men got to the top, where they broke out a flag and cheered."

Remington was reared in comfortable middle class surroundings in bucolic upstate New York. As the preeminent illustrator of the West, he

PART I — Breaking All the Rules

became a confidant of General Nelson Miles, the commander of the detachment that slaughtered a defenseless Indian encampment at Wounded Knee Creek in 1890, the last armed confrontation between whites and natives. He'd also observed from a distance the rebellion north of the Canadian border led by the half breed Louis Riel in 1885, an uprising soon put down by the Northwest Mounted Police and the Queen's Own Rifles.

The West by now was safe in both countries for the families of settlers and for the investors of Europe who were being lured to this new frontier. At every turn, they faced opportunities in railroad building, mining, land development and mercantile trade. In the drawings and paintings that Remington would create over a twenty-year period, the Old West found its greatest memorialist. In *Frederic Remington: A Biography* Peggy and Harold Samuels noted, "His drawings signaled the end of the Victorian era in illustration."

Between constant trips to the West and Mexico in search of new subjects for his paintings, and occasional hard-drinking journeys to Canada to fish and relax, Remington started writing his own accounts of outdoor adventures, the beginning of what would become an impressive literary career.

As recognition of Remington's abilities mounted, he earned a second-place medal at the 1889 Paris Exposition for *The Last Lull in the Fight*. The same year, he completed *A Dash for the Timber*, a four-foot by seven-foot commission for the industrialist Edmund Cogswell Converse.

Remington could now afford a more gentlemanly lifestyle, which he found in a brick house on three acres that he bought at New Rochelle, north of New York. He promptly named it Endion, an Ojibwa Indian phrase he had learned on a trip to Canada meaning "where I am at."

The war against Spain, it is now recognized, was as much a media creation as an act to defend a helpless people against a ruthless dictatorship. Early on the morning of February 16, 1898, William Randolph Hearst, still a bachelor, was awakened by his butler, George Thompson. Thompson had just taken a phone call from the *Journal* office. They were desperate to tell the boss of important news that had just come in. Phoning back, Hearst would later recount, he was told: "The battleship *Maine* has been blown up in Havana Harbor." Assured that the story was on the front page along with "the other big news," Hearst blustered, "There is not any other big news, spread the story all over the page. This means war."

4. Marching to a Ragtime Tune

DESTRUCTION OF THE WARSHIP MAINE WAS THE WORK OF AN ENEMY, Hearst's *New York Journal* headlined the next day. Its front page featured a large drawing of the *Maine*, anchored just feet from a Spanish mine. Hearst offered a fifty thousand dollar reward for proof of Spanish treachery and began a drive to build a memorial to the ship and its crew. He invented a card game called War With Spain and offered to personally transport a delegation of senators and congressmen to conduct an on-scene investigation. The *Journal* urged the formation of a regiment of athletes, led by heavyweight champions James J. Corbett and Bob Fitzsimmons. "Think of a regiment composed of magnificent men of this ilk!" The circulation of its two daily editions soared past the million mark.

Frederic Remington also received a telephone call on the fateful morning of the sinking of the *Maine*. When a friend phoned to break the news, he responded brusquely, "Ring off!" Within seconds, Remington had put in a call to *Harper's* in New York. His offer to cover the coming war was quickly accepted.

The battle of San Juan Hill proved to be the most costly engagement in Cuba, with twelve hundred American and nearly six hundred Spanish casualties. Teddy Roosevelt and his Rough Riders faced withering fire from the Spanish defenders. Their victory was uncertain until they were reinforced by the black Tenth Cavalry.

Frederic Remington's few days in Cuba left him ill and despondent. He fought with his fellow correspondents, wandered about the hills unsure of where he was going, and suffered from a severe cold and fever. He spent the night after the battle of San Juan Ridge haunted by images of the bodies he'd seen scattered about the hills. In this, he was not much different than most, except that he was able to get a bed on the steamer *Olivette*, which had been converted to a hospital ship, and sail back to Florida.

The war wound down quickly after American soldiers moved on to take Santiago, and soon after, Havana. Spain sued for peace on July 26. The Treaty of Paris, signed on December 10, 1898, granted independence to Cuba and turned over the Spanish colonies of Puerto Rico, Guam and the Philippines to the United States.

The American occupation of the Philippines brought on the same type of guerilla resistance the Spanish had faced in Cuba. The island nation had already declared its independence and it took a force of eleven thousand U.S. troops to put down the insurgents. It was not until 1916, with

PART I — Breaking All the Rules

Artist Frederic Remington watched black soldiers march through Tampa, Florida, to the Ragtime tune "There'll Be a Hot Time in the Old Town Tonight," then followed Teddy Roosevelt's Rough Riders to Cuba. His painting *Charge of the Rough Riders* helped establish Roosevelt's heroic role in the Spanish-American War (Remington Museum, Ogdensburg, N.Y.).

the granting of self-government and a promise of independence — ultimately achieved at the end of World War II — that the last chapter in the Spanish-American war would come to a close.

Teddy Roosevelt's Rough Riders returned from the Spanish-American War as heroes. When they camped in the fall of 1898 at Montauk, Long Island, his regiment presented him with a bronze cast of the *Bronco Buster*, the sculpture Remington had made in Roosevelt's honor. "It was the most appropriate gift the Regiment could possibly have given me," Roosevelt wired Remington. "I have long looked hungrily at that bronze but to have it come to me in this precise way seemed almost too good." As president, Roosevelt would many times invite Remington to the White House but the artist would always find an excuse not to go there.

Frederic Remington returned to Cuba to do a series of illustrated articles on the American occupation forces for *Collier's Weekly*. At Roosevelt's request, he created his famous painting *Charge of the Rough Riders* for *Scribner's* magazine.* The heroic positioning of Roosevelt as the charg-

---

*Scribner's incorrectly captioned the painting as at San Juan Hill; it actually depicts the charge up El Poso Hill.

4. Marching to a Ragtime Tune

ing officer on horseback leading a thin line of attackers helped him to become governor of New York and, in 1900, the vice-presidential candidate on the Republican ticket under William McKinley. The assassination of McKinley the next year put Roosevelt in the White House.

On Wednesday, December 22, 1909, Remington took the train into New York to pick up a painting from a bank vault. Back home that afternoon, he went to bed feeling unwell.

Dr. Robert Abbe was called in from the city. After examining Remington he decided on an emergency appendectomy operation. Remington had to be laid out on the kitchen table and given ether for the surgery. "Cut 'er loose, Doc," Remington told him. Dr. Abbe found the appendix had burst and peritonitis had begun. Remington rallied briefly at Christmas but the poison continued to spread. He died on Boxing Day at age forty-eight. The doctors later concluded that a strong laxative Remington had taken on his return from New York caused his appendix to rupture.

Remington's art and his writing added a legacy of daring creativity and rugged independence to the Ragtime era. America would forever after worship the challenge of the frontier — be it the physical frontier of rivers and mountains of the Old West, the psychic "New Frontier" of mid–twentieth century politics, or the still to be conquered frontier of space. Like Scott Joplin, Remington's life and work helped changed the culture of the world.

Part II

The Music Makers Play Main Street: The 1900s

Ragtime music filled the vaudeville theaters of North America and Europe, and the mirthful tunes of New York's Tin Pan Alley were heard by millions in the first decade of the twentieth century. The Wright brothers flew the first plane, Reginald Fessenden made the first radio broadcast, and Henry Ford built his first car. In 1900, ninety-six auto deaths were recorded, but lynchings took one hundred and fifteen lives.

Artistic interpretation broadened to include such new forms as cubism, futurism, and expressionism. France's Impressionist masters were dying off, and American names like Charles Russell began to challenge the art world.

Ragtime music moved into its second stage, as composers like Irving Berlin borrowed from the genre to write popular hits. Ragtime became the safest bet for every theatrical impresario. Thousands of musical skits were turned out every year to satisfy the crowds that filled vaudeville houses in America and music halls in Britain.

But it was the arrival of motion pictures that brought the music makers to every main street in the land. The tunes of the Ragtime era, rendered by piano players and sometimes full orchestras, added the vital element of sound to the silent cinema. New music had to be written to provide a complete theatrical experience for the audiences watching moving images in the nickelodeons — and later the ornate movie palaces — that reigned as the new temples of popular culture.

When people tired of the herky-jerky pace of the silent films, they turned either to their player pianos or their phonograph machines to listen the new tunes. And when they tired of those, they bought or borrowed

PART II — The Music Makers Play Main Street

books — by the millions — and devoured the works of writers like Joseph Conrad, Jack London, Upton Sinclair, H.G. Wells and Edith Wharton. These authors wrote with the raw taste of reality in their mouths, giving readers a sense of life and the world they'd never known before.

With America's victory over Spain, the United States was well on its way to becoming a world power. Britain's secretary of state Joseph Chamberlain welcomed the U.S. "as a colonizing nation animated by the same love of justice as ourselves." Britain's Imperial poet, Rudyard Kipling, chimed in by passing the torch of empire to Washington:

> Take up the White Man's burden —
> And reap his old reward:
> The blame of those ye better,
> The hate of those ye guard.

Still unsettled was how the new economy of technology would change human and cultural values. In this fateful first decade of the century, the battle would be joined between robber barons and muckrakers, between reformers and politicians, and between artists and the church.

5

Writing in Ragtime

> Meet Me in St. Louis ... Meet Me at the Fair.
> — *Bill Murray*

The new century broke over the United States on a wave of confidence that America was destined to become, if it was not already, the greatest country in the world. Scott Joplin was by now an established musician, which is the occupation by which he identified himself in the 1900 U.S. census. He was living with the Michael Seethaler family at 801 Washington Street in St. Louis, but was listed as the head of a household that included Belle Jones, occupation laundress.

Scott and Belle were in a conjugal relationship, but it is not known if they were married at that time or if they ever actually wed. She was the widowed sister-in-law of Scott Hayden, a young composer with whom Joplin had collaborated in writing four rags. Clearly, Hayden was Joplin's protégé, as the quartet of pieces they wrote, "Sunflower Slow Drag," "Something Doing," "Felicity Rag" and "Kismet Rag," all bear the stamp of Joplin's style. Hayden composed but one number entirely by himself, "Pear Blossoms."

The St. Louis in which the Joplins settled claimed the title of "the Gateway City," it being the historic jumping off point for the wagon trains that had taken settlers further west. Others from Joplin's circle in Sedalia soon followed him to St. Louis. Scott Hayden moved into the same row of houses as the Joplins, but later went on to Chicago where he died of tuberculosis, still the scourge of great numbers of people. Others from Sedalia who came to St. Louis on frequent visits included Otis Saunders, by now touring with McCabe's Mistrel Troupe as a singer, and Arthur Marshall, the one-time teenage runaway.

PART II — The Music Makers Play Main Street

Joplin was drawn to St. Louis partly as a result of an encounter with a prominent member of the city's cultural circle, Alfred Ernst. A German, like most of the city's cultural leaders, Ernst was director of the St. Louis Choral Symphony Society. He somehow did not share the music establishment's disdain for Ragtime, and instead found in Joplin the makings of a musical genius. The *St. Louis Globe-Democrat* of February 28, 1901, reported:

> Director Alfred Ernst believes that he has discovered, in Scott Joplin of Sedalia, a negro, an extraordinary genius as a composer of ragtime music.
>
> So deeply is Mr. Ernst impressed with the ability of the Sedalian that he intends to take with him to Germany next summer copies of Joplin's work with a view to educating the dignified disciples of Wagner, Liszt, Mendelssohn and other European masters of music into an appreciation of the real American ragtime melodies....
>
> "I am deeply interested in this man," said Mr. Ernst. "He is young and undoubtedly has a fine future. With proper cultivation, I believe, his talent will develop into positive genius....
>
> "The work Joplin has done in ragtime is so original, so distinctly individual, and so melodious withal, that I am led to believe he can do something fine in the composition of a higher class when he shall have been instructed in theory and harmony."

The account played up the likelihood that Ernst would soon be taking Joplin to Europe, where he would introduce Ragtime to that continent. There is no indication the trip ever came off. Nor is it known whether Ernst followed through on his promise to teach Joplin to add the theory and harmony to his music that would move him to a "higher class."

In St. Louis, the Joplins took a second-floor flat in a row house at 2658-A Morgan Town road. It was in a black neighborhood that also happened to house the city's red light district, the infamous Chesnut Valley, about a mile from the Mississippi River and near the Union Railroad station. Because he was earning royalties from "Maple Leaf Rag" and was teaching several students, Scott played less often at the eleven saloons and several brothels operated by blacks.

By now, Tom Turpin had his own saloon, the Rosebud, where the three-hundred-pound barkeeper had his piano hoisted onto concrete blocks so that he could play standing up. Joplin played there occasionally, or at Babe Connors' place, the Castle Club, an establishment that boasted the most beautiful black women in St. Louis.

5. Writing in Ragtime

The Castle Club was also the hangout for many of their pimps, whose fine suits and diamond jewelry — paid for by their girls — made them equally elegant. It was said that you could hear Joplin's latest compositions at Babe Connors' before he had set them down on paper. The many Ragtime players who circulated through the houses would look for Joplin, who was coming to be regarded as something of a mentor for young Ragtimers, while awaiting their turn for jobs, as described in Edward Berlin's *King of Ragtime*:

> The players would get together in the clubs and wait for calls from the houses. They were not competitive, tried to help each other. They would learn a song and try to teach the ones that didn't know it. There was plenty of work. They could pick up money any time they wanted to, were satisfied with $2 or $3 at a time. You could always get free lunches.

Joplin's output now became quite prodigious. His publisher, John Stark, had also moved to St. Louis and the new House of Classic Rags published more of his works, including "Ragtime Dance," a ballet in which a singer-narrator tells the story of an African American ball like those held at the clubs Joplin had frequented in Sedalia. Joplin also wrote and dedicated a march number, "March Majestic," to James Lacey, bandmaster in the leading black minstrel company of the day, the Georgia Minstrels. Other Joplin works from this time include "Peacherine Rag," a number with a simple opening strain that went on to finish with a flourish, "Swipesy Cake Walk" (with Arthur Marshall), "A Breeze from Alabama," and "Easy Winners." For unknown reasons, Joplin published that piece himself in 1903 rather than entrust it to Stark.

These sold well, but, ironically, a single Joplin piece published in 1902 would enjoy vastly greater success. "The Entertainer" met with instant praise, becoming an overnight favorite of black minstrel companies. The first known public comment on "The Entertainer" is from Monroe Rosenfield, a part-time music journalist, songwriter, and sometimes bum-check passer. He also limped, the result of an escape from a second storey window when he was caught trying to pass a rubber check.

Writing in the *St. Louis Globe-Democrat* in June 1903, Rosie called the new Joplin tune "a jingling work of a very original character embracing various strains of a retentive character, which set the foot in spontaneous action and leave an indelible imprint upon the tympanum." During

PART II — The Music Makers Play Main Street

the interview, Rosie had demonstrated his impression of its liveliness by hopping on his game leg. "You look like old Jim Crow," responded Joplin. "That's what they call 'buck jumping' down in the hollow where the jook joint is."

It wasn't often that Joplin broke into Negro vernacular. Because he had received more schooling than most blacks of his generation, he well understood the need to make a favorable impression on whites and always spoke carefully in their company. "He is attractive socially because of the refinement of his speech," Rosenfeld remarked.

Publisher Stark joined the praise for "The Entertainer." He hailed it for having "actually throttled and silenced the senseless knockers of Ragtime — so-called — and forced its way into the halls of the highest culture and refinement." Stark's brave assertion would be finally fulfilled sixty years later when "The Entertainer" would provide the theme music of the movie *The Sting*. The film would spark a Ragtime revival, a marrying of "a jaunty, sweetly tinkling piano soundtrack to a sepia-tinted world of shirtwaists and bowler hats."

Joplin's St. Louis compositions brought him a steady income. He and Belle were able to purchase a 13-room house at 2117 Lucas Street, which they used as a boardinghouse as well as a music studio. Unhappily, a small shadow of what would eventually be Joplin's undoing began to flicker in the background: his fingers no longer responded quite as he wished when he played his more difficult compositions. Joplin was feeling the first effects of the syphilis that was to ultimately take his life. Whether he had contracted the disease as an adult or suffered from it as a congenital infection — as some would argue — made little difference; Joplin would live and die with its consequences.

Life with Belle also was becoming difficult. Another of his protégés, Arthur Marshall, would later recall that tension and disagreements with Belle "greatly disturbed" Joplin's concentration on his musical career. Two forces appeared to be at work here: Belle had little interest in music and wished only for the comfort and steady routine of a placid household. In addition to carrying most of the load in running the boardinghouse, she had to put up with a man who played the piano incessantly, entertained frequently, and sometimes fell into grumpy moods. On top of that, Joplin tried to teach Belle to play the violin. The attempt produced yet more marital discord. She had no desire to learn the instrument. Then she got pregnant. The child, a girl born in 1903, lived only a few months. Belle was grief-stricken, suffering what in another time would be diagnosed as post-partum depression.

Joplin had natural leadership abilities that enabled him to influence the young musicians who gathered around him. In addition to helping Scott Hayden and Arthur Marshall, and later Joseph Lamb, Joplin did everything he could to bring along another young composer, Louis Chauvin. For a time, Chauvin flowered under Joplin's tutelage, writing beautiful melodies that might have put him in the forefront of Ragtime composers. Together, the two men created their memorable tune "Heliotrope Bouquet." Sadly, Chauvin preferred a dissolute life to a disciplined one. He became addicted to opium, hung out in brothels, and eventually contracted syphilis. He died from it at the age of twenty-four.

Yet another Midwesterner who benefited from Joplin's willingness to share his knowledge and contacts was James Scott, who grew up in the Missouri towns of Neosho and Carthage. He started out doing menial labor in a music store but soon demonstrated his ability to compose catchy tunes. His first published composition, in 1903, was "A Summer Breeze." He probably visited the St. Louis World's Fair, as it provided the inspiration for his 1904 number, "On the Pike," its title referring to the Fair's midway. Joplin introduced James Scott to John Stark (in 1906), who made a great success of the first Scott piece he was to publish, "Frog Legs Rag." Scott would go on to become, with Joplin and Lamb, one of the three most celebrated composers of the Ragtime era. He published thirty-eight compositions before his death in 1938.

Theodore Roosevelt became president following the assassination of William McKinley at the Buffalo World's Fair in 1901. Roosevelt turned out to be the first president since Abraham Lincoln to exhibit a genuine public empathy with American blacks. He set the pattern very early in his presidency by inviting Booker T. Washington, the most prominent Negro leader of the day, to dinner, on October 16, 1901. It was a private meal, attended only by Roosevelt's wife, Edith, and a friend from Colorado. The president saw it as natural and proper to have Washington as a dinner guest. Roosevelt was quite comfortable in accepting an inferior role for blacks in American life, but unlike the majority of people at the time, he

Part II — The Music Makers Play Main Street

saw this as a temporary condition that would be overcome by education and social evolution.

African Americans rejoiced, none more so than Scott Joplin, when it was announced the next morning that Washington had been received at the White House. The fact that Washington advocated accommodation to laws that permitted discrimination and segregation did little to still white outrage. Hate mail poured in and death threats flooded the White House. In Joplin's adopted hometown, the *Sentinel* splashed on its front page a poem entitled "Niggers in the White House." In its final line, a black marries the president's daughter. The inspiration for this invective might have been drawn in part from the fact that Roosevelt's daughter Alice often asked the Marine band to play "Maple Leaf Rag" at White House parties.

Joplin, like other young Negro men who admired Roosevelt, found it easy to relate to the president's physical prowess. Roosevelt's physical strength and his determination to struggle to achieve were important elements of his image and his approach to life. He spoke of these qualities in a speech he gave in Chicago in 1899 when he was still governor of New York:

> I wish to preach, not the doctrine of ignoble ease, but the doctrine of the strenuous life, the life of toil and effort, of labor and strife; to preach that highest form of success which comes not to the man who desires mere easy peace, but to the man who does not shrink from danger, from hardship, or from bitter toil, and who out of these wins the splendid ultimate triumph.

The speech was widely reported and it was published as the title essay in a collection called *The Strenuous Life: Essays and Addresses*. The theme caught the public's imagination. Joplin seized on it as a way of saluting Roosevelt. He quickly composed "The Strenuous Life: A Ragtime Two-Step," and told friends it was his response to Roosevelt's courageous reception of Booker T. Washington. More ambitiously, Joplin decided to honor Roosevelt by writing an opera in Ragtime based on the White House dinner. He filed for a copyright on *A Guest of Honor* early in 1903 and hired a cast of thirty singers and dancers. Joplin rehearsed them at the Crawford Theatre in St. Louis, staged one public performance, and in mid-summer set out on a tour of towns through the Midwestern states.

Joplin's optimism for his new project shines through in the item he arranged to have published in the *Indianapolis Freeman*:

5. Writing in Ragtime

President Theodore Roosevelt's invitation to black leader Booker T. Washington to dine at the White House in 1901 enraged many whites. As a result of the invitation, Scott Joplin and other African Americans became enamored of the president. Joplin wrote "The Strenuous Life: A Ragtime Two-Step" in Roosevelt's honor (Theodore Roosevelt Collection, Harvard College Library).

Scott Joplin, who is termed "the king of rag-time writers," has written a rag-time opera entitled "A Guest of Honor," which is a most complete and unique collection of words and music produced by any Negro writer. The opera is in two acts, something on the order of grand opera, with not a piece of music in the whole opera other than that from the pen of Scott Joplin,

PART II — The Music Makers Play Main Street

in which he introduces a lot of big numbers, some of which are "The Dude's Parade," "Patriotic Patrol" and many others which go on to make it grand.

The tour ended in debacle. While the cast was performing *A Guest of Honor* at the Opera House in Springfield, Illinois, on the night of September 2, a thief, probably a member of the company, stole the box office receipts. Joplin struggled on to fill other dates, but by the time his company reached Pittsburgh, Kansas, he had run out of money and was unable to meet the payroll. All of his possessions, including the musical score of the opera, were confiscated by the boardinghouse that had put up the cast. The troupe disbanded. The music has never since been seen or heard.

At loose ends after the collapse of his opera company, Joplin wandered to Chicago for a few months, returned to Sedalia, and then went to Arkansas to visit relatives. There, his wandering eye fell on a beautiful nineteen-year-old woman, Freddie Alexander. By now, his marriage to Belle had reached the breaking point. They agreed to separate. Joplin's former student, Arthur Marshall, had bought their boardinghouse. Joplin took a room in the home of his friend Tom Turpin.

By now enamored of the youthful Freddie, Scott dedicated his next work, "The Chrysanthemum," to her. He called it an "Afro-American Intermezzo," yet another attempt to lift his music above everyday Ragtime.

At the 1904 St. Louis World's Fair, Joplin introduced "Cascades," a tune he had written especially for the occasion. The music celebrated the Fair's most notable attraction, a waterfall cascading down several flights of outdoor stairs. He was not, however, allowed to perform within the fairgrounds. Joplin and other black musicians, like T.C. Bennett, whose "St. Louis Tickle" became the hit of the fair, were relegated to playing on the Pike, an avenue just outside the grounds of Forest Park.

St. Louis was the fourth largest city in the United States in 1904, although in many respects its best days as the gateway city to the West were already behind it. The Fair commemorated the centennial of the Louisiana Purchase (a year late), but the favorable attention it brought the city was overshadowed by the latest exposé of muckraking journalist Lincoln Steffans. In his *McClure's* magazine series, *The Shame of the Cities*, Steffans gave St. Louis a prominent ranking in the roll of dishonored municipalities where machine politics, graft and corruption were endemic.

Founded by French voyageurs, built up by immigrants, especially Germans — including Adolphus Busch, who started selling pasteurized

5. Writing in Ragtime

"Cascades," a tune Scott Joplin wrote for the 1904 St. Louis World's Fair, celebrated its most notable attraction, a waterfall that cascaded down several flights of outdoor stairs (The Lilly Library, Indiana University).

beer in glass bottles in 1876 — the favorite son of St. Louis was Mark Twain. He built his literary career on boyhood adventures along the Mississippi River, but never reconciled himself to the fact that when river water came through a faucet, it was "too thick to drink and too thin to plow." St. Louis finally got clear water when a new filtration plant was opened a month before the Fair.

The third of the modern Olympic Games was also held in St. Louis in 1904, an experience from which the Games almost never recovered. The Fair had brought in thousands of aboriginals from around the world to show "the development of man" and many of them were recruited for "Anthropology Days," a sideshow to the Olympics. Their failure to perform well in events for which they had no training "scientifically" demonstrated their inferiority.

Joplin, like other African Americans, saw little of the inside of the Fair. By now, he had sufficiently distanced himself from Belle — or had gotten a divorce, if they were ever married — and was ready to take up the new love of his life. He left St. Louis and on June 14, at the home of Freddie's parents in Little Rock, he and Freddie were married.

The newlyweds decided to travel the Midwest, with Joplin giving concerts along the way. By the time they reached Sedalia, Freddie was suffering from a steadily worsening cold. Local papers reported her illness in August and on September 10, 1904, a mere ten weeks after their wedding, Freddie died of pneumonia. The black *Conservator* newspaper published her obituary and noted:

> Thru-out her sickness, Mr. Joplin has administered to her every want. Her sister, Miss Lovie Alexander, arrived here last Thursday [from Little Rock] and was constantly at her side until death separated them.

Heartbroken and alone, Scott Joplin descended into a world of drift and depression. He picked up odd jobs playing piano in St. Louis and Chicago and managed to write several new works. They included two marches, "Antoinette" and "Rosebud March," and the unsyncopated "Binks' Waltz." He struggled to finish three rags, "Leola," "Eugenia," and one of his best compositions, "Bethena." His health now slowly declining, it would take a move to New York City, where he would enter into a new life around the burgeoning Tin Pan Alley of the metropolis, for Joplin to regain his position of eminence.

5. Writing in Ragtime

Joplin's insistence on being where the action was reflected the determination of artists, writers and musicians to exploit the new opportunities of the Ragtime era. Growing cities brought people together and modern communications technology made it possible to reach audiences more rapidly and in greater numbers than ever before. Authors of the day were no longer limited to crowds of a few hundred middle-class, well-educated citizens. So they began to write for everyone, in Britain, on the continent of Europe, and in North America.

A reader of a British newspaper, looking one day for an account of an anarchist bomb throwing in London, would have found it quickly:

> Ah, here it is! Bomb in Greenwich Park. There isn't much so far. Effects of explosion felt as far as Romney Road and Park Place. Enormous hole in the ground under a tree filled with smashed roots and broken branches. All around fragments of a man's body blown to pieces. That's all. The rest's mere newspaper gup. No doubt a wicked attempt to blow up the Observatory, they say.

The words were spoken by Mr. Vladimir, the First Secretary of the Russian Embassy, in an account of a fictitious event. The story appeared not in any newspaper, but in one of the most remarkable books of the time, *The Secret Agent*, by Joseph Conrad.

Conrad's ironic novel about a Soho porn shopkeeper engaged by the Russian embassy in a mission to discredit anti-czarist anarchists, was published in 1907. He used it to dissect the minds and motives of the anarchist plotters who seemed for a time to threaten law and order in all the countries of the Western world. Conrad's secret agent, Mr. Verloc, had instructions to infiltrate an anarchist cell in London and foment provocative schemes that would encourage British sympathy for the czar's resistance to rebellion.

Joseph Conrad's work bridged the gap between the classical literary tradition of such writers as Charles Dickens and Fyodor Dostoevsky and the emerging school of high modernist writing exemplified by James Joyce, Rudyard Kipling, Jack London, Emile Zola, and H.G. Wells. He was the only author writing in a language other than his native tongue. The casual ease with which his characters spoke English sprang from an upbringing in which his father, a Polish translator of English and French, instilled in him a love of literature.

PART II — The Music Makers Play Main Street

Among British writers, Herbert George Wells offered the most original ideas about the shaping of the modern world during and after the Ragtime era. He was born of a working class family and spent his youth as a shop assistant in the London suburb of Bromley. Wells attended night school to qualify for London University, where he earned a first-class degree in zoology. Wells discerned the shape of the emerging late Modernist world by his study of science, for which he was a passionate advocate. He was also a humanist, and this quality shows up in all his work.

Wells made his debut as a novelist with *The Time Machine* in 1895, a parody of the class-ridden structure of English life, as well as a foreboding forecast of a frightening future. He followed its success with such science fiction classics as *The Island of Dr. Moreau* (1896), *The Invisible Man* (1897) and *The War of the Worlds* (1898). The plot of this book would be used by Orsen Welles in 1938 to frighten millions of Americans into believing the earth was being invaded by Martians. Wells foresaw *The First Men on the Moon* (1901) and presented a prophetic description of the coming age of aerial conflict in *The War in the Air* (1908). His 1914 novel, *The World Set Free*, postulated a bomb that would use radioactive decay to set off a series of explosions.

In the United States, a new crop of writers was replacing the romantic novelists of the post–Civil War period. Mark Twain had fallen on hard times, and declared bankruptcy in 1895, the year his daughter Susy died of meningitis. Her loss helped confirm his atheism; "Faith is believing something you know ain't true," he famously remarked. Jack London, a self-taught roustabout and 1890s seaman from California, was a survivor of the Klondike Gold Rush. He launched his writing career on the wave of popular magazines that emerged when the new printing technologies became available. He wrote about his experiences in the Yukon, selling "An Odyssey of the North" to the first issue of the *Atlantic Monthly*. A short story for the *Saturday Evening Post*, "The Call of the Wild," made London both famous and controversial after it was published as a book in 1903.

Most of what London wrote came from having experienced the crude lifestyles of workers, lumberjacks and the poor in early twentieth-century America and Britain. He wrote despairingly of slum conditions in England in *The People of the Abyss*, and in 1907 he published *The Road*, a collection of stories about his hobo days. He bought into the great idea of the

5. Writing in Ragtime

time, socialism, but it was a socialism that sprang from the pain he'd witnessed in lumber camps and hobo jungles, not from the salons of the Bloomsbury set. He would write more than fifty books before his death by suicide at the age of forty.

Upton Sinclair was another rebellious writer who tackled the social issues of the Ragtime era. His novel *The Jungle*, published in 1905, exposed degrading working and living conditions in the U.S. meat packing industry. After a public uproar, Congress passed the Meat Inspection Act that set out minimum standards of working conditions and legislated humane treatment of animals. A Southerner from a comfortable background, Sinclair's 1903 work, *Manassas*, was about the Civil War. He was a frequent advocate of socialist views, and he would twice run for governor of California, without success.

Less controversial was Edith Wharton, who wrote many novels, beginning with the *House of Mirth* in 1905. It became a best seller, fascinating the American upper class — from which she sprang — with her humorous criticisms of its manners and foibles. After a tumultuous affair with the bisexual William Morton Fullerton who reportedly also had affairs with the Ranee of Sarawak and an opera singer reputed to be mistress of the King of Portugal, Wharton divided her time between America and France. During her lifetime, she crossed the Atlantic sixty-six times. She was living on the fashionable Rue de Varenne in Paris when war broke out in 1914. Her *Age of Innocence* won the Pulitzer Prize in 1920. She died in France in 1937.

The ideas of Wharton and other Ragtime-era writers broke sharply with the past by presenting environments where the possibilities of technology would override the conventions of traditional culture. Wharton realized that the aristocracy had no real understanding of the consequences their lifestyle held for the rest of society. In contrast, Joseph Conrad saw a world threatened by terrorism; H.G. Wells envisioned a universe out of control from the unintended consequences of science. Jack London and Upton Sinclair railed, as had Charles Dickens and earlier authors, against the injustices of their time and both offered new alternatives to rescue the impoverished from their fates. Others, writing in the new magazines and newspapers of mass culture that cheap printing had spawned, would take up the call for the rights of labor, the vote for women, and the protection of children on farms and in factories.

Part II — The Music Makers Play Main Street

Their writings often acted as the spearhead of a counterculture movement that challenged the accepted norms of society politically, socially and sexually. Some, like Jack London and Ragtime composer Scott Joplin, sprang from the edges of society. Uneducated and poor, they launched their assaults on conventional culture without friends or influence. In every case, their unique view of the world would soon come to be appreciated and shared by millions of people.

6

Tin Pan Alley and All That Jazz
Footloose in "Black Bohemia"

Carrying a single small suitcase, Scott Joplin left the train at Grand Central Station and mingled with the crowds in this busiest part of New York City. The long ride from St. Louis had tired him out, but he was filled with excitement at finally having reached the city where he was sure he could fulfill his dream of transforming Ragtime into a serious and respected musical form. As he walked the busy streets, he might have made inquiries as to how to reach the office of his old friend and publisher, John Stark. He knew Stark could be found somewhere in Tin Pan Alley, the name given to the burgeoning neighborhood where composers, lyricists and publishers were creating the popular music industry of the Ragtime era.

New York on this summer day of 1907 glistened with the freshness of its big new terminals — Grand Central Station, built to serve Cornelius Vanderbilt's New York Central Railroad; the Hudson Terminal, bringing trains from New Jersey through a tunnel under the Hudson River; and a new network of subways, opened just three years before. The subways served Manhattan Island, the Bronx and Brooklyn, but it is likely that Joplin was anxious to see the sights of the city, as well as save the cost of the subway fare. For these reasons, he would probably have chosen to walk.

Making his way down Lexington Avenue to his publisher's office at 127 East 23rd Street, Joplin might have wondered about the many little children that could be seen hurrying along with bundles under their arms or on their backs. He might have heard snatches of conversation wafting toward him: "Mom needs ten more yards of cotton. I've got to sew another

PART II — The Music Makers Play Main Street

dozen blouses today." Had he asked, Joplin would have learned they were among the thousands of children who worked at home, ungoverned by labor laws of any kind, in such trades as sewing clothes and making artificial flowers.

There is no doubt that John Stark was pleased to see his most profitable composer. He introduced Joplin to the local sights and took him for drinks at Ike Hines' Professional Club on West 27th Street, a favorite watering hole for the habitués of Tin Pan Alley, the stretch of West 28th Street between Sixth Avenue and Broadway. Ike's place filled the main floor of a forbidding-looking, three-storey brownstone house, and Stark had to ring the bell on the front stoop to gain entrance. Inside, Joplin found two large rooms, a luxuriously carpeted front parlor where small tables and chairs were arranged in front of windows draped with lace curtains, and a back room with a piano and ample space for dancing. On the walls were posters of leading black Americans, ranging from Frederick Douglas to Jack Johnson. The lack of a liquor license was no deterrent to visitors, who often included well-dressed white couples out for a night of sightseeing or slumming. "They have an open floor here," Stark explained to Scott. "Anyone can come in and practice or try out their latest stuff."

When Joplin arrived in New York in 1907, Ragtime music was still a novelty, although Ben Harney, the white vaudeville pianist and singer, had won celebrity status at Tony Pastor's Fourteenth Street Theater in 1896 as "the Inventor of Ragtime." Harney delighted audiences by playing semiclassical pieces in a normal manner, then "ragging" the same numbers in a syncopated style.

Joplin found a room at the Rosalline, a popular boardinghouse for musicians two blocks up from Ike's. Conveniently, it had a piano in its big front room. Joplin liked to make the rounds of the bars and brothels of the Tenderloin district where he was living, and he stopped in almost daily at the music shops of Tin Pan Alley. His favorite stops probably included the William Banks Café on West 37th, Walter Herbert's café on West 39th, and the favorite gathering spot of everyone who was anyone in the black music world, the Café Wilkins at 253 West 35th Street. Its black owner, Barron Wilkins, employed both Eubie Blake and the brother of James Reese Europe, John Reese, as pianists.

Occasionally, Joplin would have ventured north to the theater district, but he preferred to loaf around the "Black Bohemia" section where

6. Tin Pan Alley and All That Jazz

African Americans felt most at home. The neighborhood offered a friendly alternative to the segregationist practices of most of the New York's restaurants and theaters.*

Sometimes, on an evening stroll, Joplin would wander up Broadway toward the "White Light District"—the future Great White Way—where crowds gathered to enjoy the bright new electric lighting, attend plays and take in vaudeville acts. Only rarely did he make it as far as 53rd Street and the pricey dining room of the Marshall Hotel, where, when he could afford it, he rubbed shoulders with the top entertainers of the day.

When Joplin was not earning spending money by playing piano in the saloons, he hung around John Stark's office and music store. Stark could be counted on to keep Joplin in funds with the royalty payments due him for "Maple Leaf Rag" and other tunes.

One day shortly after his arrival, Joplin would have confided to Stark his main reason for coming to New York. He would have reminded Stark of his determination to raise the level of Ragtime and he might have mentioned the opera he'd written, to honor Teddy Roosevelt, *A Guest of Honor*. Of course, the tour had been a disaster and the music had been lost. But the fact he'd written it, Joplin would have argued, proved his musical versatility. Now he had a bigger plan: to write a grand opera that would encompass the essence of the African American experience. Would Stark help him raise money to finish the writing and launch the production?

It is unlikely Stark rejected Joplin's plea outright, as he would have had no wish to offend his best-selling composer. But neither did he have any interest in putting hard-earned funds into such a questionable project. The two probably discussed the opera on many occasions. Eventually, Joplin had to give up on his hope of gaining support from his publisher. Joplin's realization that he'd have to see through his dream of a Ragtime opera on his own marked the beginning of a long and slow decline, and eventual rupture, in the relationship between the two men.

As Stark had done for a time back in St. Louis, he sold both the sheet music of the day's popular tunes and the instruments needed to play them. It was in Stark's shop that Joplin met and befriended Joseph F. Lamb, a

---

*The Tenderloin extended roughly from 23rd to 42nd streets and was given its name, according to legend, by police captain Alexander C. Williams on his transfer there in 1876. Ample graft would mean he would soon be eating tenderloin, he is said to have told his friends. African Americans did not move north into Harlem until after 1900.

PART II — The Music Makers Play Main Street

young white musician from New Jersey who was to become one of Ragtime's greatest composers. Lamb had already written several rags, including "Wolper Rag," named for the hotel in Berlin, Ontario (now Kitchener), the town where he had been sent to attend a Catholic college. One suspects young Lamb had spent more time at the Wolper than at his intended school, St. Jerome's University.

An introduction by Mrs. Stark led to a quick friendship and Lamb became a frequent visitor to Joplin's boardinghouse. One evening, Lamb played several of his compositions, including one called "Sensation." Another boarder, surprised that a white man could write Ragtime, commented, "That's a regular Negro rag." Joplin convinced Stark to publish it, and suggested that adding his own name to the sheet music as its arranger would help sales. It earned Lamb twenty-five dollars up front, and another twenty-five after the sale of the first thousand copies. Lamb would go on to write thirty-six piano rags and seventeen piano novelties before his death in 1960.

Joplin continued to turn out new compositions, adding to the forty he'd already had published. Five more followed in his first two years in New York, but Joplin's real aim was to move Ragtime to a higher level of musical attainment. He was determined to give precise instruction to the students he was teaching and the followers who bought his compositions. When Joplin published "The Nonpareil" (None to Equal), with Uncle Sam pictured on the cover, he appended this stern notation: "Do not play this piece fast. It is never right to play Ragtime fast." Joplin added to this advice in *School of Ragtime*, a manual he published himself in 1908 and sold through John Stark. He made clear his views in the preface:

> What is scurrilously called ragtime is an invention that is here to stay. That is now conceded by all classes of musicians. That all publications masquerading under the name of ragtime are not the genuine article will be better known when these exercises are studied. That real ragtime of the higher class is rather difficult to play is a painful truth which most pianists have discovered. Syncopations are no indication of light or trashy music, and to shy bricks at "hateful ragtime" no longer passes for musical culture. To assist amateurs in giving the "Joplin Rags" that weird and intoxicating effect intended by the composer is the object of this work.

Joplin obviously had a sharp sense for good timing, because the interest in learning Ragtime was at its peak. An entrepreneur, Axel Chris-

6. Tin Pan Alley and All That Jazz

tiansen, had opened a chain of schools that enjoyed a booming business in teaching people how to play Ragtime music.

New works flowed thick and fast, sometimes too much for Stark to handle. Joplin found another publisher, the Jos. W. Stern Company, to put out "Searchlight Rag" and "Gladiolus Rag" within sixty days of each other in the summer of 1907.

In a frenzy of composition in 1907, Scott Joplin turned to a new publisher, the Jos. W. Stern Company, to put out his "Gladiolus Rag." Joplin's early years in New York saw him at the peak of his musical output (The Lilly Library, Indiana University).

PART II — The Music Makers Play Main Street

Joplin was always aware of happenings around him, not just among his friends in Tin Pan Alley or in other musical circles, but also in the larger world. He followed with keen interest the Panic of 1907, the latest in a series of financial breakdowns since the Civil War. Like those that came before, this debacle cost many investors their savings and thousands of workers their jobs. Joplin was perceptive enough to recognize that the financial markets passed through distinct cycles that constantly repeated themselves: panic and collapse; confidence that good times would return; fulfillment in their arrival; and finally, carefree days before another panic.

Inspired by the latest crisis, he translated these episodes to music and in 1909 published one of his most memorable compositions, "Wall Street Rag." Its four sections carried titles that evoked the atmosphere of each phase of the financial cycle. He opened the piece with "Panic in Wall Street, Brokers Feeling Melancholy," and followed it with "Good Times Coming," a segment chorded in a happier tone. Its successor, "Good Times Have Come," is filled with lift in its syncopation. The tune's closing section, "Listening to the Strains of Genuine Negro Ragtime, Brokers Forget Their Cares," restores the complacency of prosperity and harkens back to the traditional folk patterns of an earlier time. It was an altogether remarkable performance for someone with little education in financial matters. Ninety years later the Museum of American Financial History would argue that "this rag can be used to introduce a principle that has long been known on Wall Street: panics are generally followed by periods of recovery and stability."

At thirty-nine, Joplin felt he was growing musically as well as emotionally. The time had come to find a new publisher who could earn him greater prestige than either John Stark or the Stern Company. His choice was Seminary Music, a company headed by Ted Snyder, a publisher of decidedly respectable standing. The first Joplin piece published by Seminary was "Sugar Cane," followed by "Pine Apple Rag." Seminary also was the publisher of *Wall Street Rag*, which became as an immediate success. In 1910 the Zonophone Orchestra made a recording of it. It and "Maple Leaf Rag" were the only two Joplin tunes recorded during his lifetime.

Seminary also put out Joplin's "Paragon Rag," which he dedicated to the Colored Vaudeville Benevolent Association, of which he was a keen and active member. Another Joplin piece published by Seminary was "Solace," a syncopated tango subtitled "A Mexican Serenade." Despite

6. Tin Pan Alley and All That Jazz

these successes, Joplin was never entirely comfortable with Seminary. He returned to John Stark to have his next composition, "Stoptime Rag," published in 1910. The effects of his relationship with Seminary were not to end so cleanly, as would become evident later on.

While Ragtime originated in the black honky-tonks of the Midwest and the Mississippi valley and jazz was first heard in the Storyville district of New Orleans, modern popular music came of age in New York's Tin Pan Alley. This was where musicians gathered to write, rehearse and transcribe onto early phonograph records an eclectic variety of tunes. In time, it became the generic term for all publishers of popular American music regardless of their location.

According to one legend, the peripatetic songwriter and part-time newspaperman Monroe Rosenfeld coined the term on a visit to Harry von Tilzer, a publisher who had his office at 42 West 28th Street. Tilzer had written the music for "A Bird in a Gilded Cage," one of the first million copy sellers, but he still worked on an old piano that Rosie thought had a "tinny" sound. Combined with the racket from pianos being played in publisher's demo rooms along the street — he could hear them through open windows as he loafed down the block — it must indeed have sounded like pounding on tin pans.

Perhaps only Rosenfeld heard the cacophony of the street as such an orchestration. For all that, Rosenfeld's article in the *New York Herald* was the first to identify the district as Tin Pan Alley and the first to establish it as the place where popular music was being produced. In the next forty years, Tin Pan Alley delivered a succession of songs remarkable for their endurance in American culture. For verve and vivacity, none of them quite matched the nonsensical composition "I'm Certainly Living a Ragtime Life," by Robert S. Roberts and Gene Jefferson:

> I got a ragtime dog and a ragtime cat
> A ragtime piano in my ragtime flat
> Wear ragtime clothes, from hats to shoes
> I read a paper called the Ragtime News
> Got ragtime habits and I talk that way
> I sleep in ragtime and I rag all day
> Got ragtime troubles with my ragtime wife
> I'm certainly living a ragtime life.

PART II — The Music Makers Play Main Street

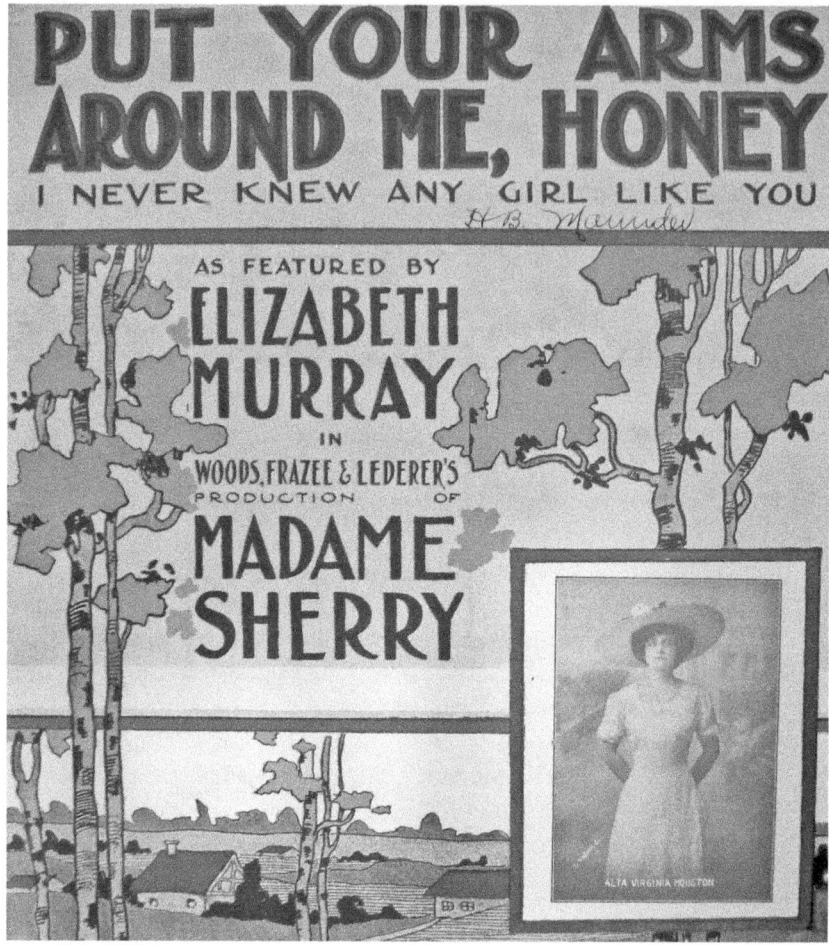

Harry von Tilzer, one of Tin Pan Alley's most successful publishers, was also a prolific songwriter. His wrote such tunes as "Put Your Arms Around Me, Honey," which made Elizabeth Murray a star in *Madame Sherry*. He had a million copy best seller in "A Bird in a Gilded Cage."

Music publishing, like most things, went through revolutionary change in the Ragtime era. Tin Pan Alley became the economic engine of the music publishing business at a time when sales of individual copies of sheet music were the mainstay of the industry, and it gained momentum as sales of song sheets gave way to recorded music.

6. Tin Pan Alley and All That Jazz

The greatest inventor of the time was Thomas Edison. His invention of the gramophone machine in 1887 brought the new age of sound to life, first on wax cylinders and then on phonograph records that spun at seventy-eight revolutions per minute. Mass production of records became feasible in 1901, when the German inventor Emile Berliner licensed the Victor Talking Machine Company to manufacture his gramophone machine that used shellacked discs. But it was player piano rolls that brought the sounds of the Ragtime era out of the cabaret and into the parlor.

The greatest tenor of the time was Enrico Caruso. In 1904, the great Italian singer made the first of his two hundred and sixty recordings. It was due to him that Victor and its Victrola player became synonymous with records. During these formative years a plethora of recording technologies competed for dominance. The U.S. Patent Office faced a variety of conflicting claims — a harbinger of the battle over industry standards that would emerge decades later with the invention of videocassette recorders and DVD players.

Carrie Jacobs Bond was a widow who tired of having her songs rejected. She started her own publishing firm in the bedroom of her Chicago boardinghouse. In doing so, she was emulating the example of hundreds of writer/publishers whose faith drove them to part with the cash to have a printer run off copies of their creations. Almost all were men, as women were less likely to be the writer of a song than the inspiration for one. Carrie Bond was a successful exception and her most successful song, "I Love You Truly," would become a standard at weddings.

A more typical Alleyman was Charles K. Harris, who started out as an eighteen-year-old music-struck kid in Milwaukee, Wisconsin. He haunted the town's music halls to catch visiting stars such as James Aldrich Libby, "the peerless baritone." Determined to be both a composer and a publisher, Harris rented a small office for seven dollars and fifty cents a month, and it was there he inveigled Harris to read one of his songs, "After the Ball." The boy had been inspired by the sight of a lonely suitor apparently abandoned by his love, and he could not dismiss from his mind the words "Many a heart is aching after the ball."

The words must have struck a chord in Libby's heart, too. For five hundred dollars and a share of royalties, he added it to his show, *A Trip to Chinatown*. Orders poured in as Libby toured from city to city, reaching the two million mark within a few months. A Boston chain ordered seventy-five thousand copies. Harris moved to New York in 1903 and was soon a leading figure in Tin Pan Alley. He would write in his autobiography that "After the Ball" earned him ten million dollars.

A Detroit businessman, Jerome H. Remick, became the biggest publisher of Ragtime music, although one of his most profitable songs was a non–Ragtime number, the Indian intermezzo "Hiawatha," for which he paid ten thousand dollars. His music was in such demand that he bought his own printing plant in 1907.

By now the waltz was being tested in popularity by new varieties of tunes, not the least of which was Ragtime. Tearjerkers like "After the Ball" gave way to happier tunes with livelier refrains, such as "In the Good Old Summertime," "Meet Me in St. Louis, Louis," and "Let Me Call You Sweetheart." Along with rags came the cakewalk, blues, animal songs (bunny hug, turkey trot, etc.) and novelty songs, all making up the vast new repertoire of modern popular music. In 1902, Hughie Cannon's Ragtime song, "Bill Bailey, Won't You Please Come Home," became a hit. It told of a man who had been kicked out of his house, returned home to his wife, and then disappeared again.* Newspapers became strong promoters of popular music, with the *New York World*, among others, stuffing their fat Sunday issues with sheet music supplements.

Singers from the African country of Dahomey (today's Benin) had been a big hit at the Chicago World's Fair. Ten years later, *In Dahomey*, a musical celebrating the traditions of the country from which it was thought many African Americans had come, became a hit on Broadway. The first full-length musical written and composed by blacks, it opened February 18, 1903, at the New York Theater. The troupe played in London, England, for seven months, where a command performance was given for King Edward VII. Other black hits followed, especially *Shoo-Fly Regiment*, a racist musical that catered to white perceptions of black incompetence.

A mainstream vaudeville act that Scott Joplin probably saw in 1907, *School Boys and Girls*, became a smash hit on the strength of its title tune, "School Days." It was the work of two of the era's greatest writers, Gus Edwards and Will Cobb. The stage lineup included such future stars as Eddie Cantor, George Jessel, Walter Winchell, Earl Carroll, Groucho Marx, Ray Bolger and Sally Rand.

---

*In the 1960s, Bill Bailey was said to have been John F. Kennedy's favorite song.

6. Tin Pan Alley and All That Jazz

Harry von Tilzer, by then one of the great publishers of the era, had begun his career as a foot soldier in the music industry—a song plugger whose job it was to gain exposure for the new numbers that were pouring out of Tin Pan Alley. Long before Tilzer's own "Bird in a Gilded Cage" became a million-selling hit, he had mastered the technique of setting up an audience for a new song. The strategy worked especially well in promoting another of his hits, "Take Me Out to the Ball Game." Von Tilzer wrote about it in a 1902 issue of *Metropolitan* magazine:

> Maybe I go to the swellest theatre in town Monday night and sit in a lower box, in my evening clothes, like an ordinary patron. During the daytime I will have fixed the orchestra and had the music run over. Between the first and second act, perhaps, I stand up in my box and begin singing. The audience is startled. A policeman comes in and walks toward the box. About the time the policeman is where he can be seen by all the audience, I step out onto the stage in front of the curtain and begin the chorus, with the orchestra playing and the audience that is now onto the game, clapping so hard it almost blisters its hands.

Around eighteen hundred Ragtime pieces were published between 1900 and 1910, the first full decade of Tin Pan Alley's prominence. More than one hundred songs each sold a million or more copies. Sheet music was bought from soda counters, furniture stores and bowling alleys, and in variety and department stores. Agents scoured the main streets of every town in North America to place their publishers' works.

Department stores, especially in the large cities, were the biggest sellers of sheet music. The Seigel, Cooper & Company store at 18th Street and Sixth Avenue ("Meet Me at the Fountain") and Macy's at 34th Street and Broadway were the most popular New York outlets. All went well between the retailers and publishers until Macy's decided in August, 1907—again, about the time of Scott Joplin's arrival—to cut its sheet music price to six cents a copy. Joplin's publisher, John Stark, knew that if Macy's won the price war, the price of sheet music would be forever debased, and with it his ability to earn a profit and pay his writers. Led by Charles Harris, five publishers created American Music Stores, Inc., to cut out Macy's. They signed fifty stores to contracts requiring them to sell their tunes at fifty cents per copy.

To really beat Macy's, however, they would have to outdo the big store for low prices. On October 12, 1907, the new cartel announced its best-selling numbers would go on sale at one cent per copy at Rothenberg & Company on West 14th Street. Shoppers were sent to Macy's, where they brandished the big store's ads claiming "We will not be undersold," and demanded similar bargains. By the end of the day, Macy's had abandoned the price war. Even so, John Stark's account books showed his average wholesale price for "Maple Leaf Rag" was still only eight and one-half cents, leaving a small margin after paying Joplin his penny per copy royalty.

The brightest stars on Broadway in the Ragtime era were not performers, but composers and impresarios like George M. Cohan and Florenz Ziegfeld, whose names ring today as among the greatest entertainers of all time. Cohan was not actually born on the Fourth of July as he liked to say — he had arrived a day earlier, in the year 1878 — but it was his patriotic tunes that brought him his greatest fame. His parents were touring vaudevillians and he made his stage debut while still an infant.

Before Cohan, musical comedy used settings from exotic locales such as the mythical Ruritania. Cohan Americanized all that, and his twenty-two musicals, most of which he would star in himself, and his thirteen dramatic plays all exemplified American themes, capturing the steadily developing spirit of nationalism in the United States. His production of *Little Johnny Jones* in 1903 had not one but three timeless hits: "The Yankee Doodle Boy," "Give My Regards to Broadway," and "Life's a Funny Proposition."

In 1906, Cohan's production *Forty-Five Minutes from Broadway* featured such songs as "Mary's a Grand Old Name" and "Stand Up and Fight Like Hell." That number shocked audiences for using "hell" and "damn." Hits followed Cohan through that decade and into the teens, including "You're a Grand Old Flag" (changed from "You're a Grand Old Rag" when Cohan was warned the title might be seen as an insult) and "Over There," the great soldier song of both world wars. President Woodrow Wilson would call the song "a genuine inspiration to all American manhood." On Cohan's death in 1942, President Franklin Delano Roosevelt would lament that "a beloved figure is lost to our national life."

Florenz Ziegfeld added the most glamorous of all elements to the stage — pretty girls, and lots of them. His Ziegfeld Follies premiered on

6. Tin Pan Alley and All That Jazz

July 8, 1907, featuring as many as fifty girls on stage clad in lavish and sexually enticing costumes. The son of a German immigrant father who ran a music college in Chicago, "Flo" first found success in New York by mounting a production to compete with the elaborate "reviews" that the Schubert brothers were staging at the Hippodrome Theater.

Ziegfeld convinced the owners of the rival New York Theater to allow him to stage a continental "revue" called *The Follies* on the theater's roof, known as the Jardin de Paris. It was a sell-out. The next year, the Ziegfeld girls appeared as mosquitoes flying from the New Jersey marshes into the Holland Tunnel, then under construction. The classic "Shine On, Harvest Moon" was introduced by Nora Bayes, and the Follies became firmly fixed as an annual event of the Ragtime era. Ziegfeld's greatest star, Fanny Brice, a one-time burlesque singer, took audiences by storm with her inimitable renderings of Yiddish-type songs such as "Second Hand Rose."

Respectable families enjoyed vaudeville and the new silent nickelodeons, but there was still a moral bias against dancing in public. That was about to change, with restaurants such as Louis Martin's Café de l'Opéra on Broadway introducing dancing at dinnertime.

The faint stirrings of something newer still than Ragtime first began to be heard and felt in early twentieth-century New Orleans. The city, an exotic locale since its founding in 1718 on the east bank of the Mississippi River, had a deep cultural history even before the Territory of Louisiana was handed over to the United States by the French in 1803. African musical celebrations were a fixture of "Congo Square" as late as the 1830s. The melodies and rhythms of the slave population found their way into the growing white community, especially through the works of Creole composer Louis Moreau Gottschalk.

By the end of the nineteenth century, New Orleans had earned a unique place in the pantheon of New World cities. Its musicians absorbed the new Ragtime themes coming out of the Mississippi and Missouri river towns further north. In an attempt to achieve respectability, New Orleans in 1898 adopted a motion by Alderman Sidney Story to restrict prostitution to a thirty-eight-block red light district adjoining Canal Street.

The district quickly became known as Storyville and attracted, as well as two thousand prostitutes, musicians who could keep brothel patrons entertained for longer than the few minutes a customer might spend with a girl. Ragtime became the standard musical fare but even it had to be given a New Orleans twist. Small musical groups began to improvise countermelodies to the chords of syncopated songs. This freer rhythmic improvisation also borrowed from the blues harp style of harmonica playing, combining blues and Ragtime into something that would become known first as jass, and later as jazz.

There are a thousand explanations for the origin of the word jazz, the melodious new fruit that the tree of popular music was about to bear. Did it come from Jasbo Brown, a Chicago trombone player whose fans would demand, "More Jasbo. More, Jas, more"? Or from a New Orleans band of the early 1900s — Razz's Band? If so, how did Razz become Jazz? Perhaps its true origin is in the plantation expression, "Jazz her up!" — a call to pep up a performance. That was certainly what the immortal Buddy Bolden, the king of New Orleans trumpeters in the early 1900s, did when his group took over a bandstand. Bolden is considered by many to be the true father of jazz, although it is uncertain that he ever used the term himself. "Before Bolden New Orleans music was still Ragtime, after him it definitely became jazz," says music historian Dave Radlauer.

Bolden's unique strength was his ability to improvise a passage when he had forgotten the original notes — a unique feature of traditional jazz. His listeners were said to enjoy his embellishments more than the original score. Bolden's career crashed before jazz became a recognized music form; he was committed to a Louisiana insane asylum in 1906, apparently suffering from schizophrenia. He would spend the rest of his life there and died in 1931.

7

They All Played Ragtime
Scott Joplin and Irving Berlin — A Case of Plagiarism?

By their nature, musicians are social creatures who crave the company of their fellows and thrive on the admiration of their followers. Scott Joplin was no exception and, even in failing health, he attended industry events and sought play dates wherever he could find them. On one of his occasional out-of-town trips, Joplin traveled to Washington where he met Lottie Stokes, a thirty-three-year-old woman with whom he would begin his third and most serious long-time relationship. It is not known exactly where or how this meeting took place. They were probably introduced when Lottie attended a party given for Scott.

The absence of records for this time period leaves both the date and the status of their relationship somewhat in doubt. What is not in doubt is that Lottie's deep love for Scott and her admiration for him as a musician eased the pain of a disease eating away at his mind and body. She also helped him confront the implacable barriers to his recognition as a great American composer.

It may have been as early as 1907, or as late as 1913, that the two met. Scott's visit to Washington could have been part of a tour that advertised a cast of twenty singers and dancers — ten of them girls — for a three-night run at the Washington Park Theater in Bayonne, New Jersey, in July of that year. The advertisement in the *Bayonne Evening Review* refers to "Scott Joplin's Merry Makers in a Real Slow Drag." This was a number from *Treemonisha*, the uncompleted opera he was working on. Again, there is maddening uncertainty about yet another detail of Joplin's life, as no review of the show was ever published. Depending on Joplin's health at the time, the tour may even have been cancelled.

Lottie would always claim they had met years earlier. According to her, they were together as man and wife from 1907. It is difficult to disprove this claim. However, it is known that Joplin was enumerated as a widower in the U.S. census of April 15, 1910. His address was that of a boardinghouse at 128 West 29th Street known to accommodate only men, but this does not mean he may not have been in a relationship with Lottie.

Little is known of Lottie's early life before she became a staunch champion of Scott Joplin. She told Brun Campbell, Joplin's young friend from Sedalia, only that they were married in New York on June 18, 1910. As Joplin seldom acted impulsively, it is probable that if they were wed on that date they must have known each other for some time.

Black musicians, their wives and girlfriends came in the hundreds to Madison Square Garden on January 28, 1910, for the first annual fundraiser of the Colored Vaudeville Benevolent Association. The festivities began with a vaudeville show but the evening soon gave way to what the guests had really come for: ballroom dancing to the tunes of black Ragtime musicians.

Scott Joplin was a strong supporter of the Benevolent Association and he had served on the arrangements committee that had organized the evening. Lottie, assuming she was with him, must have worried whether the strain of the occasion would deepen the symptoms of syphilis that were now revealing themselves in his mood swings and his difficulties with finger and body coordination.

As Joplin was the featured composer, the orchestra played five of his dance tunes, more than those of any other contributor. Included were "Paragon Rag," "Binks' Waltz," and "Gladiolus Rag." A selection of Joplin melodies was offered in a *Scott Joplin Schottische*. It was the kind of evening Joplin would have most enjoyed. It is likely that he and Lottie were dressed in their finest outfits; they would have made a handsome couple as they made several turns around the dance floor. Perhaps they sat out a few of the numbers, as Scott's nervous system, besieged by the continuing attacks of his disease, could have made it difficult for him to follow the music.

Joplin's old friend Tom Turpin showed up in New York around this time and promptly joined the CVBA, no doubt at Scott's urging. He brought exciting news from St. Louis: Tom's brother Charles had been elected as district constable, the first black man ever elected to office in that city. His victory was upheld by a local court only after recounts and challenges.

By now, perhaps, Joplin's publisher was losing interest in his work. The cover of *Euphonic Sounds* carried an old photo of Joplin that had been crudely retouched to put him in more up-to-date clothes. The picture was out of focus, and the effort to conceal Joplin's old fashioned, stiff collar was clearly visible. Why had a new picture not been taken?

Scott and Lottie are sure to have watched with interest the fortunes of the newly formed all-black Clef Club Orchestra, an outfit put together by James Reese Europe that consisted of more than one hundred performers. On May 2, 1912, the group played to the first nonsegregated audience at Carnegie Hall, but no Joplin compositions were on the program. Europe and Joplin held a common view that Ragtime represented a natural musical expression of African Americans. While Joplin sought to elevate Ragtime, Europe chose to pursue a broader body of music, perhaps because he saw this as a better strategy for gaining the respect of white audiences.

Throughout his struggles in New York, Joplin had the constant support of his younger brother Robert. They were only a year apart and although sometimes separated by jobs that Robert took in different cities, they were together whenever possible. As youths in Sedalia, the brothers had likely lived with a relative, Julius Walter Joplin. Robert held various jobs as a young man, including that of railway porter, but he too longed to make a name for himself in the music world. He and Scott had become especially close after the death of their brother Will in 1902. The same cannot be said with certainty of Scott's relationship with his older brother Monroe, who worked for a time as a railway porter, nor of another sibling, Josie. Scott is known to have kept in touch with his youngest sister, Myrtle, or Johnny.

A fine musician, Robert also had a beautiful baritone voice. He had sung in Scott's Texas Medley Quartette and had played the lead in his brother's *Ragtime Dance* production back in 1899. Robert later directed his own production of it. It is known that he lived for a time in Omaha, Nebraska, where he gained some recognition as a "professional cakewalker," being adept at performing the intricate steps of the cakewalk dance. He was in Chicago in 1905 when Scott came for a visit following the break-up of his marriage with Belle. The youngest of Scott's siblings, Johnny, is also known to have lived there.

Robert showed himself to be unusually versatile, both as a performer and as a showman. He led a company of sixteen performers in *Cuban Belle* in 1906, playing in cities from Indianapolis to Boston. He sang, danced, composed, and also went on stage in comedy roles. These gave Robert an all around understanding of the theatrical business, enabling him to win jobs as the stage director at white-owned but black-focused theatres in Knoxville, Tennessee, Columbus, Ohio, and Louisville, Kentucky. But he spent most of his life as a traveling vaudeville singer and dancer. He performed frequently in New York and had two songs published, "Since Emancipation Day" and "If I Were with My Thoughts To-Night, Sweetheart, I'd Be with You."

All the world was becoming a single stage, and the new genres of music such as Ragtime and the tango that were emerging in North and South America also found ready favor in Europe. Even so, traditional composers continued to command a fierce loyalty from their audiences, none more so than the German Richard Strauss. His one-act opera based on Oscar Wilde's daring and oft-banned *Salomé*, depicting the offering of the head of John the Baptist, confirmed his ability to create a sensation of the moment. More important, the six near-operatic works that Strauss composed in the 1890s helped Germany maintain its supremacy in classical music and established Strauss as a hallowed figure in the cultural life of the country. Listeners trembled as they absorbed Strauss creations such as *Don Juan*, *Also Sprach Zarathustra*, and *Don Quixote*.

Almost alone, Strauss enabled Berlin to preserve its favored position in the cultural firmament. Let Paris have its painters, London its high society and New York its *nouveau riche*: Germany had produced the world's musical masters, with Wagner at the pinnacle of them all. Strauss' achievement in mastering the new technique of the "symphonic poem" assured him a hallowed position in the ranks of Germanic Kultur. His brilliant

7. They All Played Ragtime

interpretation of *Also Sprach Zarathustra*, projecting into the musical sphere the inspired thoughts of Germany's most advanced philosopher, Friedrich Nietzche, gave Germans spasms of delight.

In the New World, a new musical form born in Argentina quickly became a symbol of the tempestuous Latin character. Expressed in dance as the tango, it sprang from a milieu similar to Ragtime—the world of rootless immigrants, mostly lonely men, who streamed into Argentina late in the nineteenth century, many gravitating toward the waterfront bars and houses of ill repute, the *quilombos* of Buenos Aires. It borrowed from the relentless rhythms that the African slaves beat on their drums (known as tan-go); the popular music of the pampas (flatlands) known as the *milonga*, which combined Indian rhythms with the music of early Spanish colonists; and other influences, including Latin. The name may have come from the Latin word for touch, *tangere*:

> Originally, the tango dance developed as an "acting out" of the relationship between the prostitute and her pimp. These tango songs and dances had no lyrics, were often highly improvised, and were generally regarded as obscene. Further, the early tangos not only represented a kind of sexual choreography, but often a duel, a man-to-man combat between challengers for the favors of a woman, that usually ended in the symbolic death of an opponent. Sexual and evil forces were equally celebrated in this ritual. During this time, the wailing melancholy of the *bandoneon* (an accordion-like instrument imported to Argentina from Germany in 1886) became a mainstay of tango music.

It took the blessing of Europe to win the tango acceptance in polite society. Even Raymond Poincaré, the president of France, became entranced with the Latin tempo and insisted, "Of course, we'll dance the tango." After Paris heard the music and learned the dance, the proper *portenos* of Buenos Aires made the tango their own. Argentine musicians like Roberto Firpo refined piano and double bass rhythms and combined them with the counter melodies of the *bandoneon* and the violin to create the dramatic tempos that carried the tango to the cabarets and theatres of the wealthy. With the addition of lyrics, a cadre of singers became popular idols.

Carlos Gardel was the most popular of the tango artists and his records were still in demand decades after his death. The fact that two so distinctive elements of popular culture, Ragtime and the tango, would arise at about the same time and from similar backgrounds, each to have such enduring strengths, exemplified the cultural freedom and artistic energy found among even the most economically distressed of the New World. Both would be taken up by the literati of Europe as amusing expressions of avant garde culture.

As Tin Pan Alley gathered strength as a giant music promotion machine, the feeling grew in the United States that it was time to throw off German and Viennese influences in favor of the indigenous American sounds of Ragtime, blues and the incipient birth of jazz, or jass as it was still spelled.

By now, more white musicians were composing as well as playing Ragtime. A white Chicago band leader, William H. Krell, had published "Mississippi Rag" in 1897. Joseph Lamb, the white New Jersey composer who learned the style from Joplin, wrote many hits, including "American Beauty," "Ragtime Nightingale," and "Cleopatra." Ragtime's intrusion on respectable white culture was well advanced by mid-decade when a 1905 testimonial dinner honoring Thomas Edison for his having coined "hello" as the preferred telephone greeting, saw him serenaded with "Hello my baby, hello my honey, hello my Ragtime girl." The next year, the annual meeting of Republican party women heard "frivolous music of the Ragtime brand while luncheon was being served."

Acceptance of Ragtime came finally and completely with the release of the hit Irving Berlin wrote in 1910, "Alexander's Ragtime Band." Berlin, arguably the greatest American composer of the twentieth century, integrated Ragtime styles with the classic march tempo of traditional American music when he commanded listeners to:

> Come on and hear
> Alexander's Ragtime Band,
> Come on and hear,
> It's the best band in the land!
> They can play a bugle call
> Like you never heard before,
> So natural that you want to go to war
> That's just the bestest band what am,
> Honey Lamb.

7. They All Played Ragtime

As a young tenor, Izzy Baline began singing from the balcony of Tony Pastor's Fourteenth Street Theater. At the age of eighteen, Izzy was a singing waiter at the disreputable Pelham Café ("Nigger Mike's") on the edge of Chinatown. In 1907, with Scott Joplin in town, the young Baline — only later would he take the name Irving Berlin — collaborated with "Nick" Nicholson in his first published song, "Marie from Sunny Italy." The proprietor, Mike, fired him at about this time over some imagined insult or other disagreement.

Izzy moved on to slightly more respectable locations. At one, Jimmy Kelly's café on Union Square, the publishing impresario Ted Snyder heard Berlin sing. Snyder hired Berlin for a division of his Seminary Publishing Company, paying him twenty-five dollars a week as a staff lyricist. He eventually made Berlin a partner in his firm when it changed its name to Waterson & Snyder, reflecting Henry Waterson's rise to senior partner status.

For the next ten years, most of Berlin's output was in Ragtime, earning him the title "King of Ragtime Songs." He even gave Ragtime tunes an ethnic twist, producing such numbers as "Sweet Marie," "Make a Ragtime Dance with Me" (Italian) and "Yiddle on Your Fiddle Play Some Ragtime" (Jewish). "Syncopation is the soul of every American life," he declared. "Pure unadulterated Ragtime is the best heart-raiser and worry banisher that I know."

The public first heard "Alexander's Ragtime Band" in a Broadway show, *The Merry Whirl*, that fell flat and closed after a few performances. Just the same, the tune began to catch on around the country, promoted by Waterson & Snyder's seventy-five song pluggers.

Then there were the rumors that Berlin had not written all his Ragtime songs himself. It was said he had hired black composers to create several of his works, an accusation understood to have been believed by even Henry Waterson. Berlin heatedly denied the charge.

More seriously, Scott Joplin complained that Berlin had lifted the song's verse from one of his compositions. The *New York Dramatic Mirror* went so far as to report that "Berlin has one dream.... I shall write an opera completely in Ragtime." Whether he borrowed from Joplin, the immediate success of "Alexander's Ragtime Band" (which was more a song *about* Ragtime than a Ragtime piece itself) nevertheless demolished most mainstream criticism.

PART II — The Music Makers Play Main Street

It is entirely likely that Scott Joplin and Irvin Berlin met sometime during Joplin's association with the firm, or later when Berlin was working there. Judging by sketchy accounts, their relationship was always somewhat prickly. Perhaps Berlin did engage Joplin to write a few bars for him, or possibly he paid Scott to tutor him in Ragtime styles.

Several sources lend credence to speculation that Berlin may have borrowed from Joplin with permission or taken advantage of his declining health to acquire work, either through ignorance or plagiarism.

Joplin biographer Edward Berlin repeats Lottie Joplin's accusation that Scott had to rewrite his finale for *Treemonisha*, the opera on which he was working at the time, because "someone stole the theme and made it into a popular song." That number, "A Real Slow Drag," has the cast "marching onward" in a characteristically African American slow rag. Edward Berlin also recounts an allegation by Joplin's friend Sam Patterson, who worked for Watson & Snyder, that Joplin had offered a song to Irving Berlin, only to have it rejected. When "Alexander's Ragtime Band" came out, Joplin said, "That's my tune."

Despite controversy over its authorship, "Alexander's Ragtime Band" firmly implanted Berlin as the greatest songwriter of the twentieth century. He would write more popular songs than anyone else, yet he could not read a note of music, could not write music, and could play the piano in only one key, F sharp.

Even the great composer Igor Stravinsky borrowed from the Ragtime genre; his 1917 work *Ragtime* featured a European folk instrument played with hammers to represent the clattering of a honky-tonk piano. Back in the United States, a woman composer, May Aufderheide, emerged as the most important of a number of female writers of Ragtime.

Haunting refrains of Ragtime's grudging acceptance would be heard in the 1950s when the new black-inspired musical genre of rhythm and blues would become known to white audiences as rock 'n' roll, and again two decades and more further on, when the rhyming lyrics known as rap would emerge from the black environs of New York City. They would all provide, in their sounds and in their influence on popular culture, a musical fulfillment to the promise of the Ragtime era. Our love affair with the new music of mass culture could be no longer denied. At first it was ignored. Then it was criticized and condemned. In the end, everyone played Ragtime.

8

The Girls of Ragtime and the Cult of Celebrity
Murder, Passion and Honor

When Scott Joplin published his "Wall Street Rag" in 1909, a different type of Ragtime music was being performed in vaudeville theaters and music halls in North America and Britain. Crowds that had once filled saloons to hear classic piano Ragtime now were outnumbered by those who came out to marvel at silent films, laugh at comedy acts, and applaud song and dance teams. They were hearing a new kind of Ragtime where the lyrics were as important as the syncopation and the customers were as enthralled by pretty girls who flounced across the stage in frilly pink lace dresses as they were by the tunes they heard.

Evelyn Nesbit was still in her teens when she moved to New York from Pittsburgh with her mother and brother and landed a spot as one of the Spanish dancers in *Floradora*. In London, a beauteous singer and actress born Violet Annie Markham took the stage name of Daisy Markham and began to attract attention for her performances in the city's West End theaters and in New York. These Ragtime girls came from simple backgrounds, but both were destined to shock and shame high society. They became symbols of a new type of public personality: the celebrity — famous not for achievements in the high arts of politics or science, but for scandalous behavior. Evelyn would be trapped in the intrigue of a sensational murder trial involving passion, jealously and madness. Daisy would be enmeshed in a momentous legal contest pitting honor and romance against privilege and tradition.

This could not have happened without the help of a new kind of

PART II — The Music Makers Play Main Street

media that paid less attention to the pronouncements of industrial tycoons than to cataloging the lives of actors, artists and criminals — the more blatantly shocking their exploits the better. News took on a different form in the Ragtime era; no longer were papers filled with dreary political speeches or magazines with essays of polite literary debate. Education levels had risen to create a mass audience for the printed word. The public hungered for the elemental, not the essential; amusements, crime and scandal, pseudoscience and the new art of the comic — the first comic book (forerunner of today's "graphic novel") was published in 1904 — were the main attractions for millions of readers.

The chief practitioner in Britain of the "new journalism" was Alfred Harmsworth, the future Lord Northcliffe, who turned the *London Daily Mirror*, founded as a "daily newspaper for gentlewomen," into a raucous halfpenny crime sheet filled mainly with pictures.

In the United States, William Randolph Hearst and Joseph Pulitzer brought the popular newspaper into being with their bitter rivalry for the growing masses of New Yorkers who put down their penny a day for Hearst's lurid *Journal* or Pulitzer's slightly more respectable *World*. Hearst had helped foment the Spanish-American War with lurid tales of Spanish intrigue over Cuba. Pulitzer, a more benign press lord, sent his star reporter Nellie Bly into the dark corridors of mental institutes and factories to reveal the abuses perpetrated against inmates and workers alike.

Had Evelyn Nesbit never met Harry Thaw, she would still have ranked as one of the leading celebrities of her time, admired and sought after for her beauty and recognized for her considerable stage skills. Born on Christmas Day 1884, Evelyn grew up poor in Pittsburgh, across town from Beechwood Boulevard and the mansions and leafy streets that the Thaws and the other leading families of the gritty industrial city called home.

Opposite: At 16, Evelyn Nesbit drew crowds of admirers when she became a Floradora Girl on Broadway and began posing for artist Charles Dana Gibson, creator of the Gibson Girls. Evelyn became a central figure in the "trial of the century" when her husband, Harry K. Thaw, murdered her ex-lover, architect Stanford White. She later danced in her own Ragtime show (Photographic History Collection, National Museum of American History, Smithsonian Institution, Neg. #79-11062).

PART II — The Music Makers Play Main Street

In 1900, Evelyn's mother, Elizabeth Nesbit, succumbed to her daughter's pleadings to move to New York. Evelyn quickly found work as an artist's model and was soon posing for Charles Dana Gibson, creator of the famous Gibson Girls. Still only sixteen, Evelyn was hired as one of the "Spanish Dancers" for the popular Broadway show of the *Floradora Sextette*. It was one of the sexiest acts in town, featuring six beautiful girls who paraded on stage in frilly but proper pink lace dresses, joined by six handsome men.

Evelyn's mother would pick her up after every show. It was only after much pleading that she allowed her daughter to join two other dancers in a luncheon date with a "society friend." The "friend" turned out to be Stanford White, the rich, fabulously successfully, and dissolute architect.

White had enticed the showgirls to his secret apartment on West 24th Street, where he provided a lavish lunch in a room decorated in different shades of red, set off by fine paintings, tapestries and heavy red velvet curtains. Evelyn hardly knew what to make of the place, but she was to return many times. It would later be revealed that White — Stanny, she called him — had presented her with a Little Red Riding Hood cloak and had her romp naked on a red velvet swing, kicking her feet and trying to knock aside Japanese parasols hanging from the ceiling. She lost her virginity on the night that White gave her champagne, telling her when she awoke, "Now you belong to me."

The man who would introduce himself by saying "I am Harry Thaw of Pittsburgh" came into Evelyn's life after seeing her perform as a *Floradora* girl. Flowers and notes began to arrive at the stage door, signed by a mysterious "Mr. Monroe." When Evelyn agreed to a girlfriend's urging to join the new admirer for lunch, the stranger revealed himself as none other than the famously rich Harry Thaw. He told Evelyn she was the prettiest girl in New York. He also asked why her mother permitted her to associate with "that beast" Stanford White. Shocked, Evelyn excused herself and left. When she told White of the incident, he laughed it off.

For the next year, Thaw pursued Evelyn while he curried the favor of her mother with gifts and financial support. Soon they became lovers and Evelyn found herself pregnant. After undergoing an "appendicitis" operation she sailed with her mother and Harry to Europe. There, between unpredictable temper tantrums and insatiable — and often perverse — sexual demands, Thaw finally got the truth from Evelyn of her relationship

8. The Girls of Ragtime and the Cult of Celebrity

with White. When they returned to the United States, Thaw convinced the antismut crusader Anthony Comstock to begin an investigation of White's lifestyle. A second trip to Europe in 1904 and a second attack of "appendicitis" set the stage for Harry's mother to enter the scene. She hardly approved of Evelyn, but she did feel that marriage might settle Harry down. One hundred thousand dollars was exchanged, and on April 5, 1905, Evelyn became Mrs. Harry Thaw.

Wedded bliss lasted barely more than a year. Tired of the lonely life of the Thaw estate, Evelyn convinced Harry to take her to New York. Mondays were normally quiet evenings at New York night clubs but this night, June 25, 1906, would be long remembered. The Thaws encountered White twice that evening, first at dinner at the Café Martin, and later at the rooftop nightclub of Madison Square Garden, where the new show *Mamzelle Champagne* was about to open.

As the show they'd come to see neared its end, its leading male singer, Harry Short, was singing a popular tune, "I Could Love a Thousand Girls." Thaw approached White's table, drew a gun from under his overcoat, and fired three times at the architect. White stood briefly, pitched forward, and fell amid a clatter of dishes and a woman's scream. A fireman who had been assigned to the show took the gun from Harry's hand. "He deserved it, and I can prove it," were Thaw's first words. Evelyn threw her arms about him and asked, "Oh, Harry, why did you do it?"

The "trial of the century" that followed was actually two trials. The first ended in a hung jury and the second in Harry's acquittal on the grounds of insanity. He was not to go free, however. On February 1, 1908, still in custody, Thaw was ordered committed to the Matteawan Institute for the criminally insane. He was diagnosed as suffering from chronic paranoic schizophrenia.

Evelyn's fame soared as the press zeroed in on her good looks, her saucy personality, and the obviously fatal charm she'd held for Stanford White. She became the first American celebrity of the twentieth century, serving as both an inspiration and a warning to millions of women. In Canada, a young author clipped a photo of her from a magazine and pasted it on the wall beside her desk. From that day, Lucy Maud Montgomery used Evelyn as the model for the heroine of her book, *Anne of Green Gables*, which would sell in the millions all over the world.

On a sunny Sunday morning, August 18, 1913, a day when security was at a minimum, Harry Thaw escaped from Mattewan. He took a train to Canada but was arrested by a lone policeman shortly after entering the country.

Evelyn had achieved modest success as a Ragtime singer and dancer despite the harassment of moralists who held that her performances were lewd and indecent. Her first silent film, *Redemption*—which would earn its producer two hundred and fifty thousand dollars—had just been released and she'd been a smash hit in *Hullo Ragtime* when it played the Hippodrome in London, England.

As well, she had just opened at the Victoria Theater in New York in Oscar Hammerstein's latest production, and she was scheduled to tour the U.S. and Canada, with a planned opening in Montreal in a few weeks. There were rumors the Canadian authorities might bar her as an undesirable, but with Thaw's escape she had an even bigger worry. Evelyn told police that Harry had threatened to kill her if he ever regained his freedom. She feared that with all his money and connections, he might soon find his way back from Canada to carry out the act.

Thaw's escape brought out even larger crowds for Evelyn's two-a-day performances on the Keith-Albee vaudeville circuit; she drew thirty-seven thousand dollars in one week in Chicago and was celebrated at dinner parties of the emerging film colony in Los Angeles. In Pittsburgh, Harry's mother attempted to have Evelyn's show closed on grounds that Ragtime dances were immodest and immoral. She failed, and the theater audience gave Evelyn a fifteen-minute standing ovation.

The U.S. prosecutor sent to Canada to press for Thaw's return managed to obtain a writ of habeas corpus requiring him to be freed. Three minutes after his release Canadian authorities rearrested Thaw, hustled him to the border and literally pushed him back into the arms of the United States law after ruling him an undesirable alien.

With Thaw again in custody, Evelyn sailed for Europe with her dancing partner, Jack Clifford. They were in Paris on the evening of August 3, 1914, when the First World War broke out. They watched crowds of cheering men and women shouting "*Vive le guerre! A bas les Boches!*" little realizing they were witnessing the end of an era. Before going home, Evelyn managed to lose her purse containing sixty thousand dollars worth of jewelry. There was no need to worry; movie roles and vaudeville dates awaited Evelyn's return to America.

8. The Girls of Ragtime and the Cult of Celebrity

Thaw managed to gain acquittal on a charge of conspiring to escape from Mattewan, and followed that up with yet another legal victory. After deliberating for forty-eight minutes, a jury ruled him sane. He was at last free, having killed a man without mercy, and having spent a fortune in his ten year court battle to save himself from both prison and a mental asylum. He immediately divorced Evelyn, asserting she had committed adultery with a newspaperman friend, John Francis. A crowd of more than a thousand welcomed him home to Pittsburgh.

Evelyn later married her dancing partner, Jack Clifford, and made a dozen films between 1907 and 1922, including *The Unwritten Law: A Thrilling Drama Based on the Thaw-White Tragedy*, in which she played herself. She also operated a series of Prohibition-era speakeasies, all of which would fail, and was next heard of entertaining at a high-priced brothel in Panama. She would publish her autobiography in 1934 and find herself again in the news with the release of the 1955 movie, *The Girl in the Red Velvet Swing*.* Before dying in a Hollywood nursing home in 1966, at the age of eighty-one, it would be said that Evelyn told a reporter, "Stanny was lucky, he died. I lived." She would be remembered as a symbol of the early notoriety of celebrity, a tabloid fixture and possessor of a personality and a face familiar to millions, at a time when the technology of communications was first beginning to shape the new mass culture.

The crowd that filled the British courtroom gasped as it heard the confession of William Bingham Compton, the twenty-eight-year-old marquess of Northampton, lord and master of a vastly rich estate in the English Midlands. The marquess, also known as Lord Northampton, had just inherited one of the highest-ranked titles in British nobility. Along with the title came forty-three thousand acres, two of Britain's most stately country homes, Castle Ashby and Compton Wynates, and some of the priciest properties in Islington, a fashionable district in north-central London.

The circumstances that brought the marquess before Mr. Justice Buckwill of the Court of King's Bench in London had nothing to do with real estate. It was all about love. Spectators in a courtroom "crowded with fashionable women and actresses" were taken aback as the battery of high-

---

*A modest success at the box office, the movie starred Ray Milland as White, with Joan Collins playing Evelyn and Farley Granger cast as Harry Thaw.

priced solicitors defending the marquess readily admitted to his having spurned the beautiful Ragtime actress Daisy Markham. He had dumped her, they conceded, not because he no longer loved her, but because his father had put "an absolute prohibition" on any thought of marrying her. In retaliation, Daisy launched the breach of promise suit that was being heard this day. It was a daring move for a girl from the barely respectable profession of acting.

Daisy Markham had found success as a West End actress, specializing in comedy roles that often made use of Ragtime themes. She had been to New York in 1904 where she played in two short-lived Broadway productions, *Mrs. Gorringe's Necklace* and *The Case of Rebellious Susan*. In 1906 the high society portrait photographer, Alexander Bassano, selected her for one of his most famous pictures. More recently, she had played the lead in *Glad Eye*, a comedy that toured the provinces after success in London. She had even performed at Castle Ashby Park, which is probably when she and the marquess had met.

Daisy Markham's lawsuit represented a considerable challenge to Britain's rigid class structure. It would encourage the newspapers and popular magazines of the day in what was becoming a pursuit of a new cult — a cult of celebrity in which entertainers, sports figures and other larger-than-life heroes would vie for attention with the great statesmen, landed gentry, and corporate bosses who had previously monopolized the pages of the press. The age of the celebrity personality who is celebrated not for achievement but, as the social critic Daniel Boorstin would observe, simply for "well-knownness" was about to begin.

Daisy Markham and the marquess were seated on opposite sides of the courtroom on this day in July 1913. She wore a black silk frock with a white lace collar and a black hat. The two avoided each other's glances. Not a word was exchanged between them. In all the voluminous press accounts published after the trial, never a mention was made of Daisy's pregnancy. The subject was too indelicate to mention.

The marquess was known to his family and friends as Bim, and he looked like a thousand other young Englishmen, with sandy hair, blue eyes, and a ruddy complexion from outdoor activities like riding and fox hunting. Daisy was a dark-haired divorcee with laughing eyes that could turn to embers of fire when she was angered. Born in India, she had been briefly married to a stockbroker's clerk, Harold K. Moss. She was twenty-six,

8. The Girls of Ragtime and the Cult of Celebrity

English Ragtime actress Daisy Markham scandalized British society in 1913 when she sued William Bingham Compton, the 27-year-old Marquess of Northampton, for breach of promise. She won a record settlement of £50,000 after "Bim" admitted his father had put an "absolute prohibition" on their marriage (Bassano, National Portrait Gallery, London).

Bim a year older. She waited patiently for the proceedings to begin, emboldened by the fact her case was being handled by a number of highly respected lawyers, among them Sir Edward Carson, a former Solicitor-General of His Majesty's Government.*

The presence of several dozen of Daisy's friends and fellow actors helped ease the nervousness she felt about having to testify to her year-long affair with the then Earl Compton — the title he had carried while his father still lived. She thought her humiliation and heartbreak was all the fault of the old marquess, Bim's father, William George Spencer Compton. But as today's proceedings would make clear, Bim himself was fully mindful of the danger of marrying below one's class, a reckless course that could risk the breakup of family lands and fortune. Despite the death of the old marquess, Bim still clung to the "very most solemn engagement [given to his father] that he would not pursue his desire to marry" the Ragtime actress.

The chief solicitor for the new marquess was Henry E. Duke, a member of the British Parliament as well as of the English bar, and a man who commanded among the highest fees of the day for his services. He made no effort to deny the facts. The evidence included a damning letter to Daisy, the second that the young Compton had sent her from Castle Ashby in a single, fretful day. It made it only too clear that their tempestuous love affair was finished. There would be no more nights of secret passion at their love nest in Knightsbridge or the other places he had taken her. Daisy's solicitor Sir Edward read the letter to the court in a soft but sonorous tone:

> Dearest Daisy — I must just write you a letter as I am so wretchedly miserable. I want to assure you that I am trying to do the right thing, and though you will perhaps find it difficult now, I am going to ask you to believe that I always have, and do at the present moment, love and respect you more than anyone in this world, and that you are absolutely my ideal of perfect womanhood. But, Daisy, the ways of the world are hard, and I want you to believe that what I am now doing I am doing from a sense of duty, genuinely believing it to be the best for both of us. Darling, I have known it all along. I have tried to smother my reason, to stifle my thoughts for your sake. But when my father talked to me on Friday he only faced me with the same thoughts that I told you of when I first loved you, and which I

---

*Sir Edward had acted for the Marquess of Queensbury when Oscar Wilde went on trial for gross indecency. He had been a fellow student of Wilde's at Trinity-Dublin in the 1870s.

8. The Girls of Ragtime and the Cult of Celebrity

have ever since been trying to suppress. Daisy, you don't know how these so-called "ladies" would treat you, and I really couldn't bear to see you suffering it, and with your sweet sensitive nature it would be torture to you....

Daisy, I want to beg your forgiveness for the way in which I have done it. I was so distracted between my feelings for you and my convictions of what was really best, that I am afraid I wavered in a way that was most unfair to you. I must also apologize for that hurried scrawl that I sent you this morning (it seems ages ago). I am quite mad, Daisy. I feel I have nothing left to live for. Writing that note was killing the last hope of my heart of conquering my reason. I did it in a hurry for fear of changing my mind.... You will always be my ideal and you will always be my beautiful dream.

Your broken-hearted Bim.

Daisy had carefully saved the incriminating letter. It impressed her solicitors to the extent that they were willing to take on her case in the confidence that they could win a favorable settlement. A quick consultation among the solicitors for both sides — and their clients — soon brought the revelation that the marquess was willing to settle fifty thousand pounds — an unheard of sum in matters of this sort — on the young actress. It was an offer she of course could not refuse. The news pleased Sir Edward. There would now be no need, he told Mr. Justice Buckwill, to enter into the sordid details of the case. It was an open and shut case.

There was evidence that Daisy had taken rooms at No. 2 Knightsbridge Chambers in Brompton Road, the fashionable upscale neighborhood that was home to the Harrods department store, adjoining Kensington Gardens. There was no need to discuss what might or might not have gone on there. Mr. Justice Buckwill agreed there should be no doubting the marquess's "warm, deep and sincere affection" for Daisy.

As she had undertaken to accept the settlement that the judge thought had been offered in a "generous spirit," the arrangement would have his fullest approval. The jurors who had been called to hear the case were discharged without having to deliberate the evidence. All costs would be paid by the defendant. It was the largest breach of promise settlement ever recorded in a British court (today worth two million dollars), and it made Daisy Markham a celebrity in the newspapers of both Britain and North America. She would go on to pursue her acting career and would marry her dance partner. Perhaps Daisy was after all the marquess' true love; Bim would marry three times and all his brides would be from his aristocratic circle.

PART II — The Music Makers Play Main Street

Coverage of the case ran to more than a full column in the next day's *Times* of London, headed £50,000 DAMAGES — LORD NORTHAMPTON'S BREACH OF PROMISE. Other British papers picked up the story and in North America the case was widely reported as an example of the strictures still in place in British society. The *New York Times* published Bim's letter to Daisy in full. The *Washington Post* marveled at the fact Daisy had dared to pursue her suit even though the marquess had earlier offered her ten thousand pounds. By persisting, she had enriched herself five times over. The *Philadelphia North American* ran a long essay widely reprinted in other papers: WHAT IS WOMAN'S LOVE WORTH? The Daisy Markham case, it concluded, proved that "a breach of promise suit is nothing more than an attempt to work woman's love down into hard cash. Jilted girls sit down with their lawyers and place value on that love which the villain threw from him as worthless."

For Daisy Markham, her lawsuit conferred celebrity, albeit of an unwelcome kind for her time. After bearing the twins fathered by Bim, she continued to act and sing, appearing in such early English silent films as *Candytuft*, a comedy, and *Ships That Pass in the Night*, a romantic drama based on the novel. She also performed in Paris, but died in comfortable obscurity, unmourned by a press that had gone on to celebrate other, more notorious characters.

PART III

The Dream That Wouldn't Die: The 1910s

The transformation of Ragtime into the stuff of popular musical theater thrust a legion of new personalities onto the cultural scene in the 1910s. Their verve and originality captured the spirit of a time when new attitudes about music, art, science and industry made it seem, for the first time, that everyone could dream, in a world of limitless possibility, of becoming the person each wanted to be.

In the first few years of the decade, Ragtime was being played everywhere — in dance halls that sprang up to occupy new-found leisure time, on the stage in vaudeville and musical revues, on the new phonograph discs that carried sound into parlors and drawing rooms, and as an accompaniment to the silent cinema.

"The history of the Twentieth Century will be written in Ragtime," the *Baltimore Evening Sun* prophesied. In England in 1912, the show business paper *New Era* filled its pages with news of the Ragtime invasion, declaring it "an American product [that] appeals most powerfully to the imagination of the mixture of races that make up the people of the United States and are not shackled, therefore, by musical convention."

Irving Berlin's brand of Ragtime meshed perfectly with the dancing feet of Vernon and Irene Castle, whether on the ballroom floor or in the homes of the doyens of American society. James Reese Europe, the black bandleader who claimed "there never was any such music as Ragtime," feuded with Scott Joplin while playing the very tunes that he denied existed.

The chief players of the Ragtime era all shared the dream. Stage and motion picture performers created a new category of human being — the

PART III — The Dream That Wouldn't Die

celebrity, part real, part invention. Rebels against orthodoxy, like George Bernard Shaw and Pablo Picasso, mounted irresistible challenges to convention. The shapers of new realities, like Madame Curie and Albert Einstein, saw only the future, visible in the unalterable truths of nature.

The censors did their best to prune the delights of sensuality from the cinema, stage and art. The press declared Ragtime dead, then resurrected it when it failed to go away.

It was Scott Joplin's dream to lead the migration of conventional Ragtime to a higher level of musical achievement. His medium of choice was grand opera, and *Treemonisha* was to be the instrument of his destiny. Did Joplin suspect that the Ragtime he had helped conceive would eventually wear on a public that once reveled in its new sounds? Did he abandon Ragtime in his quest to create a new American classical music? Or was he motivated to harness the syncopation that sprang from his soul for the higher mission of liberating his people through the power of education? While some dreamt of things easily obtained, his was the dream that wouldn't die.

9

Dancing in Ragtime

> When a good orchestra plays a "rag"
> one simply has got to move.
> — *Vernon and Irene Castle*

He was tall and thin, clad in immaculate evening dress, bearing a serious face that belied his love of good times. She was tiny and small-boned, with her hair cut short in a bob that revealed a headband on her forehead, both fashion innovations that millions of women would copy. When they came onstage that winter evening of early 1912 in the French musical, *Enfin ... une Revue*, the Paris crowd at first sat transfixed. In a few moments, they were wildly cheering the dancers' effervescent energy, their acrobatic leaps on and off tables, and their faultless footwork. The café-goers had never seen dancing like this. And the music? It was "Alexander's Ragtime Band," and Vernon and Irene Castle could hardly contain their delight at the ecstatic response of their audience.

Their Paris gig lasted two weeks. By the time it was over, Vernon and Irene had no doubt that their future lay in Ragtime dance, either onstage as performers, backstage as entrepreneurs, or on the ballroom floor teaching the art of the Texas Tommy, the grizzly bear, and other variations of the two-step or similar kindred gyrations. Vernon eagerly clipped reviews from the Paris newspapers and sent them to producers back in the States. He addressed his first envelope to their mentor, the Broadway promoter Lew Fields.

Vernon Castle was born William Vernon Blyth on May 2, 1887, into a family of English hotel keepers. When his sister Caroline went on stage and married into an old theatrical family, Vernon learned enough magic tricks to mount an act of his own. In 1907, Lew Fields bought the rights

PART III — The Dream That Wouldn't Die

to *The Girl Behind the Counter,* a British play in which Caroline and her husband, Lawrence Grossmith, had parts. Fields imported the British cast to New York, and Vernon came along for the ride.

Vernon's own theatrical experience had been limited to amateur magic shows, performing sleight-of-hand tricks he'd learned by hanging around magic shows at St. George's Hall in London. In New York, he got bit parts in his sister's productions and picked up the rudiments of dancing during rehearsals. There were no dance schools at the time; performers had to learn from each other or work out their own routines.

Fields, who was just turning forty, soon became a mentor and surrogate father to Vernon. He taught him the rudiments of comic acting and before long Vernon was rivaling his brother-in-law as an onstage comedian. He had sufficient income to escape the drudgery of midtown rooming houses, and moved up to New Rochelle, a tony suburb the proverbial forty-five minutes from Broadway. It was already the home of Thanhouser Film Corporation, a company that would make over a thousand films, and was becoming a gathering place for successful entertainers.

Vernon met Irene Foote, six years younger than he, when he moved into a theatrical boardinghouse in New Rochelle. They first set eyes on each other at the Rowing Club; they were both swimming in Echo Bay and ended sunning themselves on the same float. He was the first actor she'd ever met: "My heart skipped a beat." His Christmas gift to her in 1910 was a proposal of marriage, which Irene immediately accepted. They were married on May 28, 1911. After the closing of the latest Fields production, *The Hen-Pecks,* a roistering comedy about a country hick played by Vernon whose daughter runs off to the city to be married, Vernon sailed with his bride to England for a honeymoon.

Irene couldn't stand Vernon's hometown of Norwich, or his family. She thought her in-laws were a dowdy bunch and that everything she encountered in London was inferior to what she'd been used to in New York. They soon began quarrelling.

It is likely they took in some of the Ragtime shows playing in England, for the American musical invasion reached its peak in the years 1910–1912, with dozens of performers, black and white, playing in London and the provinces. The bible of British show business, the *New Era,* was particularly impressed with the American Ragtimers, a group booked into Finsbury Park Theatre. The performance of its seven men and one woman

9. Dancing in Ragtime

"consists of nothing else but the consecutive rendering of Ragtime songs including the current craze, *Everybody's Doing It Now*. We may be sure that the American Ragtimers have come to stay."

Another Ragtime show, *Octette*, offered "syncopated melodies and eccentric dancing. If we are to have a Ragtime boom the American Octette boys are the ones to produce it." The *New Era* lauded the British music publisher, Bert Feldman for having launched a company specializing in "the great Ragtime craze. Scarcely a year ago he courageously expanded the Ragtime theme — heralded it and pioneered it in Britain — amid ominous shaking of supposedly wise heads."

The popular press also took note of Ragtime. The *Daily Sketch* ran a full-page photo spread over the headline "Ragtime Craze Hits London: Real Hustle Music From America." The *Daily Mail* saw the *Octette* performance as "Hustle set to music, energy chained to a rhythm." The *Daily Telegraph* agreed they were fun and thought them "jolly as sandboys and as merry as crickets."

The Castles, however, were anxious to return to the States. Vernon realized that his wife was far from smitten with life in England and he made no effort to obtain bookings in Britain. In the U.S., they went back on the road with *The Hen-Pecks*. They were living the usual life of a traveling theatrical couple when an unexpected offer arrived from Paris. It came with the promise of a role for Irene as well as for Vernon in the French show, *Enfin ... une Revue*. They returned to Europe right after Christmas.

Little did the Castles realize as they sailed to Antwerp that they were soon to become, at a time when public dancing was still barely respectable, the most famous dancing couple in America. The moral bias against dancing in public was due in part to the popularity of Ragtime dance tunes, as Ragtime faced strong moral censure by the churches, legislators, and influential voices in the press. There were few respectable places where people could go to dance.

The new fad of "tango teas" was attracting shopgirls and clerks to some restaurants and hotels but those who went hardly dared tell their friends or families where they'd been. Dance teachers with Spanish names showed up to teach the tango, while stores sold tango shoes, tango shirts and tango corsets. Then came the Fox Trot, born of a few steps improvised by vaudeville performer Harry Fox.

PART III — The Dream That Wouldn't Die

"The Christian religion forbids modern dances," the author of a 1904 book, *Immorality of Modern Dancing*, sternly declared. That view was challenged by Caroline Walker in her tome, *The Modern Dances: How to Dance Them*. "The new dances ... are just as proper and graceful as the time-honored waltz and the two-step, and far more interesting...."

The debate spread to the press. In California, the *Oakland Tribune* opined:

> A good deal of nonsense is being written about such Ragtime dances as the Texas Tommy, the turkey trot and the grizzly bear. There is nothing indecent or even inherently indecent in these dances. It is all in the way they are danced. Because these dances in a debased form became popular in the low dance halls of San Francisco, they have been given an undeservedly bad name. There is not the slightest suggestion of impropriety in them unless the dancers disport themselves in a suggestive and indecorous manner.

Dancing also had its defenders, one of the staunchest being Elsie Janis, a dance instructor and journalist who wrote for the *Washington Post*, among other newspapers. In "How to Dance the New Steps," she wrote:

> Now, I have held back my big punch in favor of the dance, and here it is. Drinking has lost a great deal of its vogue since dancing came in. All those men who used to sit about telling stories we girls are not allowed to hear and drinking drinks we girls are supposed not to drink are now much too busy dashing about the room in what they think is a correct imitation of Mr. and Mrs. Vernon Castle, the people who wrote "The Castle Walk," to stop and get the aforesaid drink.
>
> Now let some of these anti-dance movement pushers step forward and tell me that dancing has not dome a great deal for America.

For all the moral condemnation, crowds worshipped devotees of the dance, especially the young women who were scandalizing audiences with their brief costumes and daring performances. Isadora Duncan (later to die when her long, flowing scarf became famously trapped in the spokes of a car wheel) revolted against her early ballet training to gain international fame for her Greek-inspired themes. Canadian-born Maude Allen scandalized Europe with her suggestive *Vision of Salomé*, while Ruth St. Denis became famous for a repertory of Asian-inspired solos. Anna Pavlova, the most famous ballerina of the Ragtime era, danced *The Dying Swan* in 1907 and entered ballet immortality. But all these great figures merely *danced* for their audiences; the Castles alone both performed and

9. Dancing in Ragtime

propagandized. They taught a generation of Americans, by lessons and through their books and films, *how* to dance.

Dancing had always been part of Ragtime. Scott Joplin never allowed himself to forget that the music he played as a young man drew much of its energy from the cakewalk, the traditional African American high-stepping dance that, like its dissimilar counterpart, the waltz, also was danced in couples. Respectable families had enjoyed vaudeville and the new silent nickelodeons for years, but there was still stern objection to public dancing. That was about to change, with restaurants such as Louis Martin's Café de l'Opéra on Broadway introducing dancing at dinnertime.

Vernon and Irene Castle would be among the chief beneficiaries of these new ventures. The opening of the Folies Bergère nightclub in New York in 1911 ended the separation of audience and performers by putting patrons' tables right up beside the stage. When the Castles danced at such establishments, they were invited to share customers' tables, while the customers transformed the stage into a dance floor between numbers. It was all a new and exciting experience; social barriers were being broken down for anyone with the price of admission. Champagne became the drink of choice and an evening's entertainment, including cover charge, dinner and tips could run to ten or twenty dollars, a substantial investment for even upper class spenders. Chorus girls were able to mix with wealthy men, giving both the opportunity to pursue sexual conquests.

Scott Joplin was never part of the new nightclub scene. Instead, he was pouring his energies into his lifelong ambition to create the first American Negro opera, which he would call *Treemonisha*. But he made up for his lack of newly published tunes by becoming more innovative in what he did release. His only piece published in 1910, "Stoptime Rag," showed him stretching the boundaries of Ragtime, "looking for new ways to broaden and enrich the language." Joplin sent no new tunes to market the next year. John Stark, desperate for a fresh work, retrieved an old Joplin-Hayden collaboration, "Felicity Rag."

One of the few profiles we have of Joplin at this time comes from a young white Canadian who was living in New York and who studied piano with him from about 1910 to 1912. William Sullivan was one of several students who paid Joplin fifty cents an hour, later raised to seventy-five cents.

Part III — The Dream That Wouldn't Die

As recounted later by the Canadian Ragtime pianist John Arpin, Joplin's teaching style was slow and methodical and he constantly reminded Sullivan that the first beat of each measure had to be strongly accented.

Joplin and Sullivan would often adjourn after lessons to a nearby saloon for sandwiches. At times, Sullivan found him so withdrawn that he concluded Joplin was suffering from depression due to his financial problems and frustrations over raising funds to stage his opera. On some occasions, however, Joplin was animated and high-spirited. It was unlikely anyone was aware of it, but syphilis was beginning to take its toll on Joplin's mind and body.

The Castles put their Paris exploits to good use with a letter of recommendation that got them a nightly engagement at the Café de l'Opéra in Manhattan. Louis Martin signed them at three hundreds dollars a week to appear at midnight and go through a Ragtime dance routine for the late diners. At first, the Castles didn't really know what they were doing. Vernon jotted down some notes about their steps and Irene kept her eye on her husband as he improvised through each performance. There was a good deal of clowning around, but it produced a new dance, a stiff-legged one-step that soon became the craze of New York as the Castle Walk. Its secret was a step that seemed almost a skip, with the Castles coming down on a beat when normally they would have gone up.

The engagement led to invitations to dance at society parties around New York and on Long Island. Mrs. Stuyvesant Fish, the wife of the president of the Illinois Central Railroad, presided over much of New York society from her home on Gramercy Park, a grand mansion designed by Stanford White. William Randolph Hearst became a devotee, with Irene proclaiming that once she taught him a step he never forgot it. There were also moments of humiliation, according to the Castles' biographer, Eve Golden. She recounts how they were forced to wait in a clothes closest at a Long Island home while the guests finished their dinner.

The Castles would no doubt have continued to pick up profitable gigs from society doyens, but it is unlikely they would have ever reached the level of public adoration that engulfed them without the inspired musical direction of the black composer and conductor James Reese Europe.

9. Dancing in Ragtime

Like Scott Joplin, Europe was an ambitious musician who was keen to work his way into the firmament of entertainment stardom. Unlike Joplin, he realized that Ragtime music was not necessarily a key for opening the door to American high society. He cleverly borrowed from Ragtime in his musical style and presentation, but took pains to insist that any orchestra under him would abjure the commonness of classic Ragtime. "Ragtime is merely a nickname, or rather a fun name given to Negro rhythm by our Caucasian brother musicians many years ago," Europe said. He seemed to be suggesting that it wasn't really a true musical form.

Also like Joplin, Europe was the son of a former slave, but he was even better educated. His father had accomplished the almost unheard of feat of working his way through law school at Howard University. Jim Europe was born in 1880 in Mobile, Alabama, and later lived in Washington, D.C. In 1904 he landed a job as musical director for an all-black show, *A Trip to Africa*. He later directed such African American musical successes as *Shoo-Fly Regiment* and *The Red Moon*, which was based on an unlikely plot of an Indian princess kidnapped by an African American family. When it played in Toronto in 1909, the *Globe* took pains to reassure staid theatergoers that "the music is not all ragtime."

Europe's greatest feat was his ability to mesh black music and musicians with black and white audiences. His Society Orchestra became the first African American band to obtain a recording contract when he signed with Victor Records. He took the lead in 1910 to form the Clef Club, which acted as a booking agent and a union for black musicians. His Clef Club Orchestra of more than one hundred players made history on May 2, 1912, with a performance at Carnegie Hall where all the rules of segregation were suspended. It was one of the few occasions when blacks sat with whites in the same audience.

The subtleties of Ragtime's origin or status mattered little to Vernon Castle. He liked Europe's stuff, and he and Irene jumped at the chance to dance for the twenty-five hundred people who attended a benefit evening put on by Europe's National Negro Orchestra in 1914. A firm friendship followed. The relationship introduced the Castles to some of the better black nightclubs, including the famous Cotton Club. The dances the Castles performed in Harlem inspired Europe to write new numbers and rewrite old pieces that could be marketed as tunes from the Castle repertoire. Despite what he had said about Ragtime, the titles gave them away:

Part III — The Dream That Wouldn't Die

"The Castle House Rag," "Castle Walk," "Castle Innovation Tango" and, in March 1915, the "Castle Doggy Fox Trot."

The enmity that apparently existed between Jim Europe and Scott Joplin has never been adequately explained. It is not known whether the two ever met, but their failure to do so would be difficult to credit given the tight circle that comprised the New York world of black music. "Joplin is conspicuously absent in Clef Club programs," wrote Joplin biographer Edward Berlin. So far as records of Clef Club performances show, no Joplin tunes were ever performed by the orchestra. If true, this is quite incredible. Joplin's works in the mid 1910s were being played at one time or another by virtually every musician in New York.

In three months in 1916, Joplin made seven hand-played piano rolls for two different recording companies. The tunes were cut from actual performances and included "Maple Leaf Rag," attesting to its continuing popularity. By this point, Joplin's piano dexterity was slipping and according to Berlin, the rolls were edited to modify Joplin's playing. Badly played or not, the commercial acceptance of the piano rolls demonstrates that his audience was still large. Europe would have been aware of this. Perhaps he felt that Joplin represented an earlier and more primitive era in the musical journey of African Americans from "coon" songs, cakewalk and minstrel dances, or the sentimental hogwash of white composers who depicted slaves and their descendants as contented laborers in the cotton fields. He must have seen little to gain in associating himself with Joplin's works.

Jim Europe knew his future lay in attracting white singers and dancers who would perform with his orchestra for white audiences. His skill at crossing the racial boundaries at a difficult time in American race relations stamps him as shrewd in both his business and personal relationships. The Castles admired him as a man and a musician but it was the arrangements he wrote that gave them the danceable pieces that cemented their relationship.

Another dominant figure of the Ragtime era who advanced the Castles in their career was Elisabeth Marbury, a successful literary agent and theatrical producer. She was the lesbian partner of Elsie de Wolfe, with whom she spent winters in a fine brick house on Irving Place and sum-

9. Dancing in Ragtime

mers in France. Those in the know referred to their life together as a "Boston marriage."

Marbury first set eyes on the Castles when they were performing at a party in Paris. She saw star quality in them. Becoming their agent, she used her connections to secure them many remunerative assignments. Then she hit on her biggest idea of all: to give the Castles their own unique establishment where the best people would come to dance. She found a two-story brick house at 26 East 46th Street, christened it the Castle House, and opened it for business late in 1913.

Customers paid a two dollar cover charge to dance between four o'clock and six-thirty and also to partake of tea and sandwiches. Vernon and Irene would meander through, dancing with a few favored customers who were likely to sign up for private lessons at a fancy price. Vernon's shrewd eye for business convinced him there was a future in this kind of thing. In partnership with the head waiter from the Café de l'Opera, he opened a cellar club in Times Square called Sans Souci.

The club demonstrated everything that was distasteful about the Ragtime era, especially in the way it ripped off its customers. Dishes of cold cuts and cigarettes were thrust on arrivals; only when they got the bill did they realize how they'd been overcharged. When Irene stopped by with an offer to show a customer a new dance step, the short twirl around the floor was soon followed by a bill for twenty-five dollars. The Castles didn't need the bad public relations this was causing. They must have been relieved when, after four months, the fire department ordered the closure of Sans Souci for its inadequate fire protection.

The two of them rebounded quickly. A film about the couple, *Mr. and Mrs. Castle Before the Camera*, brought in thirty-five thousand dollars a week from movie houses. The World Syndicate Co. published the Castles' book of dance instruction, *Modern Dancing*. In it, they declared: "People can say what they want about rag-time. The Waltz is beautiful, the Tango is graceful, the Brazilian Maxixe is unique. One can sit quietly and listen with pleasure to them all; but when a good orchestra plays a 'rag' one has simply *got* to move." A foreword by Elisabeth Marbury declared that the Castles "stand pre-eminent today as the best exponents of modern dancing." Their success led Vernon to buy a handsome estate on Long Island where they lived the life of the nouveau riche.

Still, they danced. Their 1914 show, *Watch Your Step*, was made up

PART III — The Dream That Wouldn't Die

of songs by Irving Berlin, hailed by the *New York Times* as "the young master of syncopation." Eve Golden, the Castles' biographer, wrote that the show "was all Ragtime, both in music and in jokes." Its success led Vernon and Irene to open two more dance clubs, both in a former music hall. The Castle Club was installed downstairs and above it, Castles in the Air offered quality cuisine and sedate dancing. They might have prospered but the mayor of New York, facing criticism over the city becoming "as wide open as Chicago," ruled that nightclubs would have to close by one in the morning. New Yorkers who partied had no desire to go to bed so early, so they simply quit coming. The Castle clubs shut down, and Vernon turned his attention to another, more fateful matter: the situation in Europe and ominous warnings of war.

When England went to war against Germany in August 1914, Vernon felt the tug of loyalty for his homeland. He was now twenty-eight and his manhood demanded that he go to its defense. He wanted to fly, and his fastest route into the air was by joining the newly formed Royal Canadian Flying Corps. Because Canada had little in the way of training facilities, Vernon paid to take private flying lessons. Then, anxious to get into action, he transferred to the British Royal Flying Corps and sailed to England. He flew combat missions in support of the Allied offensive in the Somme in France — the battle that cost both sides a million dead — and survived a crash landing near the front. He shot down at least two German aircraft.

While Vernon was at war, Irene continued to win new stage roles. Her fame was such that when William Randolph Hearst decided to produce a patriotic film series based on the adventures of a munitions heiress, he had Irene cast in the role of Patria Channing. The series, *Patria*, was highly promoted in the Hearst papers and was, in fact, well received by the public. It didn't matter that it was filled with jingoistic nonsense or that it almost caused an international incident when Japan, then a friendly country, complained to President Wilson about its unfair portrayal of Japanese evildoers. They were promptly replaced by Mexican villains.

The series won Irene a film contract from the American branch of the French film company Pathé. Irene managed to get to Europe early in 1917 and she and Vernon spent a week together in London. The end of Vernon's war came just as the United States entered the conflict in April. Another crash, again in friendly territory, sent him to a French chateau

9. Dancing in Ragtime

for recovery. From there he was invalided home and was later assigned as an instructor to a Royal Flying Corps base in Deseronto, Ontario. After a few months he was sent to Benbrook, Texas, where the RFC also had a training field. Irene by now was performing solo in *Miss 1917*, a new Broadway musical, and getting nine hundred dollars a week. On Friday, February 15, 1918, Vernon took off with a student pilot in one of the famous Curtis Jennys of the First World War. As they returned to the base, another aircraft taxied into Vernon's designated landing strip. He pulled up at the last minute, but his engine stalled at one hundred feet. The plane nosedived into the ground, killing both of them.

The last time Vernon and Irene Castle had danced together was at a benefit given for British Recruiting at the Hippodrome Theater in New York in October 1917. He was in uniform, and she wore a blue suit and a Scottish cap. They both felt the strain of the moment; war and distance had affected their marriage and Irene, and perhaps Vernon also, had found new lovers. The two had agreed to separate. Their life together, exciting, unpredictable and fun-filled, had, like the life of Ragtime itself, almost run its course.

10

The Censors and the Erotic Life

> Can't everybody ... control themselves?
> —*Anthony Comstock*

An ever-vigilant legion of moral crusaders, censors official and unofficial, and self-appointed guardians of traditional family values went on the attack against what they believed to be the decadence of music, art, and literature in the tumultuous early years of the twentieth century. The lyrics of Ragtime, even more than the music, offended many. Scott Joplin had written his share of "coon lyrics" in his early days but he spoke at length of his objection to "vulgar" songs in an interview with the *New York Age* in 1913: "I have often sat in theatres and listened to beautiful Ragtime melodies set to almost vulgar words as a song, and I have wondered why some composers will continue to make the public hate Ragtime melodies because the melodies are set to such bad words." He had more to say on this sensitive subject:

> If someone were to put vulgar words to a strain to one of Beethoven's beautiful Symphonies, people would begin saying, "I don't like Beethoven's symphonies." So it is the unwholesome words and not the regular melodies that many people hate. Ragtime rhythm is a syncopation original with the colored people, although many of them are ashamed of it. When composers put decent words to Ragtime melodies there will be very little kicking from the public about Ragtime.

The *Musical Courier*, the trade paper of the legitimate music industry, had complained as early as 1899 that "Nothing but Ragtime prevails ... it is artistically and morally depressing and should be suppressed by press

10. The Censors and the Erotic Life

and pulpit." The litany of complaints went on for years; Ragtime was an "invasion of vulgarity," merely "cheap, trashy stuff" that "overstimulates and irritates." Among young people, it "creates a distaste for that which is more staid and solid." Moreover, "In Christian homes, Ragtime should find no resting place."

As late as 1918, the University of Toronto ordered that "all music of the kind known as Ragtime be excluded" at its new student residence, Hart House. But it was neither the music nor the words of Ragtime that most bothered the moral crusaders, the police, and the courts. It was sex. Any intimation of either the joys or the tragedies of erotic life were to be crushed, quelled and extinguished from the public platform.

The mania for censorship of movies, theater, and vaudeville peaked just as the public was becoming accustomed to more explicit portrayals of the erotic on stage and screen. New York struggled over attempts to close down Sunday entertainment and regulate silent movies through a censor board. Chicago launched its own censorship board in 1907. Various states followed in rapid succession. The censors did not ignore the stage, but movies were their main focus as the industry began to turn out longer and more sophisticated films, many with morally questionable plot lines. At first, simple films like the 1902 Edison production, *What Happened on Twenty-third Street*, tantalized viewers with simplistic suggestions of sexuality; a woman walking along the street has her underclothes exposed when the breeze from a sidewalk grate blows up her skirt.

Before long, dramatic plots involving prolonged kissing, women smoking cigarettes, and suggestions of sexual misbehavior began to test the standards of conventional morality. Films that were deemed excessively violent, such as *The James Boys* and *Night Riders*, also ran into trouble; both were refused permits in Chicago in 1909 on the grounds they were immoral. The real test, however, came with Ohio's censorship law of 1913, requiring that "only such films as are in the judgment and discretion of the board of censors of a moral, educational or amusing and harmless character shall be passed and approved."

Such laws met a mixed response from an industry torn between the need to offer plots that would lure the public into empty seats, and the desire to reach a compromise with authority that would keep police off their backs. Artistic freedom was never a primary concern. Only one company, Mutual, thought the Ohio law so bad that it had to be challenged. Mutual pursued the case to the U.S. Supreme Court in 1915. The court denied the company's appeal, depriving motion pictures of the constitutional guarantees of freedom of speech and press. It made no attempt to define immorality or obscenity; the right of states to regulate commerce within their borders would override all other considerations. By now, the National Board of Censorship of Motion Pictures (NBC), an outgrowth of the New York board, had won voluntary compliance from almost all producers. It claimed to be reviewing 95 percent of all new films, delivering its edicts via weekly bulletins sent to police chiefs across the country.

The most stringent censorship was probably in Québec, where any hint of religious mockery, sex, militarism or violence would cause a film to be cut or banned. In four months in 1913, the Catholic-dominated censorship board scissored fifty-one films for reasons ranging from religious mockery, depiction of crime, too much excitement, too much shooting and gunplay, and for "depicting the downfall of a clergyman and drunken scenes with saloons and women."

Vaudeville and the legitimate stage, because they were subject to regulations long entrenched in local laws, never felt the same pressure to curb their eroticism although the industry willingly self-censored to avoid possible prosecution. Keith and Albee, operators of the biggest American vaudeville chain, issued demanding instructions to their actors to avoid "uttering anything sacrilegious or even suggestive."

They were motivated to conform to good taste by their desire to attract women and girls to their shows, as much as to obey local laws. Yet the appeal of the erotic female was not to be denied males. Acts that represented well-known works of art or classical statuary got away with presenting nude or near-nude females clad only in sheer silk or even a film of white dust. They were far more tasteful than the crude burlesque that was still being presented in some saloons and cheap movie houses.

One of vaudeville's biggest stars, Eva Tanguay, gained fame as the "I Don't Care Girl," a Ragtime tune she belted out in portraying herself as a daring New Woman whose songs seemed an invitation to riotous sexuality. She shocked audiences with her performance in *Salomé* in 1908 and once said that her costume consisted of "two pearls." Born in Québec of a French father and a *Canadienne* mother, she went on the stage as a child

10. The Censors and the Erotic Life

after her family — in the manner of many French-Canadian families of the time — moved to Massachusetts.

Eva's brassy, self-confident Ragtime songs made up in energy what she may have lacked in voice. They were all filled with sexual innuendo, from "I Want Someone to Go Wild with Me" to "It's All Been Done Before but Not the Way I Do It." She became known as the girl who made vaudeville famous, her image having been created by her sensational role in the 1904 musical *My Sambo Girl*, in which she introduced her trademark song, "I Don't Care":

> I don't care, I don't care
> What they may think of me.
> I'm happy-go-lucky, men say I'm plucky
> So jolly and care-free.
> I don't care, I don't care
> If I do get the mean and stony stare,
> If I'm never successful, it won't be distressful,
> 'Cos I don't care.

The seamier side of Ragtime was displayed in the works of May Irwin of Whitby, Ontario, who gained fame on the New York stage for her racist and vulgar "coon" songs, which at the time were regarded as amusing. She was more notable, however, for being one of the first persons ever filmed in a kissing scene, in the silent movie *The Kiss*.

Her blatant public display of eroticism was matched in the theater by Olga Nethersole, whose career depicting fallen women reached its apex in *Sapho*, a play that ran in New York in 1900. Already famous for her "Nethersole kiss" — a long stage embrace that could last several minutes — her performance in *Sapho* led to a celebrated censorship case in which she was acquitted by an all-male jury on charges of staging an obscene performance. The fact that Nethersole had herself produced the play heightened interest in the case. She based it on the nineteenth century French novel *Sapho* by Alphonse Daudet.

The attacks of the moralists on music, movies, dancing, and the stage were unrelenting, but nothing was as vicious as the campaign against birth control. Or more precisely, against the efforts of Margaret Sanger and her allies to teach women the techniques of birth control — the use of douches, condoms and cervical caps — to avoid pregnancy.

PART III — The Dream That Wouldn't Die

The thirty-seven-year-old artist and architect nervously clutched a four-page manuscript as he entered the witness box at this court of special sessions in New York City. It was September 10, 1915. William Sanger was about to testify before three judges who sat ranged behind the court's high bench. He was there to speak in his own defense to the charge of having violated the Criminal Code of New York State by giving away a single copy of a pamphlet on birth control written by his wife, Margaret Sanger, a nurse of radical political opinions. The chief witness against him was Anthony Comstock, a crusading morality censor who boasted he had convicted enough people to fill a passenger train of sixty-one coaches and had destroyed one hundred and sixty tons of obscene literature.

Sanger told the judges he would call no witnesses. Instead, he read from a statement he had prepared: "I admit I broke the law, and yet I claim that in every real sense, it is the law and not I that is on trial here today." Banging his gavel, Justice McInerney, the presiding judge, cut Sanger off with a curt admonition: this was no time for "a lot of rigmarole." He was being found guilty of circulating a pamphlet that was both immoral and indecent: "Such persons as you who circulate such pamphlets are a menace to society."

Personally, McInerney favored sending Sanger to jail. Instead, the court had decided on a fine of one hundred and fifty dollars or thirty days. "I will never pay that fine," Sanger replied. His voice was loud and shrill. "I would rather be in jail for my convictions than to be free at a loss of my manhood and my self-respect."

Sanger's accuser, Anthony Comstock, was a strapping man, not unpleasant in appearance before he began to run to corpulence in middle age. Given to wearing long red underwear and a black suit every day of the year, he had a huge influence on the perceptions of public morality that Americans held into the 1910s. As the unofficial chief censor of the United States, he possessed a fierce determination to crush the cultural qualities around him that he saw as filthy, vile, reprehensible and perverted. Almost alone, he marshaled the forces of government and the cultural establishment, including many of the country's leading newspapers, in attacking films, books, magazines and paintings; anything and everything smacking of the erotic life, including sex between husband and wife for purposes other than procreation, drew his ire. His was a battle that would never be fully won, but that would never be entirely lost.

10. The Censors and the Erotic Life

The Sanger trial was only one of the thousands of Ragtime era prosecutions of artists, writers and entertainers. Debate over the new freedoms to which people aspired reverberated through the media, the churches, the cultural establishment, and the governing classes. Drug use, domestic violence, drunkenness, gambling, and prostitution — all the problems of an emerging urban society — were now subjects of public debate.

More often than not, such open discussion was displeasing to the authorities. It was better these kinds of things not be talked about. Ibsen's play *The Ghost* spoke of upper class gentlemen contracting syphilis from whores and then passing it on to their wives. It was performed only once at a private showing in London before the authorities acted to prevent its public staging. A bitter legal battle was fought in the United States over George Bernard Shaw's play *Mrs. Warren's Profession*, about a daughter coming to terms with the discovery that her mother's involvement in prostitution has financed her exclusive university education.

Despite efforts to cleanse the popular culture of the Ragtime era, the movies, vaudeville, and popular music became more daring in their embrace of the erotic aspects of life. The loudest demand for change often came from women, still without the vote, their voices having previously been among the most silent of society. In Britain, Christobel Pankhurst, daughter of a member of Parliament, conspired with other suffragettes to burn down the houses of MPs opposed to giving women the vote. One of the era's most cantankerous personalities, Carry Nation, roared out of Kansas, taking her axe on a saloon-smashing crusade to end the abuse of alcohol. Only prohibition, she and others devoutly believed, would stop the impoverishment of working families brought on by excessive drink.

To Comstock and most of the legal and legislative establishment, writings about birth control ranked as the equal in obscenity to the rawest kind of pornography. "Are we to have homes, or brothels?" Comstock asked of a woman reporter who inquired about his opposition to contraception. "Can't everybody, rich or poor, learn to control themselves?"

Pornography had not been seen as a problem as long as its use was confined to the upper classes; the advent of cheap printing and the "dirty postcard" exposed the "the young, the vulnerable and the susceptible" to sexual temptation. It must be fought and suppressed if public order and morality were to be preserved. The age-old use of censorship for the purpose of restricting political and religious expression had been joined by a third dimension — sexual expression — an inclusion that was justified as necessary to prevent the breakdown of public morality.

Into this cauldron of controversy marched Anthony Comstock, the most notorious antismut crusader of the time. He convinced Congress to put antiobscenity legislation into the postal law and then hire him to enforce it. It served as the model for countless state laws. Backed by his New York Society for the Suppression of Vice (how similar that sounds to Saudi Arabia's Authority for the Promotion of Virtue and Prevention of Vices), Comstock unleashed the frustrations and prejudices of a society whose moral code was under challenge. Public institutions fell over themselves to conform. In 1905, the Brooklyn Public Library, under the influence of Comstock and his supporters, withdrew Mark Twain's classics *Huckleberry Finn* and *Tom Sawyer* for having set a "bad example."

The New York Public Library, guided by similar sentiments, relegated *Man and Superman*, George Bernard Shaw's philosophical comedy about capitalism, social reform, and what Shaw called the Life Force, to its restricted shelves. In New York in 1905, Comstock forced the closure of Shaw's *Mrs. Warren's Profession* after one performance. This time his efforts came to naught: a court acquitted all the actors of indecency charges even though the play dealt with "repellent things."

Comstock hardly noticed the court's verdict. He continued to pursue every miscreant he could find, including the art dealer who sold reprints of *September Morn*, the advertisements of physical culturalist Bernarr Mcfadden showing young women in form-fitting long underwear, as well as an Art Students' League catalog containing nude pictures.

Authors, playwrights, and journalists, joined by public crusaders and supported by a few enlightened judges, began to fight back. In 1907, seventy-one of Britain's leading literary figures had signed a letter to the *London Times* deploring the banning of two plays, one for its allusion to abortion and the other for depicting a woman in an affair with a married man. In 1911, a Free Speech League was launched by an American lawyer, Theodore Schroeder. In his opposition to the federal Obscenity Act, the one-time Wisconsin farm boy argued that censorship of obscenity violated the constitutional guarantee of free speech.

Schroeder was the first to articulate a position that legions of future lawyers would adopt in their defense of artists, writers and filmmakers. In another sign of changing times, the U.S. War Department in 1912 began

10. The Censors and the Erotic Life

handing out condoms to soldiers, devices that Comstock referred to as "articles for immoral purposes." In 1913, a British royal commission recommended that divorces be permitted for reasons other than adultery, but the government took no action.

Comstock's last official duty was to serve as President Wilson's personal representative to an International Purity Conference in California. The press, which had generally supported Comstock's efforts to defend conventional morality, became more critical. A 1915 cartoon depicted him hauling a prostrate woman before a judge while proclaiming, "Your honor, this woman gave birth to a naked child!" However, the muckraking magazines of the era paid him little attention. They were interested in attacking economic oppression, not moral outrage.

Comstock died at his home in Summit, New Jersey, on September 20, 1915. Newspapers recorded his passing with dutiful accounts that mixed mild criticism with cautious approval. Death was due, one said, to "overwork and over excitement." The old censor's death saved him from ultimate public disgrace; by the time of his death Comstock's blind obedience to his extremist views on sex and other lifestyle issues was facing rejection from much of mainstream society. The struggle to free writers, artists and social reformers from the oppression of cultural orthodoxy, begun in the artists' studios of lower New York, the piano parlors of Ragtime composers, the writers' garrets of London and Paris and the union halls of a hundred industrial towns, was moving into the chambers of government and the judiciary.

The erotic life now being glimpsed by audiences in England and America, as gritty as it might be portrayed on some occasions, fell short of revealing the actual reality of prostitution, drug addiction, and sexual disease. Some twenty-five thousand young women were said to be working as prostitutes on the streets or in brothels in New York alone; but their activities, often abetted by corrupt police, were an unremarkable adjunct to turn-of-the-century life. The so-called brothel dramas of the time, depicting the lives of women caught up in prostitution, coincided with the first overall study of illicit sex conducted by the Committee of Fifteen, a New York volunteer group that issued its report in 1902. It recognized that prostitution stemmed in large part from the low wages paid to women, and recommended more widespread treatment for women suffering from drug addition or sexual disease. Equally important, the report declared, would be the provision of "more elevated" forms of entertainment and the creation of a morals police — two recommendations that would never be realized.

The brothel dramas that proliferated on the stage helped spread the first great urban myth of the twentieth century — the myth of the so-called white slave trade that was alleged to entrap innocent girls, either by force or by drugging, into a life of prostitution. Plays like *White Slavery* and *Her Road to Ruin* and the movie *The Girl Who Disappeared* depicted the abduction of innocent country girls on their arrival in the city. Even more extreme in their distortion of reality were plays that put innocent white girls into Oriental opium dens or Arabian harems. An overpowering racial revulsion directed at nonwhites was evident in such plays as *Dealers in White Women*, a 1904 production of Martin Hurley, and *Slaves of the Opium Ring*, by Billy Getthore. The popularity of such plays was undiminished by the findings of the Committee of Fifteen. It had searched for evidence of an international white slave ring, but had been able to find "no trace of one."

Nor did the report quell outbursts from Progressive-style reformers who demanded action. Hysteria over the white slave trade led directly to formation of the Federal Bureau of Investigation in 1908, under the tutelage of President Theodore Roosevelt. Congress passed the White Slave Traffic Act (the infamous Mann Act) in 1910, prohibiting the transportation of women from one state to another for prostitution or other criminal sexual activity. In 1917, the act was extended to include even noncommercial travel across state lines for immoral purposes, thereby capturing private amorous trips in its net.* Even before then, the furor over supposed white slavery had largely evaporated. "There was never a joke of more huge proportions perpetrated upon the American public than this white slave joke," reformer A.W. Elliott declared in a 1913 article, "Is White Slavery Nothing More Than a Myth?" The next year, a Massachusetts commission

---

*Far from catching white slavers, the Mann Act was more frequently applied to punish male celebrities who traveled with women other than their wives. While the focus on white slavery was misdirected, it at least had the merit of treating prostitutes as victims rather than as malevolent evildoers, a role actually fulfilled by their pimps or other male masters. International traffic in women for sex trade purposes is far more prevalent today than it was a century ago, but usually involves the transfer of women from Asia or Eastern Europe to Western Europe and North America.

10. The Censors and the Erotic Life

reported that "Every story of this kind has been thoroughly investigated, and either found to be a vague rumor ... or, in a few instances, imaginary occurrences explained by hysteria or actual malingering."

The reality of prostitution at the turn of the twentieth century was that it was rampant in North America and Europe and that its sufferance was based — as in other ages — on both its tolerance and its exploitation by men. New Orleans was widely recognized as the most prostitute-tolerant city in the United States and it was here that the Hon. Thomas Anderson, a three-term representative of the city in the Louisiana State Legislature, held sway over a vast network of whores, gamblers and thieves. He owned many houses of ill fame, the largest and most profitable of which, according to a 1908 article in *Collier's Weekly*, was the Arlington Annex at Basin and Customhouse streets, "one corner of the restricted district where flourishes that wide-open prostitution peculiar to New Orleans." For twenty-five cents, one could purchase a Blue Book listing all of the houses of prostitution and the specialties of their inmates.

More typical than the civic corruption of New Orleans as a factor in prostitution was the desperation that many young women experienced as a result of family distress and economic deprivation. Maimie Pinzer grew up in Philadelphia in what was a happy home until the murder of her father in 1898 left her mother with the responsibility for raising five children. Maimie quit school to take a low-paying job in a department store and began consorting with boys to protest her mother's unforgiving dominance. She was soon arrested on a complaint of her mother and an uncle who had sexually abused her. After her release from a home for wayward girls she moved with a boyfriend to Boston, where she worked as a bit actress and a nude model for art classes.

In 1905 Maimie was hospitalized, possibly for syphilis, and had an eye removed — the first of thirty-one surgical procedures. Still attractive, she married, worked as a prostitute, became a morphine addict, and through a social worker was put in touch with a wealthy Boston socialite, Mrs. Fanny Quincy Howe. Up to this point, Maimie's life was little different from thousands of other young women caught up in prostitution, except for her even harsher than usual lifestyle. What sets her apart is a voluminous correspondence that she begins with Mrs. Howe and that runs from 1910 to 1922. The Howe family preserved Maimie's letters, which have been published as *The Maimie Papers*.

PART III — The Dream That Wouldn't Die

With the encouragement of Mrs. Howe, Maimie finally gave up prostitution and began work as a stenographer. Her employer transferred her to Montreal, where Maimie started her own business, the Business Aid Bureau, in partnership with another woman. Her main ambition, however, was to assist young women to escape from prostitution. Although her business failed during the First World War, she managed to start the Montreal Mission, a halfway house for young prostitutes. The police were distinctly unhelpful and she was forced to shut it down. By now remarried, she returned with her husband to the United States to assist her brother's family during the postwar influenza epidemic. The erotic life that Maimie Pinzer had led came to her, as it did to most others of similar fate in the Ragtime era, by circumstance and not by choice. The influence that changed her life flowed not from any social agency or institution, but from someone who cared for her as a person.

The scourge of syphilis that swept through Europe and North America in the years before the discovery of antibiotics made it the most feared — and most unspoken of — disease since the bubonic plague of the fourteenth century. During the Ragtime era, as many people — proportionate to population — may have been infected with syphilis as the forty million living with HIV-AIDS in our time. The disease ran especially rampant through groups that would be called "high risk" today — populations of low education and poor hygienic practices and those who engaged in sexually permissive behavior.*

Prostitutes would later be seen as the "Typhoid Marys" of syphilis. Given that Scott Joplin and other musicians, chiefly African American, frequented brothels for employment and found companionship among the girls that worked there, it is not surprising that their erotic experiences resulted in many of them becoming infected. As untreated syphilis can remain latent for many years after a few months of primary symptoms, it is likely that Joplin acquired the disease sometime between 1890 and 1901 when he was roaming the Midwest and playing in saloons and bordellos. Or he may have acquired it congenitally.

During Joplin's lifetime, treatment for syphilis was largely ineffective.

---

*This is not to say the wealthy were not also afflicted; famously, the father of Sir Winston Churchill died from complications of the disease.

10. The Censors and the Erotic Life

Mercury in the form of ointment that was applied to lesions was the treatment of choice for three centuries. Not until 1908 did the German scientist Paul Ehrlich discover that arsenic could destroy *Treponema pallidum*, the bacterium that caused syphilis. He called it Salvarson. It came on the market in 1910 but did not find common usage for many years. There is little likelihood Joplin ever was treated with it.

Joplin would have suffered sporadic outbreaks of rashes, fevers, indigestion and headaches during the long years in which he suffered through the secondary stage of syphilis. By 1915, he was beginning to show the effects of late stage, or tertiary, syphilis. His heart, nervous system and brain were all being affected. He entered a manic-depressive stage, with moods swings from melancholia to high excitement punctuated by periods of aggressive behavior. These would have been especially hard on Lottie Joplin. As far as is known, she never discussed his disease in public, even years after his death.

The Ragtime era pianist Eubie Blake recalled that the signs of Joplin's deterioration were tragically obvious when he met him at a reception in Washington that year. According to Blake, the guests included several pianists, all of whom wanted to hear Joplin play. At first he refused, telling Blake he was ill. Then, succumbing to requests, he sat down to play "Maple Leaf Rag." "So pitiful," Blake is said to have remembered. "He was so far gone with the dog [syphilis] and he sounded like a little child trying to pick out a tune.... I hated to see him tryin' so hard. He was so weak." Joplin's fight against the disease and his struggle to finish the great task of his life, his opera *Treemonisha*, had worn him out.

11

Reporting in Ragtime

> Ragtime Music Dead in This Town
> —New York Times

First came a timid girl in a pink dress; she was "nervous and played very poorly," according to the account in the *Dramatic Mirror*. Following her was a "fat little German," then Louis Gast, a giant of a man "who looked as though he was accustomed to eat a piano for breakfast every day." The scene was unfolding at Tony Pastor's Theater in Tammany Hall, the building on East 14th Street in New York City that served as the headquarters for the Democratic party machine that controlled local politics. It was here, past midnight on January 23, 1901, that a publicity gimmick orchestrated by Pastor with the willing support of the *Police Gazette*, a widely read but somewhat disreputable weekly magazine of sports, entertainment, and crime news, helped catapult Ragtime into national prominence.

A decade later, with Ragtime in its heyday, hardly a news cycle passed without discussion of the music and its composers and performers in newspapers across the United States and Canada. The coverage veered dramatically from the highly laudatory to the extremely condemnatory, but every article was a reminder of how Ragtime music shaped the era and how the composers and performers, from Scott Joplin to Irving Berlin, became household names in North America and Britain.

Memories of the storied evening at Tony Pastor's lingered on. It marked the annual ball of the employees of Pastor's emporium and the highlight was a piano playing contest for the "Ragtime championship of the world." The *Police Gazette* had announced it with a headline-laden flourish:

11. Reporting in Ragtime

RAG-TIME PIANO PLAYERS
IN TRAINING TO CONTEST FOR THE CHAMPIONSHIP
OF THE POLICE GAZETTE MEDAL

One of the liveliest competitions of the new year will occur at Tammany Hall, New York City, on the evening of Jan. 23 when the best piano playing talent of the country will meet to decide the rag-time playing championship, and what is by far more important, the ownership of the Richard K. Fox diamond-studded medal. This will settle a much vexed question, and one that had been raised ever since the coon melodies became popular.

After big Louis Gast performed, the raucous audience of Pastor's workers, friends and assorted hangers-on — a decidedly different crowd than the social elite who normally patronized his tony establishment — heard the master of ceremonies announce that no "gentlemen of color" would be permitted to play. The MC's manner, the *Dramatic Mirror* noted, had been "extremely officious" and his declaration set off loud protests:

> However, matters were finally straightened out and "Duke" Travers, an ebon-hued youth, with a wide smile, seated himself, while the crowd cheered. He played beautifully, without any attempt at fancy flourishes, but in perfect rag-time. His performance was greeted with uproarious applause. The next two were colored men, Lawlor and James by name, and they beat the long-suffering piano until they were stopped.

The medal that was up for grabs was sponsored by the *Gazette's* publisher, Dick Fox. It went, when the contest wound down around three o'clock in the morning, to — perhaps by prearrangement — Mike Bernard, the leader of the pit orchestra at Tony Pastor's. He had been the last to perform. When he sat down to play, he lifted the front off the piano "so that the rag-time could be seen and heard by everyone present." In the press accounts, no mention was made of what selections had been played but it would have been surprising if Joplin's "Maple Leaf Rag" had not been among them.

The music critics of the daily press were in the habit of assailing Ragtime for its unprovoked invasion of the popular music scene. But by the 1910s, the influence of Ragtime on public entertainment could be more accurately measured in what general reporters of those same newspapers wrote of their interviews with musicians, singers and other personalities. Because these reports reflected white middle class sentiments, they offered a perspective beyond that of the critics and the professional entertainment

PART III — The Dream That Wouldn't Die

writers of trade papers like the *Mirror, Variety* or *Billboard*, or writers with such leading African American newspapers as the *New York Age*, the *Chicago Defender*, or the *Indianapolis Freeman*.

Sometimes the general reporters of the white newspapers got it wrong. This was certainly the case when a spate of stories appeared in 1909 proclaiming the death of Ragtime. The *New York Times* kicked things off with a long front page article headlined RAGTIME MUSIC DEAD IN THIS TOWN. Just as Scott Joplin was having one of his most productive years and Irving Berlin was putting the finishing touches to "Alexander's Ragtime Band," foreshadowing the coming explosion of Ragtime's popularity in musical theater, records and sheet music, the *Times* was announcing, highly prematurely, its very demise.

In coming weeks, other newspapers like the *St. Louis Post-Dispatch*, whose reporters were familiar with the music scene and Joplin's role in it, picked up the theme. According to the *Post-Dispatch*, even though Joplin was studying music in New York, "Ragtime Music (Invented in St. Louis) Is Dead." Later, smaller newspapers like the upstate *Syracuse (New York) Herald* added to the clamor with a highly questionable, unattributed diatribe claiming that music publishers were about to boycott Ragtime in favor of a return to "the songs we sung in days gone by."

Nor was the African American press immune to speculation on Ragtime's death. A few weeks after the *Times* story was published, the *New York Age*, one of the largest and best black papers in the country, was in print with a column by its music editor, Lester Walton, asking, "Is Ragtime Dead?"

According to the *Times*, the patrons of New York's best hotels and cafés had lost all interest in Ragtime and were most fond of Wagner, Liszt and Beethoven and the "catchy airs from the Broadway musical shows while their popularity is at its height":

> Ragtime music is dead, according to the managers of the various hotels and restaurants in the city, and there is no longer a demand for the tunes that used to cause jig steps to come to the feet, accompanied by a desire to get up and do a cakewalk. According to the same authorities, Ragtime has been shelved to make room for the tuneful airs of the popular musical shows that last but a season and for the music of the old composers. There is also a demand for the scores of Victor Herbert, John Philip Sousa and other popular music writers.
>
> The death and funeral of Ragtime, according to John Philip Sousa, who

has the credit of being the originator of that class of music, "is due entirely to the poor class of the product turned out in latter years. Ragtime had the dyspepsia or gout long before it died. It was overfed by poor nurses. I have not played a single piece of Ragtime this season, and it is simply because the people do not want it."

Mr. Sousa's estimate of the popular taste is the result of observation on the tour of his band, and it is borne out by the hotel and restaurant managers of this city, who have entirely cut Ragtime from their musical programs.

In this, the *Times* and Sousa were half right; Ragtime was not dead but the purity of classical Ragtime as originated by Scott Joplin and other early composers had by now become corrupted with lyrics filled with vulgarities that amused partygoers. After a half column of quotes from managers at the Waldorf-Astor, the Plaza, the Gotham and the Hotel Astor, the *Times* revealed:

Cakewalk tunes have been banished from Delmonico's, and in their stead may be heard the prettiest airs of the musical shows and light operas, interspersed with music from grand opera and the older composers. Ragtime music has been made to take a back seat.

Perhaps the *Times* article was motivated by a yearning for sweet, sentimental ballads that had largely gone out of style. This certainly appeared to be the case of a report in the *Syracuse (New York) Herald* in 1912. It also presumed the demise of Ragtime, and was headlined "Call for Dreamy Lyrics Suggests End of Ragtime." The unsigned article, quoting no sources by name, claimed that music publishers "will attempt to restore to popularity the songs we sung in days gone by":

The popularity of Ragtime music that few would dare assault is in the dangerous proximity to the parting of the ways, for the music publishers have risen to revolt and are planning to restore to supremacy the unassuming lyrics of days gone by. The publishers have issued a call asking the writers to supply compositions that will relegate to obscurity *Alexander's Ragtime Band* and *Everybody's Doing It* and kindred "raves" of the season. They now want more of the dreamy type, the kind that contains love sentiments and suggestions of pastoral scenes.

The furious, catching, uneasy pace of the ordinary Ragtime melody, transformed still further by such novelties as the "grizzly," the "turkey trot," and the "bunny hug" has overdone itself and there must be a change.

"We have gone the limit of Ragtime," said one of them. "In fact, we have gone to seed. We have run the whole gamut of syncopated sensation and

PART III — The Dream That Wouldn't Die

now find that we cannot delight our progressive customers with that sort of thing anymore. To my mind, the knell was rung this winter in a vaudeville act where a young woman in appropriate costumes sang the songs of the years since 1899. The audience was delighted with such songs as *Sweet Bunch of Daisies, Doris, Doris, Oh How I Love You,* and *My Sweetheart's the Man in the Moon.*"

As she sang up the scale the applause became weaker and weaker. When she finally sang one of the latest Ragtime hits there was scarcely a ripple of handclapping. The contrast was too much for them. The producer must give the people what they want. I considered that a popular primary vote for the recall of the rag and that's what I'm attempting to do now.

Bylines were rare in newspapers of the time but the absence of named sources in the article suggests the opinions expressed might have been those of the author.

The president of Harvard University, one Lawrence Lowell had no hesitation in being quoted by name when he told the Music Teachers' Association that he was saddened when he noted "the kind of music" played at dinners of educated men. "It is Ragtime, and Ragtime of a very poor quality. These men seem to care very little for good music. What they want is a catchy song after they have exhausted their voices in organized cheering. One can hardly fail to note the progressive degeneration of the popular taste in music."

Within three years of Dr. Lowell's complaint, a ban was put on Ragtime in the Memorial Hall, the main dining room at Harvard. Waiters had been breaking dishes while trying to "juggle their trays to Ragtime," a newspaper dispatch reported. "The students, too, have added to the damage from this cause by rattling their knives and forks on the dishes in keeping time with the orchestra and chipped crockery has been the result."

In Chicago, seventy-two dancing masters voted to bar Ragtime and "permit only the old-fashioned waltz and two-step to be executed upon their floors," reported the *Washington Post* in 1912. "Ragtime is to music what the dime novel is, or rather was, to literature. It contaminates those who listen to it, spoils the taste for good music and corrupts the ancient art of dancing."

Valentine's Day that year was a sad occasion at the Alameda, California, High School, reported the *Oakland Tribune*. All the lovely cards exchanged by the students could not "restore the high school to its wanted cheerful and happy frame of mind":

11. Reporting in Ragtime

For Ragtime has to go. Yesterday afternoon Professor Arthur Agaard, the classical music expert of the high school faculty, put the ban on Ragtime with a bulletin he posted on the school board.

To him, Ragtime is something awful, a holy horror, a something to be "jumped on with both feet," throttled, to be hanged by the neck until it is dead, without even a saving clause.

It is not recorded how many other schools followed this example, but there must have been many. Perhaps Professor Agaard had been influenced by the comments of a European academic, Dr. Ludwig Brunner, of the Imperial Academy of Medical Research in Berlin. Arriving in Los Angeles in 1911, Dr. Brunner thought Ragtime was driving the American public crazy:

> Your Ragtime air jars the nerve centers and causes an irritation of the brain cells. While the roll and thump of Ragtime is exhilarating to the senses and acts as a stimulant, it has the after effects of an injurious drug that will eventually stagnate the brain cells and wreck the nervous system.
>
> I have been in this country several months, and everywhere I have visited—New York, Chicago, New Orleans and San Francisco—the little minds are crazy with Ragtime.
>
> If something be not done, the classics of long ago will be a thing of the past entirely, and they will be singing national hymns in Ragtime.

Many Americans agreed with him. Newspapers around the country repeated the plaintive cry that modern youth was being corrupted. A small Texas paper, the *Laredo Times*, added a dose of racial animosity to its critique:

> The present form of vulgar and suggestive popular song was the natural outcome of the *negro Ragtime* atrocities and the vaudeville performers soon saw that to be pleasing to an audience it was necessary to be more suggestive that would have been permitted in the old time honky tonks, which were patronized by males only and those usually of the lower class.
>
> The young girls of the land are today singing in the privacy of their homes songs that in former day would hardly have been listened to by the habitués of the lowest saloon "concert halls." And they do not seem to see anything improper in them, any more than they did in the indecent dresses, which for a time threatened to overrun the country, or than they do now in the suggestive, if not really disgusting, tango imported from the lowest haunts of vice.
>
> It is too much to expect that the young people will of their own initiative drop the modern song for the more melodious and more proper songs

of the really decent class of music. But it is to their parents and elders that we must look for the restraint of this ever-downward tendency of today.

For all the criticism, there were many defenders of Ragtime. They included some of the most celebrated figures of classical culture. A prima donna of the Metropolitan Opera, Marie Rappold, told reporters during a 1913 tour that "These songs that are called common, or this Ragtime as you would say, are sowing the seeds for a national music. Some day a few geniuses will come along and cultivate the seeds and lo and behold, this country will have a great music of its own."

"Ragtime seems to appeal only to Americans," she said, "but it is typical of America, and why should America be ashamed of what is natural to it? All music in its infancy is crude. It must be developed."

As Madame Rappold spoke, some of the steamship companies sailing out of New York reached an important decision. Their passenger liners would no longer play "Auld Lang Syne" as they weighed anchor. Instead, those aboard would hear the refrains of Ragtime music. The decision led the *New York American* to comment, no doubt sardonically, "Ragtime has its victories of utility as well as of fashion. The steamship company which has abolished the bugler's 'Auld Lang Syne' at sailing time and substituted Ragtime has undoubtedly decreased the visible supply of tears to a most pleasing extent."

The French actress Mary Garden, getting ready to sail for America to appear in Samuel Goldwyn's *Tunis*, wrote the next year in a Paris musical journal:

> All Ragtime is not necessarily bad. In fact, some of it has been particularly good. Ragtime can find its classic counterpart in some of our most celebrated and enduring music. The trouble with Ragtime is that it has not the virtue of being related to other things in life which is the symbolical significance of classical music. Lacking that its melody and rhythm may be likened to the imitation silver bells upon a Christmas tree — pretty but perishable. To like Ragtime is more an indication of joy in the ephemeral than proof of bad taste. It is the sprightliness of this class of music that has recommended it to America.

The idea that Ragtime was the music of the future was a frequently expressed theme of many newspaper articles. When "America's best composer," Charles Waxfield Cadman of Pittsburgh, went on tour in 1913, he

11. Reporting in Ragtime

told a reporter that "the swing and dash of Ragtime music is characteristic of the energy and ambition of America, and it should be encouraged. Words which are sung to the present-day Ragtime melodies are steadily becoming more degenerate and indecent, but there is bound to be a reaction from that tendency soon. The Ragtime of the future will be the predominant strain in characteristically American compositions, for syncopated music portrays America in melody better than anything else."

The same year, an editorial writer for the *Syracuse (New York) Herald* commented on "The Vogue of Ragtime":

> The continued popularity of Ragtime music must be included among social phenomena. More than fifteen years have elapsed since the popular taste for musical novelty was tickled with the first Ragtime ballads. They owed their origins to the vaudeville and comic opera stage, and their celebrity to certain rhythmical characteristics that seem to fit in with the lighter popular mood. The first batch of Ragtime compositions constituted a new type of amorous negro melody, although it afterwards took a wider and more sentimental range. The distinguishing feature of Ragtime is its syncopated swing, which lends itself admirably to dancing purposes.
>
> A great mass of poor stuff has been palmed off on the country for Ragtime. We don't suppose that one-tenth of the apparently inexhaustible compositions of this class are worth listening to. But the output has been so prodigious that the really meritorious pieces — those that combine the distinctive rhythm with fresh melody — make up a desirable addition to our store of simple popular music, the music of the masses. But in the vast production of musical ore there is enough pure and valuable metal to justify the opinion that the world is the brighter and happier for the introduction of Ragtime.

Others expressed mixed sentiments. Alexander Stewart, the director of a California chorus rehearsing for a presentation of "Old Songs of Other Days," conceded in a 1915 interview with the *Oakland Tribune* that "this so-called Ragtime music has in it some latent germ of what is to be the true American music":

> Surely no musical form heretofore has seemed to so well express the exuberant vitality of the American nation. The fact that other nations, especially the Germans and the French, have great difficulty in playing effectively our Ragtime music is also an evidence that there is something characteristically American about it. Some day a great American composer will arise who will take the germ of real music which is hidden in this mass of musical eccentricity and will mold it into some really great music. In the mean-

PART III — The Dream That Wouldn't Die

time it is a pity that we have to stand for so much musical mediocrity and so much impure and brainless sentimentality in the words of these insipid songs.

Most commentators agreed that Ragtime represented a new epoch in popular music, likely to have a long-lasting influence on the future. Casting a backward glance in 1915, a writer for the *New Republic*, asking "Is Ragtime Art?" concluded:

> Ragtime is a type of music substantially new in musical history. It has persisted, grown, evolved in many directions, without official recognition or aid. You may take it as certain that if many millions of people persist in liking something that has not been recognized by the schools, there is vitality in that thing. The attitude toward folk-music at the beginning of the nineteenth century was very similar. A Russian folk-song was no less scorned in the court of Catherine the Great than a Ragtime song in our music studios today. Yet Russian folk-song became the basis of some of the most vigorous art-music of the last century; and no musician speaks of it today except in terms of respect. The taste of the populace is often enough toward the shoddy and outworn. But when the populace creates its own art without official encouragement, then let the artists listen. I haven't a notion whether Ragtime is going to form the basis of an "American school of composition." But I am sure that many a native composer could save his son; if he would open his ears to this folk-music of the American city.

While Ragtime had no shortage of critics in the United States, press accounts from Europe told of lords and ladies dancing to the music at Ragtime parties in some of the most renowned mansions in England. The *London Standard* carried a long interview in 1912 with one of the better known English musicians, Percy Haydon. He told of playing piano at a reception given by the Duchess of Marlborough at her palatial Curzon Street home:

> I could see through the corner of my eye as I sat at the piano that everybody was listening hard, and such encouragement urges one to do one's best. The more enthusiasm I put into it the more the ladies and gentlemen appreciated it, and I know that some very stern old dowagers were swaying gently to the music, because I could see the blaze of diamonds in their tiaras moving to and fro in time with the music. In other big West End mansions Ragtime is the sign for everybody to crowd in from the other rooms to listen to it. It is also astonishing for me to discover that so many people know the extraordinary words of some of these Ragtime songs and join in the choruses. For instance, it is somewhat a surprise to discover that

prosperous and quite elderly city men (bankers) can join, word perfect in such a chorus as, "He's the hi-falutin,' shootin,' scootin,' son of a gun from Arizona, rag-time Cowboy Joe."

Ragtime not only invaded the mansions of nobility in Britain, but surrounded the king and queen at the opening of Parliament in 1913. The British entertainment paper *Musical News* voiced its objection to the inclusion of such tunes in the program of the Guards Band:

> We have plenty of fine martial music suitable for the occasion, and there was no need to go to America for inspiration. Doubtless those clever comedians, known as the "two Bobs," will feel highly complimented at their popular *Alexander's Ragtime Band* being utilized in a state procession, but to anyone who appreciates the significance in music, this selection was unsuitable and meaningless.
>
> We are not disputing the popularity of (such) tunes, but both the music and the words with which they are associated render them unfit for state pageants, and such items stick in one's throat at stately ceremonies such as the Lord Mayor's show.

The *Musical News* would no doubt have welcomed a report that appeared in a U.S. government publication in 1914. It suggested Ragtime music was a poor sell in Europe. American consular offices reported that American music in general was making its way but slowly in Italy, Spain and France, although in some German cities Ragtime was "quite popular." The editors of the *San Antonio (Texas) Light* thought this over and decided that "as the days approach when windows will remain open and doors ajar, we could heartily wish that Europe would take more Ragtime and America less."

Lester A. Walton grew up in a comfortable middle class African American home in St. Louis, the eldest son of a hotel bellman and a schoolteacher. The advantage of a stable home and a better than average education gained at Sumner High School built up his self-confidence and his expectation of a successful career. In 1902, he landed a job as a general reporter for the *St. Louis Globe-Democrat*, staying there until he switched to the *Post-Dispatch* in 1906.

Walton refused to allow the ingrained racial prejudice of the time to deter him. On one occasion, arriving at a hotel for an interview, he was told he would have to ride up in the freight elevator. He refused to do so. It was only after he got his editor on the telephone that the clerks relented and allowed him to use the passenger elevator.

Walton had a deep interest in music and was in a good position as a reporter to gain free admittance to the many musical events in St. Louis. He became friends with two of the city's leading young Ragtime composers and performers, Louis Chauvin and Sam Patterson. It is likely that Patterson introduced Walton to his close friend Scott Joplin.

Walton collaborated with Patterson on several songs, one of which attracted the attention of Ernest Hogan, the popular black entertainer and composer of "All Coons Look Alike to Me." Hogan invited Walton to write lyrics for his New York production, *Rufus Rastus* and its sequel, *The Oyster Man*. Meanwhile, an article Walton had written for the *Colored American* magazine impressed the new owner of the weekly *New York Age*, Fred R. Moore. Late in 1907, Walton was hired to become the music and stage editor of the *Age*, the leading black paper in the city.

One of the first black musical comedies that Walton was called on to review was *The Shoo-Fly Regiment*, about a young black schoolteacher who risks the love of his sweetheart by volunteering to serve with the U.S. Army in the Philippines war. Walton saw it as his responsibility to be critical of poor performance. He warned in print that *Shoo-Fly* needed to get rid of "dull and unnecessary dialogue." After struggling under three different managers, the show emerged, Walton wrote, "full of ginger, with more comedy as well as more melody."

It was this type of musical and dramatic criticism that earned Walton the respect of white reviewers as well as his fellow African American actors and singers. His reviews were among the first to offer an appraisal of the plot of a production and the performance of its players. He held that racial issues were central to black theater, and courted controversy by attacking white theater productions that he felt misrepresented blacks.

Walton also campaigned for equal treatment of black theatergoers, complaining in print whenever African American customers were denied seats or were forced to accept poorer seats than they had paid for. Not content with being just a journalist, he also became a theater manager and for a time leased the Lafayette Theater while still working for the *Age*.

On Christmas Eve 1908, Walton wrote: "If you want to learn how grossly ignorant the white man is, in general of Negro home life, of Negro mannerisms, of Negro ideals and what not, attend a theatrical performance where a Negro character is being depicted."

But Walton could also be generous with praise. When the landmark *Bandanna Land* opened at the Majestic Theatre in 1908, Walton wrote in the *Age* that he had been prepared to "tear it to pieces," but that the "energy and personal magnetism" of the company was such that he forgot he was there "as a critic." Most of the show's music had been written by Will Marion Cook, who also directed the pit orchestra. Walton called him "the greatest Afro-American composer" in the country.

During his time at the *Age*, Walton was probably the most knowledgeable journalist covering the black music scene. He paid particular attention to Ragtime, writing almost every week of new releases and the activities of prominent performers. Like white journalists, he was not above questioning the survival of Ragtime.

In Walton's 1909 interview with James Reese Europe headed "Is Ragtime Dead?" Europe is quoted as saying "there never was any such music as Ragtime." Ironically, Walton's extended coverage of the music week after week clearly demonstrated the continuing popularity of Ragtime, despite what white writers may have said of it. "Many white composers and writers do their best to disparage syncopated music, commonly known as Ragtime," Walton reminded his readers in 1912.

In the course of his work for the *Age*, Walton would have seen a good deal of Scott Joplin. They likely renewed their acquaintanceship shortly after Joplin's arrival from St. Louis in 1907. Both were active in the Colored Vaudeville Benevolent Association and Walton commented frequently in his column about Joplin's activities and his approach to composing Ragtime. His items showed great deference to Joplin and his ability, often referring to his accomplishments and his standing as a leading composer of Ragtime.

The first of several interviews Walton had with Joplin was published in the *Age* on March 5, 1908. It was headlined "Composer of Ragtime Music Now Writing Grand Opera." Walton introduced Joplin to his readers by revealing that the composer's mission in New York went far beyond simply obtaining wider publication for his rags. Joplin intended to write a grand opera, Walton reported, commenting that "from Ragtime to opera is certainly a big jump":

Part III — The Dream That Wouldn't Die

> Since syncopated music, better known as Ragtime, has been in vogue, many Negro writers have gained considerable fame as composers of that style of music. From the white man's standpoint of view he at present is inclined to believe that after writing Ragtime, the Negro does not figure.
>
> There are many colored writers busily engaged even now in writing operas. Music circles have been stirred recently by the announcement by Scott Joplin, known as the apostle of Ragtime, (that he) is composing scores for grand opera.
>
> Scott Joplin is a St. Louis product who gained prominence a few years ago by writing the "Maple Leaf Rag," which was the first ragtime instrumental piece to be generally accepted by the public. Last summer he came to New York from St. Louis and it was the opinion of all that his mission was placing several of his ragtime instrumental compositions on the market. The surprise of the musicians and publishers can be imagined when Joplin announced that he was writing grand opera and expected to have his scores finished by summer.
>
> From Ragtime to grand opera is certainly a big jump — about as great a jump as from the American Theatre to the Manhattan and Metropolitan Opera Houses. Yet we believe that the time is not far off when America will produce several S. Coleridge Taylors who will prove to the public that the black man can compose other than Ragtime.
>
> The composer is just in his thirties and is very retiring in manner. Critics who have heard a part of his new opera are very optimistic as to his future success.

Neither realized it, but Joplin was still years away from completing his opera *Treemonisha*, the project that would turn out to be his final and perhaps most enduring, if not most noted work. While Joplin's optimism would never flag, he would find little encouragement from his publishers, his friends in the music world, or in New York's African American community into which he was now immersed. There would be only a few small and insignificant press notices, including several by Walton, published to mark his progress. Joplin's struggle would go largely unnoticed while he worked in the parlor of his Harlem home, determined to construct a musical masterpiece that would surpass anything ever created by anyone of his race.

12

Dreaming of *Treemonisha*

"A thoroughly American Opera"
—Musician and Art Journal, *1911.*

Scott Joplin seldom missed a day immersed in the sounds of his music and his piano, whether he was working on a composition, giving a lesson, performing in a club, or just playing for the simple enjoyment of it. His second passion was attending theater and vaudeville, where he would soak up the atmosphere of the crowd and assess the onstage performances. He liked to compare the music with his own work, but he was more often critical than approving of what he heard. One performer whose artistry he admired was Harry Bradford, a black vaudevillian who also happened to string for the African American Midwest newspaper, the *Indianapolis Freeman.*

Joplin was not shy about discussing *Treemonisha*, the grand opera he was writing, or playing portions of its score for friends and admirers. Late in the fall of 1909, after Joplin had put at least five years into the effort, he played the overture for Bradford. His friend, who wrote of Joplin as "the Ragtime king of Greater New York," was overwhelmed. He hurried home to prepare a dispatch to his paper: "Mr. Scott Joplin, the composer of the Maple Leaf Rag, has got a new opera. I heard the overture; it is as great as anything written by Mr. Wagner ... or any of the other old masters. Not like it ever written in the United States. The public will hear all about it in a few weeks."

This was not the first time that news of Joplin's opera had appeared in print. Even before he left St. Louis two years before, a New York writer for the *American Musician and Art Journal* had interviewed Joplin at John Stark's office. The writer gave a colorful description of Joplin's habit of

Part III — The Dream That Wouldn't Die

always carrying a music pad with him so he could jot down whatever musical inspiration might come to him. Then he added: "Scott Joplin has been working a considerable time on a grand opera which will contain music similar to that sung by the negroes during slavery days, the music of today, the Negro Ragtime, and the music that the negro will use in the future.... The writer ... heard Mr. Joplin play the overture of his new opera, and to say that it was exceptionally good would be putting it mildly."

For years, Joplin had poured his energy into his dream that would be the great project of his life: a grand opera that would transcend the dreary commonality of everyday Ragtime and inspire African Americans in their struggle against social and economic servitude.

He'd prepared himself by experimenting with new forms of Ragtime music for ballet and opera, beginning with *The Ragtime Dance*, his song-rag ballet suite that was first performed in 1899. His first attempt at opera, *A Guest of Honor*, followed in 1903. In honoring Booker T. Washington, the controversial figure whom Joplin revered as the prime advocate of Negro advancement through education, he was celebrating a man often criticized by black leaders. Like Washington, Joplin saw his people's salvation in education and self-reliance, and it was this theme that provided the plot for *Treemonisha*.

This would be the great epic of Joplin's career, a mixture of Ragtime, minstrel show, vaudeville and grand opera. *Treemonisha* was developing into a complex piece of work, as any opera is, that would emerge from his fertile musical talent as something greater than an opera in Ragtime. A two hundred and thirty page opera in three acts, it ran to twenty-seven musical scores and a libretto that, while modest in its dramatic strength, powerfully expressed Joplin's reflections on his own life experience and his yearnings for a better future for his people. He made effective use of black idiom and habits and carried the story forward with melodies and dancing that tangibly brought forth the emotions of his characters.

Joplin wrote an extended preface to explain the opera's plot and setting. It tells the story of a small rural community of ex-slaves, burdened with superstition, in which a childless couple, Ned and Monisha, find a baby girl abandoned under a tree beside their home. Joplin explained:

> The year 1866 finds them in dense ignorance, with no-one to guide them, as the white folks had moved away shortly after the Negroes were set free and had left the plantation in charge of a trustworthy Negro servant named

12. Dreaming of Treemonisha

Ned. All of the Negroes, but Ned and his wife Monisha, were superstitious, and believed in conjuring.

When Treemonisha [as they named the abandoned baby] was seven years old Monisha arranged with a white family that she would do their washing and ironing and Ned would chop their wood if the lady of the house would give Treemonisha an education, the schoolhouse being too far away for the child to attend. The lady consented and as a result Treemonisha was the only educated person in the neighborhood.... The opera begins in September 1884. Treemonisha, being eighteen years old, now starts on her career as a teacher and a leader.

Treemonisha confronts the ignorance of her community by speaking in educated terms, her language sharply contrasting with the African American dialect of the conjuror Zodzetrick:

> Treemonisha: You have lived without working for many years,
> All by your tricks of conjury.
> You have caus'd superstition and many sad tears.
> You should stop, you are doing great injury.
>
> Zodzetrick: You 'cuse me wrong for injury I'se not done,
> An' it won't be long 'fore I'll make you from me run.
> I have 'dis bag o' luck, 'tis true,
> So take care, I'll send bad luck to you.

In the end, the community rallies to Treemonisha. From the beginning of the opera, its music calls America to task. "The Corn Huskers" reminds the audience of the toil of black farm workers, while the barbershop quartet-style rendition of "We Will Rest Awhile" is a tribute to their exhaustion. Pieces like "Superstition" and "Treemonisha in Peril" strip bare the fiction that there is contentment in ignorance. An almost pure Ragtime rhythm emerges in one of the opera's most ebullient numbers, "Aunt Dinah Has Blowed de Horn."

The opera's penultimate number, "A Real Slow Drag," has the heroine mustering strength for a fresh assault on life. A section called "Marching Onward" sums up the hopes and dreams of African Americans for a better future with education. It was this piece that Joplin always felt Irving Berlin had plagiarized in writing "Alexander's Ragtime Band," "the most widely sung, played, danced-to 'ragtime' song ever written." He is said to have burst into tears when he first heard Berlin's song played. Believing his music had been copied, Joplin revised "A Real Slow Drag" before

PART III — The Dream That Wouldn't Die

going to Washington in July 1913 to personally apply for a new copyright at the U.S. Patent Office.

Joplin probably completed work on *Treemonisha* early in 1911. Buoyed with the satisfaction of having finally completed the great task of his life, he set about to publicize his achievement. He still hoped to find a publisher, despite several disappointments. The greatest of these had come at the hands of his first publisher, John Stark. For years, Stark had listened patiently to Joplin's scheme to write an opera but had always declined requests for an advance. An opera by a Ragtime musician was simply too great a risk, even if it carried Joplin's name. When Stark finally told Joplin he was unwilling to publish *Treemonisha*, the news came with devastating effect. The two men hardly ever spoke again.

Their estrangement did not stop Stark from continuing to promote Joplin's rags, but he more often did so indirectly rather than directly. Perhaps recognizing the declining interest in novelty rags, Stark published a flyer in 1916 promoting "Classic Rags — Don't Let That Ever Fade From Your Memory":

> As Pike's Peak to a mole hill, so are our rag classics to the slush that fills the jobber's bulletins.... The brightest minds of all civilized countries, however, have seen the light and are now grading many of the Stark Rags with the finest musical creations of all time. They cannot be interpreted at sight. They must be studied and practiced slowly, and never played fast at any time.

Other of Joplin's publishers, including Seminary Music Company and Joseph W. Stern, who had published "Stoptime Rag," were no more interested in *Treemonisha* than Stark. Joplin would have to go ahead on his own. He published the piano-vocal score himself on May 11, 1911, and on May 22 he traveled to Washington to file a copyright application at the Library of Congress. The fee was one dollar. He also took out a British copyright.

Joplin understood the importance of publicity and still hoped that favorable press might bring around a major publisher. He first turned to his old friend Lester Walton of the *New York Age*. On May 25, the paper faithfully recorded Joplin's milestone accomplishment:

> "Treemonisha," an opera in three acts, is the latest contribution to the music world by a colored composer. Scott Joplin, who wrote "The Maple Leaf

12. Dreaming of Treemonisha

Rag" and other syncopated compositions, is responsible for "Treemonisha," words and music, which is being published by him also.

The story deals with a colored waif who was found under the trees by Ned and Monisha, and because of her inclination to play under the trees she was named "Treemonisha." The scene of the story is laid in a plantation in Arkansas. The book provides for eleven people in the cast and a large chorus. Composer Joplin characterizes the music as "strictly Negro." There are twenty-seven musical numbers and there are 230 pages to the score of the opera.

Still optimistic that he would find a publisher, Joplin agreed to attend a lunch given for him by friends to celebrate the completion of his opera. Twenty-eight people, whites as well as blacks, gathered on June 14 at the home of a Miss Christie Hawkins. The guests toasted Joplin and he played a short selection from his score. This was probably that last time that Joplin would feel content that he was close to realizing his long-held dream.

The leading music paper of the day, *Musician and Art Journal*, gave Joplin a remarkable endorsement in a long article in its June 24 issue, under the heading "A Musical Novelty." No doubt remembering its favorable report of two years before, the *Journal* hailed Joplin for having "created an entirely new phase of musical art ... a thoroughly American opera":

> A remarkable point about this work is its evident desire to serve the negro race by exposing two of the great evils which have held his people in its grasp, as well as to point them to higher and nobler ideals. Scott Joplin has proved himself a teacher as well as a scholar and an optimist with a mission which has been splendidly performed. Moreover, he has created an entirely new phase of musical art and has produced a thoroughly American opera, dealing with a typical American subject, yet free from all extraneous influence....
>
> Scott Joplin has not been influenced by his musical studies or by foreign schools. He has created an original type of music in which he employs syncopation in a most artistic and original manner. It is no sense rag-time, but of that peculiar quality of rhythm which Dvořàk used so successfully in his "New World" symphony. The composer has constantly kept in mind his characters and their purpose, and has written music in keeping with his libretto. "Treemonisha" is not grand opera, nor is it light opera; it is what we might call character opera or racial opera....
>
> To date there is no record of even the slightest tendency toward the fashioning of the real American opera, and although this work just completed by one of the Ethiopian race will hardly be accepted as a typical American opera for obvious reasons, nevertheless none can deny that it serves as an

PART III — The Dream That Wouldn't Die

opening wedge, since it is in every respect indigenous. It has sprung from our soil practically of its own accord. Its composer has focused his mind upon a single object, and with a nature wholly in sympathy with it has hewn an entirely new form of operatic art. Its production would prove an interesting and potent achievement, and it is to be hoped that sooner or later it will be thus honored.

For all the favorable publicity, no one came forth to mount a production. For the next year, Joplin vacillated between finding a way to produce *Treemonisha* or giving up and returning to writing classic Ragtime. His hopes soared briefly when a Harlem theater owner, Thomas Johnson, agreed to finance an opening in Atlantic City, then as now a playground for New Yorkers. However, Joplin had not yet completed the orchestral score, and the deal fell through before he could do so. As a diversion, and in order to bring in some money, Joplin brought forth a fresh tune in 1912 that he sent to Stern Publishing. All his flagging energy must have gone into the composition, for he titled it simply "Scott Joplin's New Rag." Despite its simple title, it was one of his liveliest and most complicated works.

Joplin's second attempt at production also went awry. Early in 1913 the *New York Age* reported that the Lafayette Theater, which had recently caused consternation by abandoning segregated seating, would stage *Treemonisha* in the fall. Joplin sent out notices saying he was looking for singers. One report said he had twenty-two people under contract. The flurry of publicity also caused Joplin some concern: it seemed as if he would have to play down his status as a Ragtime composer if he was to succeed in grand opera. He had a note published in the *New York Age*, probably written by Lester Walton:

> *Treemonisha* is a grand opera — Scott Joplin, the well known composer, says: "I am a composer of Ragtime music but I want it thoroughly understood that my opera *Treemonisha* is not Ragtime. In most of the strains I have used syncopations (rhythm) peculiar to my race, but the music is not Ragtime and the score complete in grand opera."

As it happened, the Layfayette performance never took place; the segregation controversy led to the appointment of new management. The change cost Joplin his one chance for a professional production.

Still, he was determined to press ahead. In October 1913 Joplin and Lottie Stokes (either she was still using her maiden name or it was before

12. Dreaming of Treemonisha

Scott Joplin continued to compose new tunes even struggling to complete his opera *Treemonisha*. He published "New Rag" in 1912, one of his liveliest and most complicated works (The Lilly Library, Indiana University).

they were married) signed documents to form their own company, the Scott Joplin Music Publishing Company. Later, they moved to a large home at 133 West 138th Street, deep in Harlem, where Lottie set up a boardinghouse. Joplin bought a large Steinway grand piano and this became his instrument for the classes he conducted for students of a nearby music school attended by three hundred black children. He put an ad in the *Age* advising his move and announcing that he would devote "a part of his time to instruction of pupils on the violin and piano." In another ad he offered to sell "six piano copies of any of his compositions or six assorted of any popular pieces published in New York" for one dollar.

Joplin was still struggling to generate income any way that he could. It was during this period that he wrote his last surviving composition. (Others that he was said to be working on have been lost.) His final piece was "Magnetic Rag," which he published himself and offered to sell for twenty-five cents in stamps. It was a premium price.

Finally, in 1915, Joplin in desperation put on his own production of *Treemonisha* at the Lincoln Theater in Harlem. The only help Joplin received came in the timely intervention of an old friend, Sam Patterson, of St. Louis. On arriving in New York, he volunteered to arrange Joplin's piano instrumentation for the various instruments of the orchestra. The opera called for a forty-piece orchestra, but in the end, only Joplin was there to play accompaniment on the piano. The stage was bare of costumes and sets, and the volunteers Joplin had recruited were far from professional performers.

The audience was sparse. Some eighteen friends and a scattering of locally curious spectators were in attendance. The performance received no critical reviews. It could only be described as a disaster. Aside from the futility of trying to stage an elaborate show as little more than a one-man production, Joplin had no way of promoting his great work to the urban, sophisticated audience he needed to reach. Nor had he any way of making himself known to the isolated, rural audience that was the subject of *Tremonisha*.

The collapse of Joplin's dream of *Treemonisha* left him feeling hopeless, deserted, and distraught. He had been abandoned by peers like Jim Europe and betrayed by his publisher John Stark, and now he was being ignored by music critics and theatrical entrepreneurs alike.

Whites wanted to hear only the folk music of the plantations; they had no interest in uplifting messages directed to the descendants of slaves. Urban blacks who would have been in a position to respond to *Treemon-*

12. Dreaming of Treemonisha

isha felt they had risen above the illiterate status of their rural brethren and had little wish to be reminded of their condition.

If one forgets the logistical task that would have faced Joplin in trying to stage *Treemonisha*, a more important issue remains: was Joplin creatively capable, by experience and training, to write a grand opera? Never had a major American composer acted as his own librettist and choreographer. The feat of combining a musical score with a text — the libretto — into a grand opera calls for the creation of a dramatic work that incorporates singing, acting, spoken theater, dance and staging in a single production that is a feast for the eyes, ears and mind.

To realize success would require musical mastery, literary skill and an innate understanding of African American aspirations. The latter Joplin certainly had, along with an awareness of the self-limiting roadblock of low expectations that he saw his people imposing on themselves. Joplin clearly understood the story he was attempting to put on stage, and he probably drew from his own life experience in creating its chief elements.

Treemonisha is set near Texarkana, his hometown, between 1866 and 1884, which includes the first sixteen years of Joplin's life. Like his protagonist, Joplin was taught by his mother's white employers and learned the value of an education. Treemonisha herself may have been based on Freddie Alexander, the love of his life whom he lost after barely a month of marriage. He shows a healthy skepticism toward the black church by casting Pastor Alltalk as an ineffectual goad for goodness. Pastor Alltalk is able to do little else than speak in trite generalities and he shows a lack of understanding of his community's real needs.

Tales of the German operatic master Richard Wagner, told to Joplin by his first music teacher, the German immigrant Julius Weiss, in Texarkana, had probably first inspired him. The encouragement he got from the St. Louis musical director, Alfred Ernst, would have reinforced any latent ambition to rise above the mediocrity of barroom Ragtime. However, Joplin appears not to have had the literary background to enable him to fully develop his characters or match his wonderful music with an equally compelling dramatization.

The question of whether American composers could aspire to the level of old world composers or whether there could be such a thing as an American opera were topics of lively debate in musical circles. The *American Musician and Art Journal* noted that several American operas had been

PART III — The Dream That Wouldn't Die

produced recently and that the Metropolitan Opera Company had put up a prize of ten thousand dollars for the best made-in-the-U.S.A. production. The cash would go to one Horatio Parker for an opera called *Mona*, built around a fictional princess of Britain. Another noted American writing operas at this time was Joseph Breil, although he is better remembered as the first to compose a score for a film. His work for *Queen Elizabeth*, a 1912 silent film, meant that viewers would hear, for the first time, music written specifically to accompany the images they were seeing on the screen.

After his failure at the Lincoln Theater, Joplin had neither the strength nor the resources to continue his struggle to raise Ragtime beyond vaudeville and cabaret. Fifty-seven years would pass before *Tremonisha* would be professionally produced; a revival performance in Atlanta in 1972 would be followed by productions in Houston, Seattle, and Washington before a successful appearance at Broadway's Uris Theater. *New York Times* critic Harold Schoenberg would write of "A Real Slow Drag": "Harmonically enchanting, full of the tensions of an entire race, rhythmically catching, it refuses to leave the mind."

"*Treemonisha* is America's first great opera," William Schafer and Johannes Riedel wrote in 1973 in *The Art of Ragtime*, "because it strikes a balance between the essential nonrealism of the opera form and the demands of an American audience for an entertainment which is concrete and not fantastic." They added:

> A social and historical principle seems to dictate that cultures losing track of their real needs and desires get precisely what they deserve. It is not surprising that America was not prepared to listen to Treemonisha.... After decades of unparalleled crassness, vulgarity, and social retrogression — the "Gilded Age" and collapse of Radical Reconstruction in the late nineteenth century — America was hardly prepared for a naïve, delicate, and almost translucently gentle operatic style. It was not interested in black social or aesthetic advances, and it had no curiosity about Scott Joplin, once his phenomenal success with "*Maple Leaf Rag*" faded from the popular mind. While black people were vitally interested in questions of social and political progress ... they were not especially attracted to a modest folktale set to lyrical, unpretentious music. *Treemonisha* failed to capture the imagination of its age.

At last, there was professional production and critical praise for *Treemonisha*. The fact it did not come for six decades reinforces the sagacity of Joplin's prediction that he would die before the world would recognize his genius.

PART IV

After the Rag: The Finale

The classical beat of instrumental Ragtime worked fine in vaudeville houses and rolled out melodiously from the player piano rolls of Scott Joplin and other performers. But it lent itself less well to the growing diversity of musical theater. Backup composers like Charles L. Johnson brought out such numbers as "Crazy Bone Rag" but it was Alfred Bryan's sentimental "Peg o' My Heart" that caught the fancy of Broadway and brought down the house in the Ziegfeld Follies of 1913.

Millions sat captivated in movie houses, watching glamorous men and women act out fantasies of life on flickering screens. The automobile was a common scene on city streets and there was even talk that some day anyone would be able to go aloft, just as the Wright brothers had done. Meanwhile, suffragettes marched through Washington, war clouds gathered over Europe, and something called jass (as it was first spelled) was being played by white bands who expropriated the music of the Storyville haunts of New Orleans.

In New York, the International Exhibition of Modern Art unveiled the work of a new school of realist artists at the Armory Show. Painters like John Sloan of the Ashcan school of art depicted gritty scenes of urban life: ordinary people going about ordinary lives. He was one of The Eight whose brushstrokes depicted a distinctly New World perspective on life. Their counterparts in Canada, the Group of Seven, would transfer the vast landscape of the north to small canvases that captured the grandeur of Canadian lakes and forests.

In 1914, the new mass culture that combined popular art with technology was catapulted into the hell of the First World War. The Ragtime era, illuminated by sudden discovery and breathtaking originality in music, art, science and industry, was coming to an end. The closing years of the

PART IV — After the Rag

Ragtime era were filled with all the tumult, uproar and chaos that had brought it into being a quarter of a century before. After the rag, the world was ready to move on to new experiences, having absorbed the overture, been delighted by the symphony, and entranced by the finale.

Later, when swing had succeeded jazz and rock 'n' roll permeated the airwaves and television superseded radio and the Internet all but replaced newspapers, Scott Joplin's creative genius would continue to echo across the years.

13

Little Mary and the Little Tramp
Ragtime Partners of the Silent Screen

The Blondeau Tavern was little more than a tacky booze joint and cheap hotel at the corner of Sunset Boulevard and Gower Street in a desolate section of Los Angeles when David Horsley, a pioneer filmmaker from New Jersey, came upon it. The Blondeau was mostly boarded up, the paint peeling from its shutters; but Horsley decided that its barbershop would well serve the purpose he had in mind, which was to set up the first permanent film studio in California. He rented it at thirty dollars a month.

Good outdoor shooting weather enabled Horsley to turn out a new one-reel Western every week for his Nestor Film Company, beginning with *Law of the Range* in 1912. It was something that would never have been possible in the damp and cold of the East. Within a year, fifteen other film companies had followed him to Hollywood. It was in this sleepy coastal suburb — founded by a dedicated prohibitionist — that Cecil B. DeMille would make *The Squaw Man*, the first feature-length motion picture. The most powerful new cultural medium of the Ragtime era had found the place where it would flourish.

The California coast, empty except for a few small settlements that harkened back to the days of Spanish missionaries, proved hospitable to the silent film industry. By the mid–1910s, it was home to thousands of actors, writers, directors and producers who were pursuing fresh ways of manipulating the new technology of film. On a cool winter evening of early 1917, the upper echelon of filmdom gathered to celebrate an industry that by now knew few limits and had imposed little in the way of social or moral restraint on its members. Although tonight's "movie ball" was being held not in Hollywood but in another coastal village, Long Beach, the greats of this swaggering new world of motion pictures had come out to entertain and be entertained. In the crowd were the two highest paid performers in history, a brash young Cockney born in poverty in London, England, and a graceful, soft-spoken but very assertive young woman from Toronto, Canada, both bound for greatness.

Mary Pickford's millions of followers called her Little Mary for her gifted performances as an innocent golden-haired gamine, and they gave her the title of "America's Sweetheart." As Mary watched Charlie Chaplin perform shoeless that night in giving his impression of another silent film notable, J. Warren Kerrigan, his act more than anything reminded her of Chaplin's famed Little Tramp of comedic genius. Mary thought him "very young and aesthetic, all eyes, with a great big black cloche (ascot) necktie." Looking at him carefully, she noted "the sensitivity of his face, and the smallness of his hands." When they were introduced, she found his handshake limp: "What my mother used to call a cold-fish hand." They eyed each other comfortably; the substantial heels of her dancing shoes put her five-foot frame on an almost equal level with his five-foot four-inch height.

There were more than twenty thousand theaters showing silent films, but something more was needed to satisfy the audiences who turned up to see the images of their new idols cast on flickering screens. It was music, and Ragtime music especially, that provided the vital missing link by adding sound that gave the pictures meaning and emotion. Charlie Chaplin spent hours writing compositions for his films. Other producers simply sent along a list of pieces to accompany different segments of a movie: for love scenes, for chases, for moments of suspense. In Montreal, a young pianist named Willie Eckstein became so proficient at playing Ragtime for shows at the Strand Theater that he became known as the "Boy Paderewski." He commanded fifteen thousand dollars for a year's tour of American silent film palaces. Eckstein went on to write both rags and patriotic songs, including "Delirious Rag" and "Perpetual Rag" and the World War I hit "Good-bye Soldier Boy."

13. Little Mary and the Little Tramp

Mary Pickford and Charlie Chaplin were children of the motion picture age, born three years and an ocean apart, just as the wondrous new technology of casting moving images onto screens was about to come into being. Charlie was born in the grungy Limehouse district of London on April 16, 1889, and Mary in a small but comfortable home on Toronto's leafy University Avenue, on April 8, 1892. They were the first and greatest stars of the silent film era and together they made the movies the most powerful medium of communication the world had ever seen.

Despite what Mary would call Charlie's "strange and unpredictable" behavior, they would be loyal business partners in the first actor-controlled film company, United Artists. Its role was to distribute the films that each of its four owners — Mary, Charlie, Mary's swashbuckling husband, Douglas Fairbanks, and the great pioneer director David W. Griffith — would produce independently. The UA distribution formula would eventually become the dominant model for doing business in Hollywood.

Charlie's parents, Charles Sr. and Hannah, were modestly successful vaudeville performers on the English music hall stage. He was a baritone and comedian, she a singer, dancer and mimic. Hannah brought an older son, Sidney, into the marriage and Hannah was faced with supporting two young children after she and Charles Sr. separated following years of abuse brought on by his heavy drinking.

Young Charlie's efforts were not enough to keep Hannah and the two children from the Lambeth workhouse, one instance of a uniquely British institution that provided a refuge for destitute families in the Victorian age. Charlie would eventually bring his mother to the United States and would recall that as far as acting went, "I learned from her everything that I know. She was the most astounding mimic I ever saw."

Mary, whose real name was Gladys Louise Smith, was the product of the Anglo-Saxon and Celtic stock that filled Toronto with English, Irish and Scottish immigrants in the nineteenth century. Her father, John Charles Smith, was a descendant of British Methodists and her mother, Charlotte Hennessy, came from an Irish Catholic family. Their marriage was notable, at a time of considerable religious prejudice, for bridging the Protestant-Catholic divide that was sharply visible in Canada. Gladys was their first child, born in their small house at 211 University Avenue, then

PART IV — After the Rag

a quiet street that led south from Queen's Park, the site of the provincial parliament buildings.

Mary's father secured the candy concession on the *Corona*, a steamer that traversed Lake Ontario. He died from a cerebral hemorrhage brought on, it was thought, by a blow on the head from a dangling pulley as the ship was coming into dock. He also drank too much. Mary would later write, "I can close my eyes and still hear the scream of Mother's at the moment Father passed on."

Mary and Charlie both performed throughout their childhoods, learning the skills of mimicry, song, and dance and mastering ways of gaining the attention of their audiences with a skilful stage presence. Charlie got his first continuing role in 1900, when he was only eleven, as one of the eight Lancashire Lads in the pantomime *Cinderella* at London's Hippodrome.

Mary Pickford, still Gladys Smith, was often ill as a child. In 1899, when she was seven, she was befriended by a doctor at the Children's Hospital. Dr. G.B. Smith was no kin, but he and his wife offered to adopt her. Charlotte left it to Gladys to decide. She decided against it: "A determination was born in me that day that nothing could crush. I must prevent anything from breaking up my family."

That same year, Mary found her way onto a Toronto stage on the invitation of her mother's boarder, who was the stage manager for a local stock company. Gladys played the role of Big Girl in a children's production called *The Silver King* at the Princess Theater. Her success led to roles in other light melodramas popular among Toronto's theatergoers at the time. Charlotte saw the possibility of a better future in her daughter's acting skill and trained her other children to follow Mary's example.

It was inevitable that Mary and Charles would find their way to the United States where there were more theaters to play and where the silent film industry was moving from unsatisfying one-reel mini stories to full-length features. Mary got there first, touring with her siblings and mother as a family act, playing rag-tag melodrama roles in one-night stands.

After six years of surviving seedy, third-rate hotels, the family arrived in New York in the summer of 1907 — the year that Ragtimer Scott Joplin had moved from St. Louis — with Gladys determined to either get a decent role or quit show business. Every move in her life was controlled by the

13. Little Mary and the Little Tramp

Syndicate, the powerful trust that made bookings, set actors' salaries and determined what theaters they would play. "I made up my mind that if I couldn't appear in a Broadway play this fall I would give up the theater forever," she said.

Just fifteen, she went to the office of one of the city's top producers, David Belasco, insisting "My life depends on meeting Mr. Belasco!" Her determination won her a part in his Broadway production, *The Warrens of Virginia*. It was written by William C. DeMille, brother of Cecil B. DeMille, who would go on to movie fame. But Belasco laid down one condition: Gladys needed a new name. She chose to become Mary Pickford, a name taken from her maternal ancestors.

Never anxious to get into films, Mary went for a screen test only on the urging of her mother, who saw the new fad as a way of bolstering the family's finances. "It's only to tide us over," Charlotte assured her daughter. Movie actors were considered even less respectable than theatrical people, and Mary had little desire to mix with such riffraff. When she went for a screen test at the Brooklyn office of Biograph Pictures, the leading film company of the day, David W. Griffith told her, "You're too little and too fat, but I may give you a chance." She convinced Griffith to pay her ten dollars for a day's work, twice the going rate. In 1910 Mary moved to Los Angeles to join a Biograph shoot there, beginning a silent film career that would make her one of the world's richest women. Film historian Tino Balio described her uncanny ability to project her personality onto the screen: "She invented acting for film. She understood that you have a close, intimate relationship with the camera, and more subtle, more naturalistic gestures would be very effective. She stands out because she has more vibrancy, she has more immediacy, and she actually conveys more emotion in the process."

Charlie Chaplin arrived in New York on October 2, 1912. Now twenty-three, he traveled with one Art Jefferson, who would become known as Stan Laurel of Laurel and Hardy fame. A Chaplin performance in *A Night at an English Music Hall* caught the attention of Mack Sennett, one of the greatest of the early silent film directors. He wired Chaplin's troupe: "Is there a man named Chaffin in your company or something like that" and would he get in touch with Sennett's New York office?

The summons reached Chaplin, and when he arrived at what looked like a law office, he thought he might be about to receive an inheritance.

Part IV — After the Rag

Instead, he was offered a one-year contract paying one hundred and fifty dollars a week to go to Hollywood and make films with Sennett.

The second film Charlie made for Sennett saw the launch of his career-defining character, the Little Tramp, a tragicomic figure whose optimism was undimmed by constant hardship and misfortune. The tramp figure would remain a central component of every Chaplin movie up to *Modern Times* in 1936.

Marital success eluded Mary for a time, and Charlie until late in his life. She had a short, tempestuous marriage to a hard-drinking silent film actor, Owen Moore, before commencing an affair with Douglas Fairbanks about 1915. They married in 1920, created the marvelous Pickfair estate in Beverly Hills, and divorced in 1936. Mary was married for the last time that year, to actor and bandleader Buddy Rogers. Chaplin married four times, but had hundreds of affairs. On his first tour of America, he proclaimed that he'd found the most beautiful whores in Butte, Montana, and the most brazen ones in Chicago.

Mary, in contrast, lived a life largely free of scandal. There was never any suggestion of an affair with anyone other than Fairbanks; certainly she had no intimate liaison with Charlie Chaplin. While still married to Owen Moore, she underwent what was reported to be an appendectomy, the well-known euphemism for an abortion. She blamed her later failure to bear children on a fall she'd had from a horse. Given the primitive nature of abortions at the time, this could well have been the cause of her sterility.

Born amid a jungle of cut-throat competition, the motion picture industry harnessed new technologies in cameras, projectors and film production to cast its spell over Ragtime era audiences. The science of it came first. Everyone knew the images you saw were not scenes of continuous motion but thousands of individual photographs, or frames, projected rapidly one after another to create the illusion of motion. After much experimentation, a rate of sixteen frames per second, shot on film thirty-five millimeters wide, was found to function best.

The reason the system worked, the scientists reasoned, was the brain's ability to retain an image for a fraction of a second longer than it had actually been viewed. This persistence of vision, as it was called, made it pos-

13. Little Mary and the Little Tramp

sible for early inventors to bemuse viewers with devices that rapidly flipped drawings of objects such as horses, birds or people, making them seem to run, fly or dance. Eadweard Muybridge, the photographer who had taken serial pictures of galloping horses to prove they lifted all their hooves off the ground while running, did this with a projector he invented called the Zoopraxiscope.

Who were these people who were flocking to the new nickelodeons to see simple renditions of make-believe life? Far from representing a cross section of the American population, they came almost entirely from the working class, many of them newly arrived immigrants. The educated class, the bastion of traditional culture, had little time or interest for the superficial offerings of the motion picture companies peddled by the disreputable, usually dirty and uncomfortable nickelodeons.

Police raids on the nickelodeons were common occurrences, with exhibitors being charged either with presenting immoral performances or with violation of safety codes. In New York, where nickelodeons paid a license fee of only twenty-five dollars while vaudeville houses faced a levy of five hundred dollars, Mayor George B. McClellan, Jr.— son of the Civil War general — ordered all six hundred shut during Christmas week of 1908. "The Christian Sabbath is one of the civil institutions of the state," declared Justice James A. O'Gorman. After two weeks of civic uproar — thousands thronged Times Square to make clear their desire to take in Sunday shows — the city backed down.

"Charlie Chaplin gets laughed at in one week by more people than any man in history. Chaplin is excruciatingly funny. He can make fun at a funeral. It's worth $1,500 every week of the year. They pay him every seven days one year's salary just because he's Charlie Chaplin." So read the hand-out from Chaplin's studio, the Essenay Film Manufacturing Company, published in the *Atlanta Constitution* on February 28, 1915.

Chaplin had gone to Essenay after making thirty-five films in his year with Mack Sennett. He'd become disenchanted with the comedic producer after learning that his costar in *Tillie's Punctured Romance*, the Canadian actress Marie Dressler, was being paid twenty-five hundred dollars a week. Charlie took with him everything he'd learned working for Sennett, including his Little Tramp character, who became the central figure of his main effort in 1915, *The Tramp*. It did only moderately well at the box office, but those who saw it loved it, especially the closing frames in which Charlie — after realizing he'd never win the hand of the farmer's daughter with whom he'd fallen in love — sets off dejectedly down the road, his shoulders squared for whatever other misfortune life can throw at him.

Chaplin by now was writing his own film scripts, but he was still looking for the kind of financial windfall he felt he deserved, given his rapidly growing popularity. He found it with the Mutual Film Company, where on February 26, 1916, he signed a contract that would pay him ten thousand dollars a week, on top of a one hundred and fifty thousand dollar signing bonus.

Chaplin usually worked without a script. He'd shoot hours of action and then decide to change the plot, or even cut the film he was working on into pieces, using each piece in different pictures. He reduced his famous 1916 production, *The Immigrant*, from twenty-four hours of raw footage into twenty-one minutes of screen time. Charlie also worried about the music that theaters would play with his films, and insisted on personally handling the musical "cue sheet" that would give precise directions on what the audience was to hear.

The First World War posed problems for Charlie, still a British subject, and he was widely criticized in Britain for not returning home to join up. He received white feathers in his mail, symbols of cowardice. The fact that he flunked a U.S. Army physical in 1917 did little to quiet the criticism. Chaplin toured with Mary Pickford and Douglas Fairbanks in a massive Liberty Bond drive that raised hundreds of millions of dollars to support U.S. involvement in the war. "I'm only five feet tall," Mary would tell enthusiastic crowds, "but every inch of me is a fighting American!"

In fact, Mary had mixed emotions about the war. Canadian-born, she felt a strong tug of loyalty to the British Empire and empathized with the ordeals of her relatives back in England. Her immense popularity led E.E. McClure, the founder of McClure's Newspaper Syndicate, to sign her up in 1915 for a ghost-written newspaper column of Daily Talks. The writing was done by Frances Marion, who also ghosted for Marie Dressler, but the ideas were usually Mary's. As to the war, Mary expressed a typical feminine response: "Can you imagine women — mothers of girls and boys — going out to kill one another with the strange deadly fatalism that

13. Little Mary and the Little Tramp

seems to seize our soldiers?" Her readers considered her the supreme authority on most other topics, asking her in hundreds of letters a day for beauty tips, advice in the workplace, or how to get along with their mates.

The films Mary made for David Griffith made her more famous than ever, but she was still not sure whether her future lay in the movies or the Broadway stage. When David Belasco offered her the lead in his new play, *A Good Little Devil*, Mary finished up work on her final film for Griffith, *The New York Hat*, and went off to rehearse her role as a blind child whose sight is restored by a magic queen. The play was a success, but acting for the stage failed to match "the exciting jigsaw puzzle of a motion picture in progress — the novelty, the adventure, from day to day, into unknown areas of pantomime and photography."

The film that locked Mary Pickford forever in the hearts of moviegoers was an eighty-minute production released in 1914, *Tess of the Storm Country*. It was tailor-made for her capacity to play indomitable adolescents, this time the heroic Tess, who nobly undertakes to provide for the baby born to a suicidal unwed mother named Teola. Battling a heartless landlord and a cruel priest who refuses to baptize the baby, Tess has to steal from Teola's rich family to feed the child.

She struggles on until finally Teola comes to her senses and confesses, "He is my baby!" The press idolized Mary's performance, movie magazines rhapsodized about her moral qualities, and fan letters came in from all over the globe. *Photoplay*, one of the first fan magazines, saw her acting style as one of "luminous tenderness in a steel band of gutter ferocity." It all led B.P. Schulberg, who was doing publicity for Famous Players, to dub her "America's Sweetheart" after hearing the conversation of a couple buying tickets for the film. "My little sweetheart," the husband said in pointing to a picture of Mary. "She's not just your little sweetheart, she's everybody's sweetheart," his wife responded.

The silent films of Mary Pickford and Charlie Chaplin entertained and amused moviegoers and established the two — although they never played together — as the greatest cinematic performers of the Ragtime era. Their talent in dramatic and comedic acting gave the motion picture camera, a new device in the repertoire of the theater, a raw emotional force that could send viewers into paroxysms of delight before reducing them to tears. Their presence at the birth of motion pictures gave this new

PART IV — After the Rag

medium a life and purpose it would never otherwise have realized. They had changed the culture of the world, irretrievably and permanently. The lives of Mary and Charlie ran long past the Ragtime era but covered virtually identical spans. He died on December 5, 1977, age eighty-eight, she on May 29, 1979, at eighty-seven. They had played their life roles to near perfection.

14

The Rites of Spring
The Martyred Saint of the Ragtime Era

The railway station in the small southern town of Tutwiler, Mississippi, is stuffy and hot the day that William Christopher Handy, the young white leader of a black band called the Knights of Pythias, waits for the next train for Clarksburg, the band's home base. His dozing is interrupted by the sound of a "lean, loose-jointed Negro ... plucking a guitar beside me while I slept." The man, running a knife against the strings of his instrument, slowly sings a line that he repeats three times: "Goin' where the Southern cross' the Dog."

The song refers to two railway lines that cross. Handy would later recall it as "the weirdest music I had ever heard." What he was listening to was a distinctive sound that Handy would master in becoming the "Father of the Blues." Like Ragtime and jazz, the blues emerged — all three at almost the same time — as fresh variants of the folk songs that African American laborers and farm workers sang to escape, at least for a few moments, the tortures of their daily lives.

Like Scott Joplin, W.C. Handy had played the cornet in pick-up bands at the 1893 Chicago World's Fair. By the 1910s he was well established in Memphis with his own outfit. He kept in mind what he'd heard at the railway station in tiny Tutwiler when he wrote a campaign song for a candidate for mayor, Edward Crump — the future revered, and hated, Boss Crump. That song became the "Memphis Blues," and Handy sold all rights to it for one hundred dollars. His next creation, he decided, he would publish himself. It was the even more memorable "St. Louis Blues."

Part IV — After the Rag

Few who have heard this song can forget its immortal first two lines: "I hate to see de ev'nun sun go down, Cause my baby he done lef this town."

For centuries, "the blues" had been a synonym for melancholia and is the term still in use today when we talk about someone undergoing mild depression. Blues as applied to African American music covered a far more nuanced range of experiences. The songs of the blues began in the oral traditions of black slaves and often recounted the painful experience of undergoing great physical strain, usually the consequence of hard labor. Harvesting, hoeing, hauling and breaking rocks all took their toll on black males. The black writer Ralph Ellison saw the appeal of the blues as stemming from "an impulse to keep the painful details and episodes of a brutal experience alive in one's aching consciousness."

Songs like these, along with traditional Ragtime favorites such as "Alexander's Ragtime Band" and "Maple Leaf Rag" were played at the hundreds of fairs that towns all over North America staged each spring as salutes to the rebirth of nature and the expectation of fresh bounty. Those who relaxed and played at these Rites of Spring were largely oblivious to other rites being played out far beyond their borders.

The titled, the moneyed and the parvenu of the English upper class gathered on June 4, 1913, for the Epsom Derby, the greatest of all of Britain's Rites of Spring. These crowds also were largely oblivious to the great social upheaval going on around them, as clouds of war gathered over Europe and English suffragettes became more militant in their demand for the vote.

As the fifteen horses thundered around the final, sharp left bend of the grass track at Epsom Downs, a woman suddenly dodged under a railing and onto the course, flinging herself among the galloping thoroughbreds. In an instant, the big bay Anmer, owned by the new king, George V, bore down on her. The jockey, Herbert Jones, tried desperately to dash past the woman. It was impossible, on this bright Spring day, to avoid a collision. The horse struck the woman full force, then stumbled and fell, throwing Jones to the ground. Beside him lay Emily Wilding Davison, a well-known suffragette who had been jailed seven times in the campaign to win women the right to vote. She was bruised and battered and would die four days after her suicidal act, a revered martyr to the cause of women's

14. The Rites of Spring

rights. She had decided, according to suffragette leader Emmeline Pankhurst, that only her death "would put an end to the intolerable torture of women."

Meanwhile, *tout Paris* was caught up in feverish discussion of another Rite of Spring, the controversial ballet of that name — *Le Sacre du printemps* — which had been performed less than a week before at the Théâtre des Champs-Élysées. The performance by the Ballets Russes at this newest of Parisian entertainment palaces, built especially for the staging of contemporary music and dance, staggered cultural circles for it brazen impertinence. Depicting the primitive dance of a pagan tribe — complete with the ritual sacrifice of a chosen maiden — the complexity of Igor Stravinsky's musical score and the violence of Vaslav Nijinsky's choreography puzzled and upset many in the audience. Laughter, followed by loud arguments, broke out all over the theater and quickly descended into fistfights. The police were called and Stravinsky, just twenty-eight and still learning to deal with the fame that had come from his 1910 success, *Firebird*, fled the theater in dismay.

Clearly, this radical new ballet was seen as a scandalous attack on traditional high culture. It was entirely too lustful and sexual for public presentation. *Le Sacre du printemps* would finish out its six performances, surprisingly without further trouble. The Ballets Russes would perform later in the year in London, but the controversial production would be forever remembered as a landmark of modern composition.

All during that Spring of 1913, the ferment of cultural as well as political protest bubbled through the established order, while the specter of an oncoming war cast its darkness over Europe. Ragtime music had peaked in North America and had swept across the Atlantic. Britons loved nothing more than an afternoon or an evening at the music hall. England's Harry Lauder sang the suggestive "It's Nice to Be in Bed" and Julius Lenzberg turned Liszt's *Hungarian Rhapsody* into *Hungarian Rag*. In the U.S., Irving Berlin scored with a half dozen popular melodies, including "International Rag" and "They've Got Me Doin' It Now."

The first International Exhibition of Modern Art — the Armory Show — ran in New York from February 17 to March 15, creating as great a stir as that which would greet Stravinsky's *Rite of Spring* in Paris. Crowds came to see eight works by Pablo Picasso, each of distinctly modernist creation. None of them compared, some clients complained, with his 1907

PART IV — After the Rag

work, *Les Demoiselles d'Avignon*. That eye-catching depiction of the various moods of the prostitutes in a *maison de tolerance* scandalized proper French society, although few who had the opportunity of gazing at it missed doing so. In its place, it fell to Marcel Duchamp's *Nude Descending the Staircase* and Henri Matisse's *Luxury* to signal the breaking of the old boundaries of artistic tradition. The American artists of the Ashcan school made their presence known, but even the grittiest of their depictions of urban life were tame compared to the scandals of Duchamp and Matisse.

The shadows cast by World War I had a sudden and overwhelming impact on popular culture. Patriotic songs rapidly replaced the Ragtime tunes that had been favored by vaudeville acts and music hall performers. In Canada, which went to war automatically when Britain declared hostilities against Germany and Austria-Hungary in 1914, patriotic songs like "Stand by the Union Jack" spurred recruiting:

> Great Britain needs more Warriors!
> The cry rings far and near —
> And in recruiting centres
> How quickly men appear.

More famously, British troops in that first enthusiastic summer of 1914 marched off to battle singing "It's a Long Way to Tipperary":

> It's a long way to Tipperary
> To the sweetest girl I know!
> Goodbye Piccadilly,
> Farewell Leicester Square!
> It's a long long way to Tipperary,
> But my heart's right there.

Tin Pan Alley joined the fray even before the United States was in the conflict. But by 1917, with America preparing reluctantly to join the war in Europe, the country was rocking to the martial airs of such George M. Cohan compositions as "Over There":

> Over there, over there,
> Send the word, send the word over there —
> That the Yanks are coming,
> The Yanks are coming,

14. The Rites of Spring

And we won't come back till it's over
Over there.

Irving Berlin, who would be conscripted into the U.S. Army in 1917, turned the experience of having to get up at five o'clock in the morning into a musical hit, "Oh! How I Hate to Get Up in the Morning!"* He used it in the patriotic recruiting show he mounted, *Yip Yip Yaphank*, a

Irving Berlin's patriotic hit, "How I Hate to Get Up in the Morning," headlined his 1917 recruiting show *Yip Yip Yaphank*. The show was also notable for his final Ragtime composition, "Ragtime Razor Brigade."

*Berlin would reprise the number for his World War II show, This Is the Army.

PART IV — After the Rag

production that was also notable for his final Ragtime song, "Ragtime Razor Brigade." By now, Ragtime's rapid fading had opened space for a new entry in the cultural lexicon — jazz: "A new kind of Dixie had come to New York and this jazz baby was making Miss Ragtime look like an old maid." Sophie Tucker was suddenly being hailed as the Queen of Jazz.

The strains of jazz had been first heard in New Orleans, where small bands were improvising syncopated Ragtime melodies as early as Buddy Bolden's time. Sometime in 1916, the first jazz band (or jass, as it was then spelled) to move north reached Chicago, where it played at Schiller's Café and then at McVicker's, a leading vaudeville house. Its rendition of "Walkin' the Dog," a number by the Canadian-born black pianist Shelton Brooks, caused a sensation.

The all-white group performed under the name of the Original Dixieland Jass Band. (The spelling was changed to jazz when it was discovered that youthful miscreants were deleting the first letter of jass from their posters.) The singer Al Jolson heard the band on a visit to Chicago. He was enthusiastic and encouraged the theatrical agent Max Hart to recruit the band to play in New York. Hart had to outbid other agents who also had heard of the new outfit. A flurry of telegrams passed back and forth between Hart, his rivals Marvin Welt and Max Lowe, and Dixieland trombonist Eddie Edwards, who was acting as the band's manager. For whatever reason, the band chose to go with Hart. Consisting of Edwards, cornetist Nick LaRocca, clarinetist Larry Shields and pianist Harry Ragas, the ODJB broke in at the Reisenweber's Café on Columbus Circle on January 27, 1917.* It is said customers sat in their seats for the first two nights, afraid to get up and try to dance to these strange new sounds. Hart finally took over the microphone on the third night and announced, "This music is for dancing." A few of the braver patrons then moved to the floor.

The fledgling recording industry moved quickly to appropriate jazz. The Columbia Gramophone Company brought the ODJB to its New York studio in January 1917, but the historical record is unclear as to whether it was for a recording session or merely an audition. One version has it that the musicians were handed two songs they'd never heard before — Shelton Brooks' "Darktown Strutters' Ball" and James Hanley's "(Back Home Again in) Indiana." Both would become enduring hits, but because

---

*Ragas would die in the influenza epidemic of 1919.

14. The Rites of Spring

most of the band couldn't read music, their improvisations had to be played over and over again. If a recording was made, Columbia for some reason chose not to issue it.

Columbia's indecision gave the Victor Talking Machine Company the chance to be first on the market with a jazz recording. In March 1917 it issued *Sensation*, the historic Victor 18255 record containing a medley of the band's best numbers, "Dixieland Jazz Band One-Step" backed by "Livery Stable Blues." The inclusion of a strain from Joe Jordon's 1909 rag, "That Teasin' Rag," in "One-Step" led to claims of copyright infringement. The rules regarding intellectual property were still unclear and, perhaps more to the point, still largely unrecognized and unenforced.

Black performers also began making records about this time. One of the earliest was Wilbur Sweatman, who had made the first recording of "Maple Leaf Rag" around 1903. He modified the sound of his Ragtime band to accommodate the strains of jazz and issued several records with Columbia in 1917.

W.C. Handy did his best to keep Ragtime alive with a new composition, "Ole Miss Rag." But Ray Nunez of Stein's Dixie Jass Band had a bigger hit with "Livery Stable Blues" and Will Hart touched patriotic hearts with "When Yankee Doodle Learns to Parlez Vous Francais." Broadway's big hit of the year was *Maytime*, the Sigmund Romberg musical that ran for four hundred and sixty-three performances. In London *The Maid of the Mountains* ran for more than thirteen hundred performances at Daly's Theatre. War-weary Britons forgot for an evening the horrendous casualties in France as they sat entranced by the music and song of a love affair set in a bandit camp high in the mountains of Italy.

While the Original Dixieland Jazz Band was being introduced to northern audiences, Scott Joplin was struggling to finish his final compositions. He was receiving meager royalties and on many days he was unable to give lessons due to illness. One of his adult students, Martin Neiderhofer, had been paying him a dollar a lesson and when he offered Joplin an old coat and a fedora, the composer was so broke that he was pleased to travel to the Bronx by subway to collect the offerings.

In September 1916 Joplin completed the score for a musical comedy, *If*, and claimed to be making progress on his *Symphony No. 1*. Still mindful of the value of publicity, he sent out a notice that he was going to his sister's home in Chicago to recover from "a serious illness," but that he would be "back in the Metropolis in time to get off several new numbers for various big productions, especially ... *Symphony*." The *Indianapolis Freeman* published Joplin's hand-out on October 21.

By now, it was too late for him to be going anywhere. The syphilis that Joplin had lived with for as long as twenty years finally brought on dementia paralytica, a complete deterioration of his physical and mental faculties. He became impossible for Lottie to manage. His fevered mind provoked outbursts of anger and aggression and he began to destroy his manuscripts, declaring they were worthless trash. By Christmas of 1916, Joplin was unable to speak or walk and was forced to stay in bed.

Lottie scarcely noticed the arrival of Christmas or the advent of the New Year. Her boarders attempted to cheer her up by offering small gifts and treating her to food and drink. Joplin's condition deteriorated further as he slipped into incoherence and mindlessness. In mid–January 1917, Lottie had him taken to the Bellevue Hospital in New York. Doctors there were unable to do anything for him and on February 3 they transferred him to Manhattan State Hospital on Ward's Island where he was put in a mental ward.

The medical staff, handicapped by an unmanageable patient load and bereft of medication to treat such an advanced case, could do nothing more than maintain an around-the-clock watch on their patient. It was then only a matter of time. Joplin died on April 1, 1917. He was forty-nine. His death certificate listed the cause of his demise as "Dementia Paralytica—cerebral form"—the outcome of his long battle with syphilis.

In a rite almost as old as the human species, Joplin's body was interred on the beautiful spring day of April 5 in Saint Michael's Cemetery in East Elmhurst, Queens County.* There was no crowd of mourners at the funeral. The few friends in attendance wanted to have Joplin's music played at his graveside, but Lottie refused, a decision she apparently later regretted. On the same day as Joplin's burial, the *New York Age* reported:

SCOTT JOPLIN DIES OF MENTAL TROUBLE
Scott Joplin, known throughout the United States as the composer of syncopated music, died Sunday at the Manhattan State Hospital, where he had

---

*Plot 5, Row 2, Grave 5.

14. The Rites of Spring

been confined for a number of months for mental trouble. His death was not a surprise to friends, who had been informed that his malady was incurable. Funeral service will be conducted from the undertaking establishment of G.O. Paris, 116 West 131st Street, Thursday at 1 o'clock.

Scott Joplin first came into prominence as the writer of "The Maple Leaf Rag," which was published in St. Louis about eighteen years ago. He was born about 150 miles from St. Louis some forty odd years ago, and resided in New York about ten years. The deceased is survived by a widow, Mrs. Lottie Joplin.

In the same issue of the *Age*, Lester Walton wrote his last item about his respected friend. He put his own particular slant on the cause of Joplin's demise:

> Scott Joplin's burning desire to have produced a ragtime opera he wrote many years ago was responsible for the composer's death, is the opinion of his friends. About twelve years ago in St. Louis Joplin started to write the book and music to an opera which he had finished when he came East ten years ago. One of his missions to New York was to interest someone in producing his ragtime opera.
>
> He was advised by musicians of ability to rewrite the opera, which he enthusiastically set out to do; but even after making numerous changes in the book and score found it a herculean task to interest people with money in the opera's production.
>
> His failure to have his opera produced weighed heavily on his mind, and a few months ago he was taken to Ward's Island, where he died Sunday,

As a writer, Walton would have understood the feeling of despair and rejection that passes through the mind of an author, whether of books or of music, when one's work is rejected. His reference to Joplin having set out to rewrite his opera at the behest of others would ring true with those of his readers — and they were probably legion — who had dealt with publishers disinclined to publish their work.

Walton's view that Joplin's death resulted from the strain and frustration of trying to mount his opera was shared by many. W.C. Handy, in his 1941 autobiography, declared that Joplin "was driven insane by overwork and underpay." There is no doubt Joplin suffered from both these misfortunes, but perhaps the reluctance to recognize the true cause of Joplin's death reflected the sexual repressiveness of the times as much as the goodwill of his friends for his reputation and legacy.

They should not have been so loathe to face the facts. Joplin's condition — G.P.I., or general paralysis of the insane — was the most common

Part IV — After the Rag

cause of mental illness requiring institutionalization in the first half of the twentieth century.

There is no record of a will by Joplin or of the holding of a probate hearing to recognize the authority of his trustees, who included his wife, Lottie, and his long-time friend Wilbur Sweatman.

A week after Joplin's death, President Woodrow Wilson sent a War Message to Congress:

> The present German submarine warfare against commerce is a warfare against mankind. It is a war against all nations. American ships have been sunk, American lives taken....
>
> We desire no conquest, no dominion. We seek no indemnities for ourselves, no material compensation for the sacrifices we shall freely make. We are but one of the champions of the rights of mankind. We shall be satisfied when those rights have been made as secure as the faith and the freedom of nations can make them.

The United States was in World War I on the side of Britain and France. The Ragtime era was at an end. Joplin had struggled in his final years to bring Ragtime into the realm of serious composition, but the world was not ready for anything beyond the patriotic wartime tunes of Tin Pan Alley. Lottie Joplin was reduced to renting out the upper rooms of her Harlem home to prostitutes. Ragtime historian Scott Kirby would give Joplin this epitaph: "Scott Joplin spent his life trying to get out of the whore house, and he died in one." Lottie Joplin would remember her husband in different terms:

> You might say he died of disappointments, his health broken mentally and physically. But he was a great man, a great man! He wanted to be a real leader. He wanted to free his people from poverty and ignorance and superstition, just like the heroine in his Ragtime opera, *Treemonisha*. That's why he was so ambitious; that's why he tackled major projects. In fact, that's why he was so far ahead of his time.... You know, he would often say that he'd never be appreciated until long after he was dead.

Now he was dead, the martyred saint of the Ragtime era.

15

Ragtime in Revival

> Ragtime dead? Hell, I didn't even know it was sick!
> — *"Ragtime Bob" Darch*

The First World War ended nineteen months after Scott Joplin's death. The combined might of America and the British Empire had made the world "safe for democracy." After the war, the illusion cast by what the politicians and economists called normalcy put the stock market in an upward spiral. With the new prosperity of "the roaring Twenties" the American public transferred its interests to jazz, the blues, and the emerging new sound of swing.

In Europe, where the Ragtime craze arrived later, interest lasted longer than in North America. In 1920 Igor Stravinsky, attracted to Ragtime since creating "Golliwog's Cakewalk" in 1905, published *Piano-Rag Music* two years after having written a rag movement in the popular *l'Histoire du Soldat*. When the Prince of Wales, Britain's future king, Edward VIII, visited Canada in 1919, he insisted on having Ragtime played at a formal dance held in his honor in Halifax.

After Joplin's death, his widow, Lottie, continued to operate her Harlem boardinghouse, attracting such guests as the clarinetist and bandleader Wilbur Sweatman, pianist Willie "The Lion" Smith, and Jelly Roll Morton. Many years later, Smith would recount how the residence often seemed more like an "after-hours" joint, with people "sitting around talking or playing the piano in the parlor." Other reports describe people wandering around clad only in towels, giving credence to the suggestion that the house may have been used for purposes other than those normally carried on in a boardinghouse.

Lottie kept a stack of Joplin's manuscripts in the cellar, but most were

PART IV — After the Rag

eventually lost. She was fastidious in renewing copyrights on much of his work, including "Maple Leaf Rag" and *Treemonisha,* and continued to draw royalties from "Maple Leaf." Some who had known Joplin sought Lottie out with a view to preserving his works and firming up his legacy. One who did so was Brun Campbell, who as an aspiring teenage Ragtimer had been befriended by Joplin. He established a Scott Joplin collection at Fisk University, a noted African American institution.

It is not difficult to understand Scott Joplin's long-postponed but ultimate emergence as an icon of popular musical culture. Ernest Hemingway observed that all of American literature can be traced back to Mark Twain. Arguably, the roots of all modern American musical forms can be found in the revolutionary techniques of melody, texture, rhythm, and instrumentation that Joplin employed in his Ragtime compositions.

Mimi Blais, hailed as the "Queen of Ragtime" at festivals around the world, calls Ragtime "the trunk of the tree of modern music." Her assertion, with which few would disagree, would make Joplin the musical godfather of such later icons as Buddy Holly, Elvis Presley, Bruce Springstein, and Eminem. All fell under the influence of black music and no genre was more influential as a progenitor of jazz, blues, swing, rock and roll and hip hop than Ragtime.

For a time in the 1920s, what Ragtime was heard consisted of vapid songs that were momentarily popular but had none of the staying power of Scott Joplin's classic instrumental rags. One of the reasons for the abandonment of pure Ragtime was that much of it was too difficult for people to play themselves. Contemporary performers whose enthusiasm and proficiency brought Ragtime into revival understood this very well. Bob Darch, whose incessant promotion of Ragtime festivals helped keep the music alive, urged his fans to treasure the original sheet music and piano rolls of Ragtime era artists.

Jack Hutton, a recipient of the Bob Darch Memorial Award at the 2006 Alexandria Bay, N.Y., Jasstime Festival, says, "People today have a lot of mistaken ideas about Ragtime." This Canadian virtuoso adds, "To some, it conjures up images of spittoons, musicians in striped shirts, and a partly-inebriated piano player working an out-of-tune piano. In the technical demands Ragtime puts on a player, it is the exact opposite. It is closer to chamber music than any other genre." Lawyer Ted Tjaden who keeps the Website www.ragtimepiano.ca, says he found Ragtime "more

15. Ragtime in Revival

intoxicating as well as more demanding" than the classical music he studied as a boy at the Royal Conservatory of Music in Toronto.

As Ragtime receded from notice, the blues came to the fore in the 1920s on the strength of popular hits like Mamie Smith's "Crazy Blues." The dollar platter sold seventy-five thousand copies in its first month, mostly to black buyers. Its success reminded producers of the market they could tap if they could reach white audiences. Ethel Waters met their need with classic blues songs like "Down Home Blues." By the 1930s, she'd migrated to popular songs and was one of the biggest stars on Broadway.

But it was jazz that had captured the public's imagination, and it was jazz that sent Ragtime into oblivion until its first, short-lived revival in the 1940s and its later, longer-term renaissance that began in the 1970s. Victor recording executives recognized that, just as in the case of Ragtime, the biggest market for jazz was to be found on the dance floors of America. They took pains to describe both tunes on their first jazz record as "for dancing." The company pressed the theme in its publicity. A 1921 release of "Broadway Rose" and "Sweet Mama" announced: "Here are two numbers, which, if danced properly, are guaranteed to keep the participant at least two jumps ahead of gloom and disaster."

Louis "Satchmo" Armstrong joined the Fletcher Henderson band in 1924, bringing the trumpet artistry that he exhibited in numbers like the "Lindy Hop," the first swing dance to achieve widespread popularity. That success led bandleader Benny Goodman to buy a clutch of "hot jump" jazz arrangements from Henderson. He played them during a coast-to-coast tour that ended with an engagement at the Palomar Ballroom in Los Angeles.

Arriving at the Palomar on August 21, 1935, Goodman was unaware that the California audience had been prepped by radio broadcasts of his tour performances. But it was only when the audience failed to react to a selection of "sweet" tunes that Goodman switched, in desperation, to Henderson's arrangements. They were what the audience had been waiting for. That night marked the arrival of swing as the standard music Americans would listen to for the next twenty years. Goodman became known as the "King of Swing." More than any other music, the sound of swing boosted the morale of Allied soldiers throughout the Second World War.

Part IV — After the Rag

An interesting footnote to the arrival of swing came when Louis Armstrong, asked what swing was during an appearance on the Bing Crosby radio show, responded: "Ah, swing, well we used to call it syncopation — then they called it Ragtime, then blues — then jazz. Now, it's swing. Ha! Ha! White folks yo'all sho is a mess." Armstrong was obviously having fun with Crosby, but his point was well made: the common roots of modern music were to be found in Ragtime.

The advent of "big bands" that played swing left Ragtime in dormancy despite occasional successes. A white composer, Euday L. Bowman, wrote the most popular rag of the inter-war years, "12th Street Rag," recorded in 1927 by Louis Armstrong. A number that was even more popular but was not true Ragtime was "Tiger Rag," introduced by the Original Dixieland Jazz Band.

Ragtime enjoyed its first, hesitant revival in the 1940s. A young white jazz trumpeter and former cruise ship musician, Lu Watter, formed the Yerbas Buena Jass Band in San Francisco and began to mix Ragtime numbers with popular jazz. The band was a New Orleans-style combo outfit and Watter recorded such traditional numbers as "Maple Leaf Rag" and "At a Georgia Camp meeting." His pianist, Wally Rose, made a sensationally popular solo recording of the 1908 work of George Botsford, "Black and White Rag," and attracted national attention. A number of imitators sprang up; but when the group dissolved, its members found their interests focused more on Dixieland jazz than on Ragtime.

In 1950, Rudi Blesh and Harriet Janis, co-owners of Circle Records, published the first Joplin biography, *They All Played Ragtime*. A proliferation of Ragtime-style pianists followed, including Johnny Maddox and Bob Darch. Max Morath, a devoted Ragtime historian and musician, combined performing with broadcasting. He had been taught to play by his mother, who had been a professional Ragtime pianist. Morath headlined two television shows, *The Ragtime Era* and *Turn of the Century*, which played on U.S. public television in 1959 and 1960. By then, musical journals were publishing the recollections of pioneers such as Eubie Blake and were running articles on Ragtime.

The power of Tin Pan Alley to dictate American music tastes fell into sharp decline in the postwar years. It was finally done in by the same thing that allowed it to emerge in the first place: new technology that changed audience, access and attention. Upstart record makers at first refused to

15. Ragtime in Revival

Pianist Bob Darch roamed North America for nearly forty years, keeping alive the syncopated music of Ragtime. He was instrumental in the launch of the Scott Joplin Ragtime Festival in Sedalia, Missouri, in 1983. Seen here playing on a Yukon riverboat, he entertained crowds at such far-off locations as Dawson City (Dawson City Museum).

pay publishers for use of their tunes; it had taken a new Copyright Act in 1909 — the last bill signed into law by Theodore Roosevelt — to award publishers a payment of two cents per song for every record or piano roll sold. The law generated far more money than the publishers expected, but little did they realize they were ceding control of songwriting to a Frankenstein monster they had helped create — the gargantuan recording industry of the future.

By 1950 six major record companies controlled the music industry, with business tactics growing ever more ruthless in the struggle over artists, air time and marketing. Tin Pan Alley had surrendered the market to the recording industry, radio broadcasters, and the thousands of new artists who sprang up far from the canyons of Manhattan, determined to bring their own brand of musical culture to the world. Sales of sheet music virtually evaporated as radio popularized hit songs for the record industry, which was no longer confined to New York but was now prospering in places like Nashville, Detroit, Los Angeles, and Toronto.

A single announcer, Martin Block who hosted *Make Believe Ballroom* on WNEW in New York City, became the most powerful arbiter of popular music. The songs he played became hits. Along with the new songs, new audiences arose. American blacks listened to their own stations playing local artists versed in rhythm and blues. Inevitably, white listeners heard and liked them and in 1951 a disc jockey in Cleveland, Ohio, Alan Freed, got around his station's prohibition on playing black rhythm and blues records. He simply called them rock and roll. Other stations followed his example. Singer-composers like Bo Diddley, Chuck Berry, Little Richard and Elvis Presley quickly entrenched themselves in the musical consciousness of a new generation.

Soon, a British "invasion" would shake the American music industry to its core. The regime of Tin Pan Alley was over, but not its contribution to musical culture. A saga that took flight on the wings of the technology of cheap printing and player pianos in the 1890s was grounded by the technology of mass broadcasting and the advent of low-cost records in the 1950s.

Scott Joplin wrote hundreds of pages of music during his lifetime and assembled notebooks filled with information about his compositions and his life. All of these have disappeared. What happened to them is a mystery. The last trace of a roomful of Joplin manuscripts and memorabilia, carefully kept by Lottie Joplin for more than forty years, vanished in 1961 following a legal hearing on the tax value of the properties.

Lottie tried hard throughout her life to preserve her husband's legacy. After her marriage to a man whose last name was Thomas but about whom nothing more is known, she established the Lottie Joplin Thomas Trust. On Lottie's death in 1951, control of the trust passed to Wilbur Sweatman, the long-time friend of Joplin whom Lottie had appointed as trustee.

Sweatman operated a small publishing company, to which he assigned the rights to *Treemonisha*. He is presumed to have distributed royalties from Joplin's music to Lottie's three siblings and a niece. He began work on an autobiography that friends said contained a lot of detail about Joplin

15. Ragtime in Revival

and their relationship. On Sweatman's death in 1961, his daughter Barbara took possession of his apartment and all his belongings, including original Joplin material.

There had been no will. Its absence sparked a legal battle when Sweatman's sister Eva challenged Barbara's right to the Joplin works. At a court hearing, Barbara testified that papers containing Joplin's compositions and music had filled half of a small room in her father's apartment, from the floor halfway up to the ceiling. The court ruled that because Barbara had been born out of wedlock she had no rights to the estate. She was ordered to turn everything over to Eva's lawyer, Harry G. Bragg.

From there, the trail goes cold. Eva discharged Bragg as the executor of the Sweatman estate and Lottie's niece, Mary Wormley, became executrix. For several years she drew royalties of between one thousand and fifteen hundred dollars a year. Joplin biographer Edward Berlin leaves the issue unsettled in *The King of Ragtime:* "Do Scott Joplin's manuscripts still exist, and if so, who has them?" He could find no answers.

Formal recognition of Joplin's historic contribution to the music of mass culture finally arrived in the 1970s, a half century after his death. Joshua Rifkin, the noted musicologist, had become familiar with Joplin's rags and in 1970 he played a selection of them, *Piano Rags by Scott Joplin*, for Nonesuch Records, a classics label. Rifkin refused to corrupt the tunes by improvising in what his producers thought would be a more captivating style. He remained true to the classic intonation of Joplin's music and the album became a best seller.

The production of *Treemonisha* in Atlanta in 1972, followed by other productions around the country, brought on an upsurge in interest that finally gained Joplin the appreciation and fame he'd predicted would follow his death. The productions also brought on new legal hassles between Mary Wormley and the Joplin Trust, and theater and record producers. In a settlement in 1978, the trust won a settlement of $177,980 from Olympic Records and its parent, Crown Publishers, for unauthorized use of *Treemonisha* excerpts in a five-record set entitled *Scott Joplin — His Complete Works*. The producers, apparently unaware of who held the rights, had neglected to obtain permission from the William Sweatman Publishing Company.

In 1976 the Pulitzer Prize committee awarded Joplin a posthumous Bicentennial Medal in recognition of his lifetime contribution to music.

PART IV — After the Rag

In 1983 a twenty cent U.S. Postal Service stamp bearing Joplin's portrait was issued in commemoration of Black Heritage. A letter from a Kentucky congressman, Romano L. Mazzoli, had made the case: "This multi-talented Black American never received the true recognition he deserved during the Ragtime era. It is fitting to give posthumous recognition to him for his outstanding contributions to American art and culture."

Two films, *The Sting* and *Scott Joplin*, finally brought his music and his personality to life for millions of moviegoers. Director George Roy Hill selected Joplin's "The Entertainer" as the musical theme for *The Sting*, starring Robert Redford and Paul Newman, in 1974. Hill had supposedly heard a recording of the tune coming from his son's bedroom. The score hit the top of the musical charts that year.

The Sting is a lighthearted comedy that featured two very good actors in a rollicking film about a pair of poker-playing, Depression-era crooks. But it was Joplin's "The Entertainer," run as a ubiquitous soundtrack whenever there was a break in the action, that made *The Sting* memorable. Many who saw the film assumed the soundtrack was of the same name; it took time, and considerable effort by Joplin loyalists, to identify him with the tune.

The movie *Scott Joplin* was one of those "B" efforts that Hollywood is so capable of producing in the wake of a genuine artistic triumph. This 1977 version of Joplin's life, with Billy Dee Williams in the title role, builds on many fictitious scenes in patching together a weak story line that is compensated for by some very good Ragtime scores. It depicts the troubled relationship between Joplin and John Stark (played by Art Carney) and covers Joplin's obsessive quest to produce *Treemonisha*. There are amusing scenes where Joplin outperforms his rivals in "cutting contests" of

Important recognition for Scott Joplin came after his death, as he had often predicted to his friends. Joplin was awarded a posthumous Pulitzer Prize Bicentennial Medal in 1973, and in 1983 a 20-cent U.S. Postal Service stamp bearing Joplin's portrait was issued in commemoration of Black Heritage.

15. Ragtime in Revival

piano virtuosity of the type promoted by the *Police Gazette* early in the century. But its most remarkable footage may be the cameo appearance of a then–90ish Eubie Blake.

That modern measure of artistic success, the fan club, sprang up for Joplin in the 1960s. Most of them published newsletters of varying qualities. One of the best was *Ragtime Review*, put out by Trebor Tichenor and Russ Cassidy between 1962 and 1967. In Toronto, the Ragtime Society issued the *Ragtimer* from 1962 to 1986 and a Maple Leaf Club was set up in Los Angeles that published *Rag Times* after 1967.

Back in Sedalia, a series of concerts by Bob Darch led to a growing appreciation for the achievements of a hometown son. Darch, born in Detroit, Michigan, acquired a taste for Ragtime music in the 1950s. He traveled the continent as an itinerant pianist and for several years was based in Virginia City, Nevada, where he performed regularly and had his own publishing company. His Ragtime compositions ranged from "Delta Saloon Rag" to "Opera House Rag," commemorating the famous Piper's Opera House of that gold mining town. Joseph Lamb had came out of retirement to arrange that number for him.*

At Darch's urging, the Scott Joplin Memorial Foundation was set up, initially as sponsor of his concerts. That led to the launching of a four-day Scott Joplin Ragtime Festival in Sedalia, Missouri, in 1983. It has continued on an annual basis except for a brief interruption shortly after its founding. Inspired by its success, some two dozen Joplin festivals are held every year, including one in Hungary. All the festivals feature readings by Ragtime researchers and historians, in addition to a full slate of performances by musicians.

The West Coast Ragtime Society, based in Sacramento, California, does for the Pacific Coast states what the Joplin Festival does for the Midwest. It claims to be "the biggest and best" Ragtime festival in the world. At nearby Sutter Creek, the Mother Lode Society sponsors a lively festival each summer. The Original Blind Boone Early Ragtime and Jazz Festival enlivens the streets of Columbia, Missouri, every year. Smaller events like the Charles Templeton Ragtime Musical Festival at Mississippi State University support the serious pursuit of Ragtime knowledge.

The greatest Ragtime renaissance is the one occurring right now,

---

*Darch died October 20, 2002, in Springfield, Mo.

PART IV — After the Rag

thanks largely to the omnipresence of the Internet. The web has become the repository of an immense volume of Scott Joplin and Ragtime material, with thousands of sites containing articles, pictures, MIDI files and other data. A Google search for Ragtime yields nearly seven million results, while a Joplin inquiry generates one and a quarter million responses. There is even an around-the-clock radio station featuring Ragtime and related music, *Rocky Mountain Ragtime*, operating out of Longmount, Colorado.*

Responding to the new demands aroused by the Internet, musicians and producers have brought many new Ragtime arrangements to market. Nearly four hundred Ragtime musical products, including CDs and DVDs, are offered at amazon.com. They range from Ragtime piano roll performances ("Please Don't Shoot the Piano Player") to selections by the Paragon Ragtime Orchestra (*Black Manhattan*, including such numbers as "Castle House Rag" and "The Clef Club March"). Scott Joplin's music has been recorded by dozens of artists, including Mimi Blais, James P. Johnson, John Arpin, Claude Bolling, Max Morath, and such groups as Terry Waldo & the Gutbucket Syncopators and the Canadian Brass.

What accounts for the longevity of Ragtime and the renewal of interest by each generation in this music that ushered in the modern era of culture and technology? For some, the nostalgic appeal of an earlier period may be their chief motivation; for others, it is a desire to know and appreciate the rhythms of a unique genre that is at the root of modern music. Yet others simply like the stuff.

Ragtime music draws enthusiasts of all ages, but this writer's unscientific observation—attendance at festivals and responses to my writings—leads me to think that it's a mature audience (aged forty-five to sixty-five) where Ragtime finds its greatest following. But to soak up the vibrancy of Ragtime as it is celebrated in the twenty-first century and to see people from nine to ninety enjoying the legacy of Scott Joplin, the best place to go is the Scott Joplin Festival in Sedalia, Missouri, in June of any year.

---

*http://www.live365.com/stations/rmragtime

16

Echoes of the Music
We're All Still Playing Ragtime

Nowhere do the echoes of the Ragtime era resound more clearly than in the small town of Sedalia, Missouri, where Scott Joplin spent his most formative years. The best time to visit this pleasant town is in early June when the Scott Joplin International Ragtime Festival is in full flower.

Sedalia is reached by traveling Route 50 from either Kansas City or St. Louis, passing towns that perch as relics of the Ragtime era, their main streets little unchanged from that time. Not far away, time vaults into the twenty-first century at Whiteman Air Force Base, from where Stealth bombers took off to drop their deadly cargo on Afghanistan and Iraq.

The festival begins with the Strenuous Life Parade and March Majestic Strut, followed by a welcome from the mayor and some suitable remarks by Scott Kirby, Ragtime musician and historian. Two of our fellow guests at the Georgetown Inn, the home built by General Smith, the founder of Sedalia, were a couple from Colorado who marched in the parade and won prizes for their Ragtime outfits. It is the kind of neighborly celebration you'd expect from a community where, if the people don't all know each other, they at least feel linked by a special connection, in this case their love of Ragtime music. Dances, concerts and seminars filled the next three days, with a star of the Festival being the "Queen of Ragtime," Mimi Blais, of Quebec, Canada.

For all the celebration, it is hard to ignore the fact that late in the Ragtime era, around the First World War, the soul of Sedalia slowly vanished and the spirit of the city changed. Like air escaping through a pinprick in a balloon, it whooshed away almost imperceptibly, taking with it

Part IV — After the Rag

Mural on the wall of a building in Sedalia, Missouri, celebrates the years Scott Joplin spent in the small city where he wrote "The Maple Leaf Rag." Sedalia hosts the Scott Joplin International Ragtime Festival every June (Scott Joplin Ragtime Festival).

the enterprise — and perhaps the opportunity — of what had seemed to be a limitless future.

No longer were the citizens banding together to raise money to attract corporations and the jobs that came with them, as did they did in the time of General Smith and the generation that followed him. It was the donations of Smith and his neighbors that brought the Missouri Pacific railway to Sedalia. Later, the town raised another hefty contribution to gain its biggest employer, the Katy railroad workshop and its thousand jobs.

General Smith's daughter Martha, touring Europe at that time, received an urgent cable from the town appealing for money. Her response was to promise "three thousand if necessary." Her business manager got her off with a two thousand dollar donation. "Our money goes rapidly, whether wisely we do not know," Martha jotted in her journal. That same year, Sedalia's visionary town fathers drew on municipal funds to purchase fifty acres from farmers Joseph and Frank Sicher to establish Liberty Park, putting up a racetrack and a hotel and constructing a five-acre lake.

Most of Sedalia's substantial buildings were erected between 1880 and 1910: the Farmers and Mechanics Bank, with its cast stone window frames,

16. Echoes of the Music

the Italianate-style Sicher Hotel now an industrial building, the Commerce Building built in French Renaissance Revival, the Missouri Trust Building and its Romanesque turrets, the Community church noted for its handsome stone arches and the First United Methodist church for its medieval-looking asymmetrical towers, the terra cotta and stone Carnegie Public Library and the Anheuser-Busch bottling works, used for many years as a saloon.

The town's builders favored classical architecture, and they left many fine structures along Ohio Street, the short main stem. *Life* magazine, writing about Sedalia as a typical American community in 1940, recalled that the town had "one of the midland's most notorious red light districts." The magazine also made note of Sedalia's "claim to having been the town second hardest hit by the Depression [after Gary, Indiana]. Three of its four banks closed during the worst days and three leading bankers killed themselves in quick succession."

Early photos show the main street of Sedalia clogged with traffic and people, depicting a scene that vanished long ago. It wasn't that the folks remaining in Sedalia weren't good and virtuous and hard-working; they were. It was that America had changed. With the advent of the automobile and good roads, there were too many Sedalias. While places like Kansas City and St. Louis forged ahead, other good towns stagnated, losing people and business to their larger competitors.

Sedalia had fifteen thousand people in 1890; more than a century later the population barely tops twenty thousand. By now, there are more people in its cemeteries than walking its streets. This has become a pattern of small town life across the United States and Canada, yet another change among all the other changes from the Ragtime era. In 2003, permits were issued to build only twelve new homes in Sedalia. Its median household income is twenty eight thousand dollars a year, below the Missouri state average. It also records less than one murder per year.

We left Sedalia for St. Louis in the late afternoon, our destination the Scott Joplin House at 2658A Delmar Boulevard. When Joplin and his first wife, Belle Hayden, lived there, it was but a stone's throw from the honky-tonks and dives of the notorious Chestnut Valley district. This city reached its zenith over one hundred years ago when, in 1904, it hosted both the World 's Fair and the Olympics. At that time, St. Louis was the fourth largest city in the United States. The population peaked in 1950 at

Part IV — After the Rag

850,000. Today, it ranks 52nd among American cities, at slightly more than 350,000.

Just when everyone thought the city's fortunes had bottomed out, St. Louis received its greatest blow in 2008 when the Belgian-based international beverage giant, InBev SA, paid fifty billion dollars to buy out the symbol of the city (no, not the Gateway Arch): the storied brewer, Anheuser-Busch Companies.

Anheuser-Busch has been the greatest corporate citizen to St. Louis that any city could ever have. After the buy-out came fears that this legacy of enterprising German immigrant Adolphus Busch might not survive the inevitable corporate cost-cutting and rationalization. Or that the company might even be moved away entirely, as has happened with such one-time St. Louis stalwarts as Ralston Purina, May Department Stores and McDonnell Douglas. Could the St. Louis Cardinals be next?

One of the things that made St. Louis great before and during the Ragtime era was its immigrant German population. Mr. Busch was but one example. Joseph Pulitzer, one of the great figures of American journalism, got his start on a German language newspaper in St. Louis. It was Alfred Ernst, the German-born director of the St. Louis Choral Symphony, who gave Scott Joplin a great boost in 1901 by declaring him "an extraordinary genius as a composer of Ragtime music."

Today, the Scott Joplin house stands almost alone among the few buildings left intact in its part of St. Louis after one of the greatest urban clean-outs ever orchestrated in the United States.

Fountain Park, an old district adjacent to the Joplin House, and Gaslight Square, once a vibrant entertainment district, are among the north St. Louis neighborhoods most victimized by the flight of white population and by corporate disinvestment after the Second World War.

In the last fifty years, a city that boasted a densely packed and almost elegant urban core has lost hundreds of once magnificent buildings and tens of thousands of housing units, leaving behind vast swaths of wasted landscape that give the appearance of a devastated war zone. Perhaps more than any city, St. Louis displays the tragic legacy of the fact that America was not ready in the Ragtime era — nor for many years thereafter — to deal with the aftermath of slavery.

16. Echoes of the Music

By the 1960s the migration of African Americans to the border and northern states was largely complete. Few had yet achieved the education or the opportunities that Scott Joplin had dreamt for them in his opera *Treemonisha*. Their arrival, colliding with the postwar dream of the white middle class for homes of their own in the suburbs, emptied the hearts of great American cities, none more so than St. Louis. Public housing projects that were built to replace the slums of the inner city failed disastrously.

The most spectacular failure, the thirty-three buildings of the Pruitt-Igoe project, each rising eleven stories — but with elevators that stopped only on every third floor — became crime and vermin-infested, its tenants hating the place. Erected between 1951 and 1956, the last of them was demolished by 1976. The land remains vacant, the cost of removing the buried concrete foundations of the buildings a deterrent to redevelopment.

St. Louis, to its credit, has not forgotten either Scott Joplin or the Ragtime era. A nonprofit organization, The Friends of Scott Joplin, promotes the memory by sponsoring Ragtime concerts, the Scott Joplin Birthday Party, and the Rosebud Ball & Cakewalk Competition. It provides continuing support to the Scott Joplin House State Historic Site. A TV show, *Ragtime St. Louis*, at one time ran on local cable.

Scott Joplin House is not really a house but part of a low-rise commercial structure that has been fitted out with furniture from the Ragtime era, but with none of Scott Joplin's belongings. They were all lost, given away or sold off when he divorced Belle and began his wandering years. The memory of him has been kept intact, however, with vintage posters, a player piano that faithfully repeats his most popular tunes, the icebox in which the day's food would have been kept at an edible temperature, and the other accoutrements of family life — a bed, a kitchen table, a parlor sofa.

The inevitable museum shop offers Joplin books and paraphernalia. Next door, a reconstructed Rosebud Café reminds one of the smoky saloon in which the giant barkeep, Tom Turpin, stood playing Ragtime at a piano mounted on concrete blocks.

My visit to Scott Joplin House recalled for me the turbulent twenty-five years before the Great War — as it once was called — when a generation of creative artists and skilled inventors brought the modern world into being. In music, Joplin and his contemporaries wrought the kind of revolution that Pablo Picasso ignited in art and Jack London and Upton

PART IV — After the Rag

Scott Joplin and his first wife, Belle, moved into this building at 2658A Morgan St. (now Delmar Blvd.) in 1901. Known as the Scott Joplin House State Historic Site, its rooms are outfitted as they would have been when the Joplins lived there. The wing at the right contains a replica of Tom Turpin's famous Rosebud Café, which Joplin commemorated with his "Rosebud March" (Missouri Department of Natural Resources).

Sinclair brought on in literature. They gave us new ways of listening to, looking at, and understanding the world. The new technologies of Thomas Edison, Henry Ford, and the Wright brothers delivered us from isolation by giving us freedom and mobility. But they also changed us from participants to spectators in the creation of our culture; it became so much easier to play a record (or a CD) at home than to join a community concert where everyone was expected to add one's voice.

The pace of change in the Ragtime era equaled anything we are seeing in the world today. By 1915, more than 30 percent of American households had telephones in their parlors. Twenty per cent of U.S. households had electric light, and car production passed the one million mark. Movie houses reached into every downtown.

It is said that each generation builds on the groundwork laid before it. The achievements of Scott Joplin and others of his generation went far beyond merely continuing what their parents had started. They changed the culture of the world through their invention of new forms of music,

16. Echoes of the Music

art and literature. The new technologies of the time enabled them to reach incredibly larger numbers of people than ever before. The artists and technocrats who fashioned the new era of mass culture came to their tasks with passion, and for the most part, fulfilled the promise of their generation.

The same cannot be said of the era's statesmen, who may have faced a more onerous duty but who blundered into an unnecessary war that set the stage for a century of tension and disaster. Perhaps a new scenario is now being written. When Scott Joplin died, women could not vote and it would be another twenty-five years before a black man would again sit in the U.S. Congress. In our time, the ascendancy of Barack Obama has gone a long way toward eroding the barrier of race, just as John F. Kennedy's presence rendered one's religion largely irrelevant in American public life.

The achievements and the misadventures of the Ragtime era still echo today, as does the faint tinkling of the piano keys that one imagines hearing from the Rosebud Café. The journey that began in such places in the twilight past will go on and our dreams will endure, into the future. Whether we realize it or not, we're all still playing Ragtime.

The Life and Times of Scott Joplin

1868   Scott Joplin born Nov. 24 near future Texarkana, Texas.
Thomas Edison patents electric vote recorder.

1893   Joplin takes his Texas Medley Quartette to Chicago World's Fair.
U.S. Marines land in Hawaii; Queen Liliuokalani overthrown.

1899   Joplin's "Maple Leaf Rag" earns him $4.00 royalty in first year.
U.S. Senate ratifies peace treaty to end Spanish-American War.

1902   Joplin's "Entertainer" and "Strenuous Life" published.
First movie theater in U.S. opens in Los Angeles.

1905   Joplin in despair after death of 2nd wife, Freddie Alexander; wanders in Midwest.
Einstein publishes 4 papers that revolutionize scientific knowledge.

1907   Joplin moves to New York; works on "Wall St. Rag."
Financial panic grips U.S.; stock market falls 50%.

1910   Joplin struggles to finish *Treemonisha*, unable to find a backer for opera.
Teddy Roosevelt is first president to fly in an airplane.

1915   Joplin produces opera on his own; it is a disaster.
Trench warfare in World War I; Germans use poison gas.

1917   Scott Joplin dies at 49 in mental hospital; Ragtime era is at an end.
U.S. enters World War I; jazz and blues emerge as new musical styles.

Scott Joplin's Compositions

INSTRUMENTALS

1896
Great Crush Collision
Combination March
Harmony Club Waltz

1899
Original Rags
Maple Leaf Rag

1900
Swipsey Cake Walk (with Arthur Marshall)

1901
Sunflower Slow Drag (with Scott Hayden)
Peacherine Rage
Augustan Club Waltz
The Easy Winners

1902
Cleopha
A Breeze from Alabama
Elite Syncopations
The Entertainer
March Majestic
The Strenuous Life

1903
Something Doing (with Scott Hayden)
Weeping Willow
Palm Leaf Rag

1904
The Favorite
The Sycamore
The Cascades
The Chrysanthemum

1905
Bethena
Rosebud March
Leola
Binks' Waltz
Eugenia

1906
Antoinette
The Ragtime Dance

1907
Lily Queen (with Arthur Marshall)
Heliotrope Bouquet (with Louis Chauvin)
Searchlight Rag
Gladiolus Rag
Rose Leaf Rag
Nonpareil

1908
Fig Leaf Rag

Scott Joplin's Compositions

Sugar Cane
Pine Apple Rag

1909
Wall Street Rag
Solace
Pleasant Moments
Country Club
Euphonic Sound
Paragon Rag

1910
Stoptime Rag

1911
Felicity Rag (with Scott Hayden)
Treemonisha (Opera)

1912
Scott Joplin's New Rag

1913
Kismet Rag (with Scott Hayden)

1914
Magnetic Rag
Silver Swan Rag (Piano Roll)

1917
Posthumous publication
Reflection Rag

Songs

1895
Please Say You Will
A Picture of Her Face

1902
I Am Thinking of My Pickaninny Days (4)

1903
Little Black Baby (Louise Bristol)

1904
Maple Leaf Rag (Sydney Brown)

1905
Sarah Dear (Henry Jackson)

1906
Good Bye Old Gal, Good Bye (Darden & Taylor, arr. by Scott Joplin)

1907
Snoring Sampson (H. La Mertha, arr. by S. Joplin)
When Your Hair Is Like the Snow (Owen Spendthrift)

1910
Pine Apple Rag (Joe Snyder)

1911
Lovin' Babe (A.R. Turner, arr. by S. Joplin)

Known Lost Works

1901
A Blizzard

1903
A Guest of Honor (Opera)

Scott Joplin's Compositions

1905
You Stand Good with Me, Babe

1915–16
Morning Glories
For the Sake of All

Syncopated Jamboree
Pretty Pansy Rag
Recitative Rag
If (Musical Comedy)
Symphony No. 1
Piano Concerto

PIANO ROLLS

Maple Leaf Rag
Magnetic Rag
Weeping Willow

Something Doing
Pleasant Moments
Ole Miss Rag (by W.C. Handy)

Sources of Quotations

Chapter 1

Page 6: The Chicago World's Fair attracted more journalists and generated more newspaper and magazine space than any single event in the United States up to that time. The problems of the Fair's orchestra conductor were featured in hundreds of stories. Our account is from the August 3, 1893, issue of the *Alton (Illinois) Weekly Telegraph*. Alton was typical of Midwestern cities which sent thousands of visitors to the Fair.

Page 6: The Texas Medley Quartette was a loosely organized group with a constantly changing membership. Scott Joplin shepherded it through several difficult years, probably from about 1891 to 1897. Joplin's premier biographer, Edward A. Berlin, wrote in his *King of Ragtime: Scott Joplin and His Era* (25) that "the only tangible evidence of the Texas Medley name was during the 1894–95 period." However, the *Cedar Rapids Evening Gazette*, apparently not known to Berlin, places the group in that town in 1893. Another author, James Haskins, reports in *Scott Joplin* (81) that Joplin formed his first band in Chicago, consisting of a cornet, clarinet, tuba and piano. Berlin has it consisting of eight members, which is more likely the case given that the four Joplin took to the newspaper's office were all singers. Given the date and location of the Cedar Rapids gig, it is evident it was the Texas Medley Quartette that Joplin took to the Fair. However in this, as in most other details of Joplin's life, direct evidence is lacking.

Page 12: The *New York Sun* report on Ben Harney and the supposed origins of Ragtime was reprinted in the *Alton (Illinois) Evening Telegraph* on August 24, 1901.

Page 14: For more information on Ragtime in Canada, see the author's article, "Rocking with Ragtime," *The Beaver*, June-July 2008.

Chapter 2

Page 16: "My Kind of Town, Chicago Is" a popular tune by Jimmy Van Husen, with lyrics by Sammy Cahn, was first featured in a 1964 musical, *Robin and the Seven Hoods*.

Page 19: Files of the *Chicago Defender*, preserved at the Chicago Public Library, reveal in great detail the struggle of the city's African American community. The reference to "rag-time piano playing" appeared May 30, 1914, and is cited in Allan Spears' *Black Chicago: The Making of a Negro Ghetto*.

Page 21: John Philip Sousa's quote about his European tour is from the *New York Times* of April 24, 1900. The reference to "talking and playing machines" is from *Appleton's Magazine*, September 1906. Sousa would have been even more shocked by later technological developments such as the Moog synthesizer or the advent of digital recording.

Sources of Quotations — Chapters 3–4

Page 22: E.L. Doctorow's *Ragtime* placed immigrants at the center of emerging entertainment media. The United States exercised little control over immigration until 1892, when an Immigration Bureau was established. A 1911 commission blamed festering social problems on "inferior" migrants from southeastern Europe. In the same year, Dr. C.B. Davenport relied on the now-discredited science of eugenics to argue in his book, *Heredity in Relation to Eugenics*, that "the population of the United States will, on account of the great influx of blood from South-eastern Europe, rapidly become darker in pigmentation, smaller in stature, more mercurial, more attached to music and art [and] more given to crimes of larceny, kidnapping, assault, murder, rape and sex-immorality."

Chapter 3

Page 29: Edward A. Berlin, the author of *King of Ragtime: Scott Joplin and His Era*, recounts that Joplin made frequent use of his line about becoming famous twenty-five years after his death, which was picked up and repeated by his widow, Lottie Stokes.

Page 29: On racial relationships, Berlin reports that in 1891 Joplin got a lesson in how easily the feelings of his own people could be chafed. The Texarkana Minstrels made their debut at Ghio's Opera House in July of that year, apparently unaware that the evening had been organized as a benefit to raise funds for a monument to Jefferson Davis, the late president of the Southern Confederacy. They were attacked for this in the colored newspaper *Southwestern Christian Advocate*, where the wife of the editor wrote that "their action dishonors their race." No one, she added, should "feel like building monuments for anybody that fought to keep them in slavery, under the lash, and that sold their children, parents, and husbands and wives from each other. The thing is unnatural." The Minstrels apologized; pointing out that none of their 40 percent of the take went toward the monument. Their apology made her even angrier.

Page 29: The effect of the 1896 Plessy decision was to officially sanction a form of apartheid in American life. The decision provided a legal and moral justification for oppressing African Americans by sanctifying segregation in transportation, accommodation and education. It would stand until 1954 when the U.S. Supreme Court, in *Brown v. Board of Education*, rejected the principle of "separate but equal" and held it a violation of the Constitution. In 1955, the Court ordered that school desegregation proceed "with all deliberate speed."

Page 31: In 2004 filmmaker Ken Burns, producer of *Unforgiveable Blackness: The Rise and Fall of Jack Johnson*, filed a petition with the U.S. Department of Justice asking a presidential pardon for Johnson on the grounds that his conviction was racially motivated.

Page 33: The supposition that the Williams brothers were Canadian and that their Maple Leaf Club was named for the Canadian maple leaf is likely a myth. There is no Canadian record of their origin and the 1901 U.S. census lists Missouri as their birthplace. Maple trees are common to the area.

Page 36: The report from the *New York Medical Journal* of the value of Ragtime music as an antidote to depression was published in the *Engelwood (Illinois) Times* on November 19, 1915.

Page 37: The complexity of Ragtime music is discussed at length by James Haskins in his *Scott Joplin: The Man Who Made Ragtime*.

Chapter 4

Page 39: The song "The Black KPs" was written by Eugene Hillman and Sidney Perrin. They also composed such hits as "Black Annie," "Mammy's Little Pumpkin" and "Colored Coons."

Sources of Quotations — Chapters 5–6

Page 42: Samuel Brunson Campbell's description of Scott Joplin is from his autobiography, cited in *Scott Joplin* (89) by James Haskins with Kathleen Benson. His comment on how "Maple Leaf Rag" "blew the lid" off the musical world is cited by Rudi Blesh in *They All Played Ragtime*.

Page 42: The quote about Joplin's compositional habits from the unnamed New York music journal appears in Katherine Preston's book, *Scott Joplin: The Composer*.

Page 43: Remington's description of the Battle of San Juan Hill was published in *Harper's Weekly* of July 15, 1898.

Page 44: The reference to Remington's work having signaled the end of the Victorian era in illustration is from *Frederic Remington: A Biography* (62) by Peggy and Harold Samuels.

Chapter 5

Page 52: Scott Joplin's first home in St. Louis is now a historic site, Scott Joplin House. Furnished in the style of the period, it is lit by gaslight. None of the furniture or artifacts belonged to Joplin but the house contains exhibits interpreting Joplin's life and work. The Rosebud Café has been re-created in a building next door. The street where he lived is now named Delmar Boulevard. See www.mostateparks.com/scott joplin.htm.

Page 53: The description of Ragtime piano players waiting their turn for jobs is from Berlin's *King of Ragtime* (93). Joplin's reaction to Monroe Rosenfield's impulsive dance during "The Entertainer" interview is cited by Ian Whitcomb in *Irving Berlin and Ragtime America*. The Rosenfeld reference to Joplin's refined speech is from Berlin's *King of Ragtime* (206).

Page 54: David Wondrich wrote of "the jaunty, sweetly tinkling soundtrack" of "The Entertainer" in the *New York Times* of January 21, 2001.

Page 54: The Rosenfeld reference to Joplin's refined speech is from Edward Berlin's *King of Ragtime*, (206). The description of "Alexander's Ragtime Band" as the most popular Ragtime song ever danced to is cited by David Ewe in *The Life and Death of Tin Pan Alley* (176).

Page 57: The *Indianapolis Freeman* published its item on *A Guest of Honor* on September 12, 1903. Edward Berlin, in *King of Ragtime* (128), suggests the notice was written by Joplin.

Page 60: Belle Jones, or Joplin, is believed to have died in Chicago in 1930.

Chapter 6

Page 66: Ike Hines' Professional Club is described in James Weldon Johnson's 1912 novel, *The Autobiography of an Ex-Colored Man*. The book exploring the taboos of racial intermarriage and miscegenation was originally published anonymously; by the time Johnson allowed his name to be attached to it in a 1927 edition, he had become widely respected as a poet, diplomat and pioneering anthropologist of black culture. Johnson was a founder of the National Association for the Advancement of Colored People (NAACP).

Page 70: Joplin's music is discussed in the article, "The Panic of 1907 and The Wall Street Rag: Art Imitates Life" by Brian Grinder and Dan Cooper, *Financial History* (Summer 1997).

Page 75: Harry von Tilzer's article in *Metropolitan* magazine is cited by David A. Jasen in *Tin Pan Alley* (Donald I. Fine, 1988).

Page 78: A fictionalized version of Bolden's life forms the basis of Michael Ondaatje's 1976 novel, *Coming Through Slaughter*. It veers from fact, however, in presenting Bolden as a barber and as publisher of a salacious scandal sheet called *The Cricket*, of which no copies have ever surfaced. A more realistic picture is presented in Donald Marquis' *In Search of Buddy Bolden: First Man of Jazz* (Da Capo, 1978).

Sources of Quotations — Chaptesr 7–8

Chapter 7

Page 80: Brun Campbell, Joplin's young friend from Sedalia, retired from the music business in 1908 and moved to California, becoming a barber and a part-time piano player of Ragtime music. He was one of the last living connections with the Scott Joplin era and died in 1952. Before his death, he wrote dozens of articles about Ragtime and helped launch a 1940s revival. Campbell recalled that the first Ragtime tune he'd ever heard was the first one published in 1897, "Mississippi Rag." He found a copy of "Maple Leaf Rag" in an Oklahoma City music store in 1900 and immediately hitchhiked the three hundred miles to Sedalia to meet Joplin. In *Classic Jazz: A Personal View of the Music and the Musicians*, Floyd Levin quotes Campbell as having said, "After hearing me play, he (Joplin) agreed to become my teacher."

Page 83: The extract on the origins of tango is from History of Tango, www.gardelweb.com/tango_history.htm

Page 83: The French President's remark about dancing the tango is from the *Syracuse (New York) Herald*, November 23, 1913.

Page 84: Edison's use of "hello" to answer the phone was reported in the *New York Times*, April 14, 1905, and April 25, 1906. Prior to Edison's adoption of "hello," most people answered the phone with variations of "Who is there?"

Page 85: The *New York Dramatic Mirror's* quote about Berlin's Ragtime opera dream is from Warren Forma's book, *They Were Ragtime* (196).

Page 85: The Irving Berlin comment about "Syncopation is the soul of every American life" can be found in Lawrence Bergreen's *As Thousands Cheer: The Life of Irving Berlin* (60). Bergreen also quotes Berlin as confessing, "I never did find out what Ragtime was."

Page 86: Except in cases of wholesale literary theft, plagiarism is often difficult either to prove or defend against. It is well known that Shakespeare borrowed from the works of earlier writers, ranging from the unknown original author of *Hamlet* to his reworking of Sir Thomas North's translation of Plutarch's life of Marc Antony for *Antony and Cleopatra*. Judge Richard A. Posner, author of the delightful *Little Book of Plagiarism*, concluded that in the case of Shakespeare's treatment of the North translation, "If this be plagiarism, we need more plagiarism."

Chapter 8

Page 93: Following Harry Thaw's acquittal on insanity charges, he was rearrested eighteen months later and charged with kidnapping and assaulting nineteen-year-old Frederic Gump, Jr. Thaw was sent to the Pennsylvania State Hospital for the insane, where he remained until 1924. Freed again, he would take up his old lifestyle much as before. He would die in Miami of a heart attack in 1947, at the age of seventy-six.

Page 93: Evelyn married her dancing partner, Jack Clifford, shortly after Thaw divorced her in 1915. She made a dozen films between 1907 and 1922, including *The Unwritten Law: A Thrilling Drama Based on the Thaw-White Tragedy*, in which she played herself.

Page 93: Evelyn also operated a series of Prohibition-era speakeasies, all of which would fail, and was next heard of entertaining at a high-priced brothel in Panama. She published her autobiography in 1934 and was in the news again with the release of the 1955 movie *The Girl in the Red Velvet Swing*. Before dying in a Hollywood nursing home in 1966, at the age of eighty-one, it would be said that Evelyn told a reporter, "Stanny was lucky, he died. I lived."

Page 94: Daniel Boorstin's comment about the "celebrity personality" is cited by Amy Henderson in "Media and the Rise of Celebrity Culture," *Magazine of History* (Organization of American Historians, Spring 1992).

Page 97: The reference to Daisy Markham's twins is from Marcus Binney in the *Times* of London, December 1, 2006.

Sources of Quotations — Chapters 9–10

Page 97: For Bim Compton, the Marquess of Northampton, ahead lay a life of aristocratic security but not, apparently, marital happiness. He would marry Lady Emma Thynne in 1921, divorce her in 1942, wed Virginia Heaton the same year, and finally marry Elspeth Whitaker in 1958. He would follow in his father's footsteps as an Egyptologist, or amateur archeologist interested in Middle East ruins. He would also adhere faithfully to the doctrines of the British Israelites, preaching a mix of racist supremacy and conservative politics.

Page 98: Daisy Markham was not the first woman of the theater to gain the favor of a titled British peer. The frequency of such liaisons led the quasi-official court journal, *The Throne*, to suggest in 1913 that any peer marrying an actress should be deprived of his seat in the House of Lords so that it would not pass to a son as "he may have inherited the moral, mental and physical blemishes of his mother's unknown ancestry." In fact, any woman who could summon the courage and self-assurance to perform on the stage probably possessed greater mental acuity than the average peer. In many such marriages, it was the actress who rescued her doltish husband from the mediocrity of his genes.

Page 98: The marital track record set by Bim would be bettered by his son Spenny, who would take four wives. The latest marquess would also take desperate measures to cover the maintenance costs of the family's country homes, converting Castle Ashby into a conference center while keeping Compton Wynates, "regarded as one of the world's finest examples of Tudor architecture," as the family's private home.

Chapter 9

Page 104: The idea that dancing was incompatible with good Christian behavior was commonly held by many religious sects in the early part of the twentieth century. The book, *Immorality of Modern Dancing*, was published around 1905 by a New York firm, Everitt & Francis.

Page 104: The *Oakland Tribune* editorial "Decency and Ragtime Dancing" appeared on February 22, 1912. Elsie Janis' article in the *Washington Post* appeared November 2, 1913.

Page 105: William Sullivan's recollections of Scott Joplin are mentioned by Edward Berlin in *King of Ragtime* (213).

Page 107: James Reese Europe's comment on Ragtime music is in Berlin's *King of Ragtime* (197). Berlin also notes Joplin's absence from Clef Club programs.

Page 109: In her biography, *Vernon and Irene Castle's Ragtime Revolution*, Eve Golden asserts that *Watch Your Step* incorporated all the elements of Ragtime music (125).

Page 111: Irene Castle married the well-to-do Robert Tremaine on May 21, 1918, just three months after Vernon's death. They had met when he came to her home in response to an ad for the sale of Vernon's car. She made several inconsequential films, played vaudeville briefly, and divorced Tremaine in 1923. She later remarried, had two children, and, inadvisably, became involved in the anti–Semitic, isolationist America First movement.

Page 111: A 1939 film, *The Story of Vernon and Irene Castle*, did well at the box office. It starred Fred Astaire and Ginger Rogers, he the natural inheritor of Vernon Castle's dancing crown. Irene published her memoirs, *Castles in the Air*, in 1958. Irene died on January 25, 1969, at the age of seventy-five.

Chapter 10

Page 114: Rulings that prohibited the showing of certain films in the Province of Quebec are recorded in records of the Régie du cinema Québec, the censor board that continues to function today, although largely as a review body.

Page 114: By 1917 Eva Tanguay was

Sources of Quotations — Chapter 11

working in the movies, making *The Wild Girl.* Commanding fees of thirty-five hundred dollars a week, she accumulated a small fortune, invested it in California property and bonds, and lost most of it in the 1930s Depression. The *Mansfield (Ohio) News* carried an NEA dispatch on September 13, 1932, that she "ended up working in a small and obscure night club on a Brooklyn side street — far from the glamorous picture in which she was once framed. Her act was tossed in with a $1.25 dinner." Arthritic and nearly blind, Eva Tanguay died in 1947. She would be memorialized in an uninspiring and soon-to-be-forgotten film, *The I Don't Care Girl,* released in 1953.

Page 116: Among other newspapers, the *New York Times* reported the trial of William Sanger in great detail. His declaration that he would go to jail rather than pay a fine is from the *Times* of September 11, 1915.

Page 120: The findings of the Massachusetts commission on white slavery are recounted by Katie N. Johnson in *Sisters in Sin: Brothel Drama in America, 1900–1926* (116).

Page 121: Maimie Pinzer's story of her life as a prostitute and recovery through the help of Fanny Quincy Howe is told in *The Maimie Papers,* edited by Ruth Rosen and Sue Davidson for the Feminist Press (1969).

Page 123: Eubie Blake's recollection of his 1915 meeting with Scott Joplin has been recorded by several sources. Some are cited by Edward Berlin in *King of Ragtime* (236).

Chapter 11

Page 124: The *Police Gazette* sponsored its Ragtime piano contests for several years. Events of this type would provide the inspiration for the piano playing "cutting contests" featured in the 1977 film *Scott Joplin.* The *Gazette* story appeared January 20, 1900; the follow-up account in the *Dramatic Mirror* was published February 3, 1900. Founded in 1845, the *Gazette* published its last issue in 1982.

Page 125: I obtained most of the various newspaper articles cited here from the digital online database www.newspaperarchive.com, a resource not available to previous researchers of Ragtime era books.

Page 126: "Ragtime Music Dead in This Town," *New York Times,* March 16, 1909; "Ragtime Music (Invented in St. Louis), Is Dead," *St. Louis Post-Dispatch,* April 4, 1909; "Call For Dreamy Lyrics Suggests End of Ragtime," *Syracuse (New York) Herald,* July 7, 1912; "President of Harvard University Criticizes Ragtime," *Washington Post,* December 29, 1910; "Harvard dining hall bans Ragtime," *San Antonio (Texas) Light,* April 19, 1913; "Chicago teachers ban Ragtime," *Frederick (Maryland) Daily News,* November 2, 1912; "Valentine's Day Ragtime ban," *Oakland Tribune,* Feb. 14, 1912; "Dr. Brunner's attack on Ragtime," *Frederick (Maryland) Post,* October 9, 1911; "Criticism of suggestive and vulgar songs," *Laredo (Texas) Times,* February 15, 1914; "Marie Reppold on Ragtime," *Frederick (Maryland) Daily News,* February 13, 1913; "Ships playing Ragtime," *New York American,* in *Syracuse (New York) Herald,* July 24, 1913; "Mary Garden interview," *San Antonio (Texas) Light,* August 5, 1917; "Charles Cadman comments," *Connellsville (Pennsylvania) Daily Courier,* October 25, 1913; "Alexander Stewart interview," *Oakland Tribune,* May 2, 1915; "Is Ragtime Art?," *New Republic,* in *Syracuse (New York) Herald,* November 19, 1915; Peter Haydon interview in *London Standard, Oakland Tribune,* January 26, 1913; "Criticism of Ragtime at opening of Parliament," *Musical News,* in *Washington Post,* May 23, 1913; "Europe cool to Ragtime," *San Antonio (Texas) Light,* May 10, 1914.

Page 126: Lestor Walton's articles appeared in the *New York Age* over a period of several years:

Page 135: Walton's review of *Bandanna Land* is cited in *The First Black Actors on the Great White Way,* by Susan Curtis (University of Missouri Press, 1998), 48. Other Walton articles: "On ignorance of the white man," December 24, 1908; "Is Ragtime

Sources of Quotations — Chapters 12–14

Dead?" April 8, 1909; "White writers disparaging Ragtime," May 9, 1912; "Composer Writing Grand Opera," December 24, 1908.

Chapter 12

Page 137: While Harry Bradford was working in New York and stringing for the *Indianapolis Freeman* (a well-regarded black newspaper of national circulation) he often wrote of the activities of his friend Joplin. Tragically, Bradford died just a week after his story on *Treemonisha*. Coverage of Joplin in the *American Musician and Art Journal* was more sporadic but usually favorable. The accounts here are from issues of June 17, 1907, and June 24, 1911.

Page 146: The staging of *Treemonisha* in the 1970s led to an entanglement of legal actions involving the producers and members of the Music Trust of Lottie Joplin Thomas. The trust later turned down an offer by Columbia Records to record the full opera, and by Twentieth Century–Fox to reproduce some portions in a television movie. The disagreements centered largely on the artistic arrangements of Joplin's musical score.

Chapter 13

Page 150: Joyce Milton described Mary Pickford's first impression of Charlie Chaplin in *Tramp: the Life of Charlie Chaplin* (113, HarperCollins, 1966).

Page 153: Mary Pickford's declaration that she would quit the theater if she couldn't get a role in a Broadway play appears in her autobiography, *Sunshine and Shadow* (93, Doubleday, 1955).

Page 153: Film historian Tino Balio credited Mary Pickford for having "invented acting for film" when he appeared in American Experience's *Mary Pickford* on the Public Broadcasting System.

Page 157: Mary Pickford's comparison of movie and stage acting is from *Sunshine and Shadow*, (157).

Page 157: The careers of Mary Pickford and Charlie Chaplin of course extended well beyond the silent film era. Mary's strong voice and forceful personality made for a relatively easy transition to sound, and she won the first Academy Award for her performance in the 1928 talkie *Coquette*. She would retire from filmmaking in 1933 and sink slowly into obscurity, selling her shares in United Artists in 1956, a year after Chaplin had left the company. "Little Mary" returned to the spotlight in 1976 when she accepted an Academy Award for lifetime achievement. Charlie would resist the sound era and continue to make what were largely silent films well into the 1930s, including his memorable *City Lights* and *Modern Times*.

Page 158: Later sound pictures such as *The Great Dictator* and Chaplin's final Hollywood film, the 1952 *Limelight*, would continue to display his acting genius. Exiled from the United States, Chaplin's achievements would finally bring him great honors late in life: an Academy Award for lifetime achievement in 1972 (he'd won an Oscar for his 1929 work, *The Circus*) and a knighthood from Queen Elizabeth in 1975.

Chapter 14

Page 159: William Christopher Handy (1873–1958) published his autobiography, *Father of the Blues*, in 1941. In it, he describes the incident at the Tutwiler railway station that inspired him to write "Memphis Blues" (74). He also tells of writing the "St. Louis Blues" in September 1914 after having concluded that Ragtime "was passing out." His aim was to "combine Ragtime syncopation with a real melody in the spiritual tradition."

Page 164: The reception given the ODJB at the Reisenweber Café, one of many celebrations marking the group's introduction in northern cities, is recounted by Stephen M. Stroff in *Discovering Great Jazz* (13).

Page 168: Lottie Joplin's summation of her husband's life first appeared in an article she wrote with Kay Thompson in *The Record Changer* (October 1950). It is cited by Susan Curtis in *Dancing to a Black Man's Tune*.

Page 168: In 2005, a group of musicians gathered at St. Michael's Cemetery in the Bronx for an outdoor concert dedicated to Joplin's memory. Pianists Reginald Robinson, Peter Muir and Aaron Diehl played selections from Joplin's repertoire while Edward Berlin gave a belated eulogy. The event concluded with a graveside performance by the Vince Girodano Trio.

Chapter 15

Page 169: Willie Smith's recollections of life at Lottie Joplin's boardinghouse are from the autobiography he wrote in collaboration with George Hoefer, *Music on My Mind: The Memoirs of an American Pianist*

(90). Numerous accounts of the house at 163 West 131st Street suggest that either prostitution was conducted there or that prostitutes lived there and worked elsewhere.

Page 172: The anecdote about Louis Armstrong explaining the Ragtime roots of jazz to Bing Crosby is from W.C. Handy's autobiography, *Father of the Blues* (292).

Chapter 16

Page 180: I have drawn on the unpublished journal of Martha Smith, daughter of Sedalia's founder, for her account of how the community raised the money to bring in the Missouri Pacific Railroad. I am grateful to Lorene Downing of the Georgetown Inn, Sedalia, for supplying me with a copy.

Page 181: The reference to Sedalia's red light district was published in *Life* magazine, October 21, 1940.

Appendix: Ragtime in the Newspapers

Cedar Rapids (Iowa) Evening Gazette, August 22, 1893:

LOCAL NEWS

The Texas Medley Quartette (colored), en route from Chicago to the Pacific coast, favored The Gazette force with some of its choice melodies this afternoon. The names of the singers are: Please Jackson, first tenor; Scott Joplin, second tenor; R. Denson, baritone; G. Minor, basso. They will remain in the city a few days and will be heard at the hotels and other public places. Their singing is excellent.

Marshall (Michigan) Daily Chronicle, December 11, 1897:

NEW MUSIC
**Louisiana Rag Two-Step —
For Piano or Orchestra**

Composed by Theo. H. Northrup, the greatest living Ragtime Pianist. This piece has made an instantaneous hit and has become a great favorite everywhere. Price 50 cents. Ask your dealer for it or send 25c for sample copy to:
The Thompson Music Co., 26 Wabash Ave., Chicago, Ill.

Lincoln (Nebraska) Daily News, April 5, 1899:

AT THE FUNKE

We have had ragtime operas, ragtime farce comedies, but never before ragtime hypnotism. Last night Flint, the only hypnotist, presented at the Funke hypnotic ragtime singing and dancing, which was the best band most comical bit of work presented by him during any of his previous engagements in this city. Long before the doors opened crowds packed the lobby to such extent that the entire force of the Funke were called upon to hold the crowds back. All records are again being broken this week. The advance sale is crowded all day by those securing seats in advance. Seats are selling for each performance and the Saturday matinee at a lively rate.

Fort Wayne (Indiana) News, September 14, 1899:

TIRED OF RAG-TIME MUSIC
Writers Find a Difficulty in Disposing of Their Compositions

Ragtime music is doomed. This statement was made by a music writer of this city who had made a thorough canvass of the principal music publishing houses of the country. A year ago this writer had no trouble disposing of ragtime music to any of the leading houses that buy music outright but of late these houses have notified their contributors that hereafter they will not buy ragtime compositions. In doing so they say that while ragtime music will perhaps continue in popularity for a year or so, its day is about over and the end of the craze is not far off. The only houses publishing any of the ragtime compositions are those that do so on royalties.

Tyrone (Pennsylvania) Daily Herald, September 22, 1899:

RAG-TIME MUSIC POPULAR

Rag-time coon music and words have become very popular the past year and writers of that class of songs have been viewing with each other to produce those catchy rag-time airs which become immediately popular with the masses. We have before us a sheet of music which to use a slang expression, "Takes the Cake." The music is strictly rag-time and the words have evidently been written to suit the music thus reversing the usual method of producing songs. "She'll Never Live to Love Another Coon" is the title and Claude Melnotte the composer. It is published by the Kansas Talking Machine Company of Kansas City, Missouri, at the price of fifty cents per copy.

Sandusky (Ohio) Daily Star, October 4, 1900:

WINTER'S NEW DANCES
The Five Latest Are Stately and Mark Radical Change
UNDIGNIFIED RAGTIME DOOMED

Five new dances will hold the attention of society during the approaching winter season. A striking and radical change will be instituted by dancing masters, and there will be another return to the slow, stately measures of the minuet, says the Chicago Tribune. The Pembroke, the Debut, the Fantasia and the Polonaise complete the list of new conceptions in the art. Dignity and grace will characterize the ballroom dances this coming winter. The undignified ragtime and cakewalk will be strictly eliminated from programs. The ban thus put upon one time favorite dances for amusement is the outcome of the five days' convention of the American Society of Professors of Dancing held at Saratoga, N.Y.

The dancing masters declare the ragtime type of dancing destroys all the grace and beauty which should represent the terpsichorean art, and they are loud in their denunciation of what they call a "deep-rooted evil." With accord they proclaimed its undesirability in the ballroom and declared they would take measures to eradicate its influence from the realm of good society.

Dancing authorities say the two step waltz will be even more popular this season than ever before, but a careful watch will be kept lest it degenerate into the peculiar eccentricities of the ragtime. For it is claimed that the graceful two step in its original form is always in great danger of losing its aesthetic properties through the reign of excessive ragtime. The degree of disgrace into which the two step has fallen by the departure from its former beauty and grace has won for it from the disgusted professors the well deserved title of the "bear dance." The death of ragtime will be sounded with long drafts of relief from the dancing masters. The waltz, glide polka, two step and gallop will largely help to make up the program for this season's dancing.

Moberly (Missouri) Democrat, March 10, 1901:

THE WAR ON RAGTIME

The safe rule is to like what you please, and if you like ragtime music or unmusic, like it and bid those who would interfere with you go hang. It is better to be tolerant than to be learned. But ragtime strains are delightful, all the same. We doubt if the man who haughtily turns his ears upon them can really appreciate either Bach or Handel. — *New York Sun.*

Musicians cannot suppress ragtime. Airs set to that measure will be published so long as there is an active popular demand for them — aye, and they will be played, too, or the very musicians who are now protesting against such "unmusical trash" will render ragtime on their instruments or go without audiences or, what is worse, without salaries. The people, after all, determine what sort of music shall or shall not be played. — *Kansas City Times.*

Atlanta (Georgia) Constitution, July 18, 1902:

DOWN IN THE DANCE HALLS OF DECATUR STREET

Notorious Dives and Dens Where the Pool Tables are Center of Attraction and Ragtime Music Reigns Supreme

By Gordon N. Hurtel

As it was in the old days before the war, when the best study of the negro character was made while "toil remitting lent its aid to play," so now in this day if one would get a true insight into the character of the post-bellum darkey he must find him when he is out for a frolic.

It is at night, when the work of the day is done and cares and troubles are thrust away, that the darkey finds his true enjoyment, and nothing gives him more pleasure than a dance. Next to the dance comes the pool table with the city negro. It is said that those who have conducted dance halls and run pool halls in the city for the negroes have laid aside considerable fortunes.

There are, of course, different grades of negro dance halls. Some are for toughs, and others for the negroes who pride themselves on "social status." All kinds are liberally patronized every night in the week.

Down in the "Dives"

The lowest class of these dance halls are called "dives," probably from the fact that they are generally located in cellars or basements. In the "dives" everybody is welcome who has his or her nickel to spend. Ex-convicts, rounders, crap shooters, tapers and sneak thieves all congregate in a "dive" and dance as if they had not a single care or bad record to contend with. The "dive" music is not very inspiring, but it makes a note and that is all that is wanted. A wheezy old piano and a fiddle with half the strings gone grind out a ragtime tune, while a negro man sits on a platform and slaps his hands together as he calls out the figures. The dancers are not at all careful about their poses. The fumes of beer, the odor of pipes or bad cigars, in the close, hot atmosphere is sickening. These "dives" are tolerated by the police because criminals are often caught by simply raiding the places.

The second-class negro dance hall is on the upper floor of some building on either Decatur or Peters street. Very fair music is furnished and toughs and convicts are kept out.

One step higher in the Darktown Terpsichorean scale and you come to the dance hall where etiquette and decorum are painfully emphatic. Only the "elite" of Darktown can enter these halls, and cigarettes and razors are barred. There is a grotesque exaggeration of politeness, and affection runs riot with the dance.

"Will you give me the extinguished pleasure, Miss Mandy, of leading you through the mazy walt?" some Darktown beau will ask, and he will be told:

"Mister Jones, it will be my most delightful experience of this evening's function to allow you to dance this waltz with me."

The contrast between the reckless abandon of the "dive" and the stilted and pompous ethics of the swell dance hall is striking. And after all there is more amusement is seeing the dancers of the "dive" "cut the pigeon wing" and do the "double shuffle" than to look upon the higher set.

Of course this list does not include the private dances by the more respectable negroes in the city. It is only about the public dance halls, where are more or less under police surveillance, that I write.

Where They Play Pool

If the Darktown citizen does not care for the dance, but wishes to leave his family at home and spend the evening for his own pleasure (like many do who live in Darktown, alas) he seeks a pool room. I do not think there are any billiard tables. The negro pool player shoves a cue at the balls as if his whole life depended upon it. Some of the players are very good shots, considering the kind of tables they have to use. It is said that one of the old tables in a negro pool room had a hen sitting in one of the pockets and the owner closed up the pocket for three weeks, but kept the table in use.

Close to the "Beer"

There is just one more point that must not be overlooked in this account of the dance "dives" and pool rooms, and that is the fact that "dives" and rooms are all conveniently located in reference to the saloons. The ex-convict as he swings corners with the stockade belle must have his beer, and the pool player has to have a little liquor to keep his nerves steady.

There is now a new fad called "slumming," and the way you "slum" is to spend an evening viewing the slums of a big city. The fad has reached Atlanta and the dance "dives" and pool rooms are coming in for a fair share of attention. "Slumming" in Atlanta without taking in a "dive" is like Hamletting without a Hamlet.

Ogden (Utah) Standard, September 30, 1903:

RAGTIME ENJOYED

The lovers of classical music are disposed to frown upon those who declare a desire to hear ragtime, but the American music is destined to survive the opposition of the exacting and critical. Bandmaster Sousa, who has just toured Europe, relating his experience, says: "Of course, I don't mean to compare them musically, but ragtime has become as firmly established as the others, and can no longer be classed as a craze in music. Nearly everybody likes ragtime. King Edward VII liked it so well that he asked us to play more if it, and we gave him 'Smoky Moke' and 'Georgia Campmeeting.' Emperor Wilhelm and the Czar were also converted to ragtime. It is just as popular everywhere as it ever was, and I see no reason while it should not remain in favor so long as music is played." If kings and czars, the favored of all people, who hear the best of musicians, appreciate ragtime, it certainly is excusable for the unpretentious to encore a melodious American air.

Washington Post, August 14, 1904:

NEGRO'S PART IN MUSIC

Time was when "coon songs," whether of the old plantation variety or the modern ragtime kind, were written by white men, but a great change has come about in the last few years, says a writer for the New York *Sun*. The negro composer has now almost a monopoly of ragtime and is reaching out into more classical work, and there has hardly been a musical play in the last two or three years which hasn't contained one or more songs of negroes.

Some of the work is done by negro sketch teams, who write their own songs on the road, make them popular and collect the royalties when they are published. But most of it comes from the negro quarter of New York, where a dozen composers make their headquarters.

Most of these men are musicians of education and high musical ideals. If pinned down to it, they admit that they write ragtime not so much for the love of the thing as because it pays.

Take Cole and the Johnson brothers, for example. They have on their list a long string of ragtime successes. Yet, of the three authors two are university men — one of them a master of the arts — and the third is finished student of music.

The Johnson brothers come from Florida. Sons of a Baptist minister, they entered Atlanta University to work their way through. Rosamond Johnson had the musical bee in his bonnet, so he cut loose after a time and entered the New England Conservatory of Music, where he studied for three years.

James Johnson stayed with his books and was graduated with honors. He became principal of the Colored High School of Jacksonville, Fla., and in his odd moments he wrote for various publications and has had poems and short stories in the big magazines.

Cole was also at Atlanta University, where in the college glee club he learned that he had talent for the stage. He drifted into a minstrel show, and from there into the Black Patti Troubadours. All that time he had been struggling with composition, but he was handicapped by a lack of technical knowledge.

One day in Boston he ran against Rosamond Johnson, who had decided that he had had about enough of the Conservatory. Together they patched up a song or two, threw an act together, and played the vaudeville circuit for two or three years. Then, one summer, Rosamond Johnson went South for a vacation and found his brother James working on the libretto of a comic opera.

Rosamond liked the idea and set music to it. James became so enthusiastic that he threw up his job and came to New York with the manuscript under his arm.

"We didn't sell it," says James Johnson, "at least, not then; we have been selling it in stove lengths ever since. We've got the libretto yet, and we're thinking of putting in a new set of songs and trying it again."

Cole and the Johnson brothers now have a bank account, of which wonderful stories are told in the negro quarter. They are taking care of their parents, and two Johnson sisters are in college now, all on the proceeds of ragtime....

Another negro composer is Will Marion Cook, who has been in London with "In Dahomey," for which he wrote most of the songs. He comes from Washington. His father was a prosperous man. The boy showed an early bent for music and was given a thorough education in it. He studied the violin and harmony under Dvorak and finished off with a course under Joachim.

Then, one day his father went broke. Thrown on his own resources, the youngster began to write ragtime. He has gone in for whole scores rather than single songs. The scores of "The Southerners," most of the songs in "The Casino Girl," and "Chlorinda, or the Origin of the Cakewalk," are his. He is another composer who has made it pay.

On the other extreme is Al Johns, who hasn't any musical education at all, but a wonderful memory and ear. He composes his songs, gets them fixed in his head, and then plays them off to some other musician, who puts the score on paper. While Rosamond Johnson, the scholarly musician, writes ragtime, Johns the natural musician, goes in for the classical. His reputation rests mostly on ballads like "The Afterwhile" and "The Darling of My Dreams." Once, needing the money, he burst into ragtime and made more money than he ever got from all his ballads, with "Go Way Back Down and Sit Down."

Williams and Walker are better known as actors and managers than as composers, but they write a part of the music for their own songs. In that same class of actor-

Appendix

composers is Ernest Hogan, who set the whole country singing his "All Coons Look Alike to Me." He is also responsible for "I'm Goin' to Live Anyhow Till I Die."

Will Dixon hit town with a hard-luck story. When the ragtime craze was booming he bethought himself of several songs which he had made up "out of his head" to sing to the neighbors. He went to a white musician, he says, and sang them over to him several times.

"Do you think there's anything in them?" asked Dixon.

"Not much," said the white man; "they'll hardly do." So Dixon gave it up. But two or months later along came his songs to the music score, published under another name.

The most famous negro composer of popular songs was Gussie L. Davis, now dead. And he never wrote a negro song — at least not one that made a hit. He belonged to the era of the "story song." "The Lighthouse by the Sea," "The Fatal Wedding," and "The Baggage Coach Ahead" were his. He was a performer, too, and used to sing his own songs.

The great composer of the negro race isn't claimed by America. He is S. Coleridge Taylor, of England, who was born in Africa, and is half Scotch and half native. Oratorio is his specialty. "The Atonement" is his best known long work. He has written also "Hiawatha," not the late popular two-step, but a cantata of that name. "By the Waters of Babylon," an anthem often heard in American churches, is also his.

American Musician, New York, June 17, 1907:

Scott Joplin
It Was He Who Gave Us That Cleverest of Rags, "Maple Leaf" — Other Clever Numbers From His Pen

The subject of this sketch, Scott Joplin, is a negro who is considered to be one of the greatest composers of ragtime music in this country. He gave us that clever and best of rags, "Maple Leaf," which has sold for years, and will sell for years to come.

One of his recent efforts is a march entitled "Antoinette," written in 6-8 time. It is an excellent composition and one which should become a favorite with bands and orchestras.

Scott Joplin has been working for a considerable time on a grand opera which will contain music similar to that sung by the negroes during slavery days, the music of today, the negro ragtime, and the music that the negro will use in the future.

While in St. Louis the writer paid a visit to the John Stark Company, where he met and heard Mr. Scott play the overture to his new opera, and to say that it was exceptionally good would be putting it mildly.

Scott Joplin considers it too hard work for him to sit at the piano and compose. He gets his inspirations while walking along the street or in his bed at night, and when a melody comes to him he immediately puts it down on music paper, which he always carries with him.

He is unassuming and never has much to say, and seldom speaks of his music. The Stark Music Company, of St. Louis, Missouri, publishes his compositions.

New York Times, March 16, 1909:

Ragtime Music Dead in This Town
John Philip Sousa Says the People Have Had a Surfeit and Are Sick of It

Old Composers in Favor
Hotel and Restaurant Orchestras Have Cut Out Ragtime Altogether — New Composers Also Popular

Ragtime music is dead, according to the managers of the various hotels and restaurants in the city, and there is no longer demand for the tunes that used to cause jig steps to come to the feet, accompanied by a desire to get up and do a cakewalk. According to the same authorities, Ragtime has been shelved to make way for the tuneful airs of the popular musical shows that last but a season and for the music of the old composers. There is also a demand for the scores of Victor Herbert, John Philip Sousa, and other popular music writers.

The death and funeral of ragtime, according to John Philip Sousa, who has the credit of being the originator of that class of music, is due entirely to the poor class of the product turned out in latter years.

"Ragtime had the dyspepsia or the gout, long before it died," says Mr. Sousa, who is now touring in the South with his band. "It was overfed by poor nurses. Good ragtime came, and half a million imitators sprang up. Then, as a result, the people were sickened with the stuff. I have not played a single piece of ragtime this season, and it is simply because the people do not want it."

Mr. Sousa's estimate of the popular taste is the result of observation on the tour of his band, and it is borne out by the hotel and restaurant managers of this city, who have entirely cut ragtime from their musical programs.

"Our orchestras have not played ragtime in a long time," said manager Barse of the Waldorf-Astoria last night. "We have always made it a rule to furnish the music our patrons wanted, and most of the programmes have been made up by request. The people have simply stopped asking for ragtime tunes. Mr. Boldt, the proprietor, is particularly fond of music, and he always supervises our programmes before they are played, but he has always been perfectly willing to let the people have a proportion of good ragtime when they asked for it."

At the Plaza Hotel Naban Franko said that his clientele did not care for ragtime, and he is never asked to play it. "The people like high-class music, and are fond of Wagner, Liszt, among the old composers, and Victor Herbert and John Philip Sousa among the new. They like the catchy airs from the Broadway musical shows while their popularity is at its height, but take it through and through, the general public is being better educated in music and the standard works are growing more popular."

Manager Hahn at the St. Regis, Manager Wood at the Gotham, and Mr. Muschenheim of the Hotel Astor, all joined in the same opinion as to the death of ragtime and the desire of the people for high-class music.

"We find that our patrons prefer French and Viennese music," said the manager of Sherry's, "and we have an imported orchestra to meet their desires. Our musicians know absolutely nothing about ragtime and are, of course, never asked to play it."

Cakewalk tunes have been banished from Delmonico's, and in their stead may be heard the prettiest airs of the musical shows and light operas, interspersed with music from grand opera and the older composers.

A trip through Broadway, where the after-theatre parties had assembled for supper, showed the same condition to exist at Rector's, Churchill's, Shanley's, Martin's, the Hotel Knickerbocker, Murray's, the College Inn, the Marlborough, Imperial, and Victoria Hotels, while in the table d'hote dining rooms ragtime music has been made to take a back seat.

Reno (Nevada) State Journal, November 15, 1910:

Phonograph and Records Purchased by Sheriff for County Jail
RAGTIME IS THE FAVORITE
Eighty Per Cent of This Sort of Canned Melody is Selected

Realizing that music is a necessary adjunct and essential to jail birds, Sheriff Ferrel yesterday purchased a $60 Victor phonograph and 25 records for the amusement of the prisoners in his charge.

The sheriff knew that the element of time was very important to his charges so he added that of tune to make the slow hours of captivity pass swiftly by and to soothe the savage souls of the more intractable.

The 25 records invested in by the sheriff as a starter were in the nature of an experiment into the temperamental requirements of his charges. Shutting his eyes, he demanded 80 per cent of ragtime and this he will try on the defenseless prisoners. Classical music he was averse to as he knows that there is something in the constitution about cruel and unusual punishment being forbidden.

Prison rules will be somewhat amended to conform to the music box. Music will be dispensed between daybreak and sunset and after the prisoners get acquainted with the names of the selections, choice will be by ballot. The duty of operating the machine has not yet been assigned.

Winnipeg (Manitoba) Free Press, February 11, 1913:

RAGTIME DANCING POPULAR IN ENGLAND

London — Although several persons in high places have shown a disposition to set their faces against the present craze for ragtime, so far as the ball-room is concerned, society now seems determined to set the seal of its august approval on ragtime dancing. One of the most interesting and elaborate functions of the season now beginning will be a ragtime ball to be given at the Savoy hotel. Already extensive preparations are in progress and a large part of society will certainly be present. The dancing will be exclusively ragtime, and handsome prizes will be bestowed on the best dancers in the various compositions. Both of the ball rooms at the Savoy will be utilized, and a novel scheme of decorating is being designed. Judging from the applications already received, it will be impossible to accommodate even one half of those desirous of being present.

Oakland (California) Tribune, May 2, 1915:

RAGTIME POINT WAY?
Stewart Praises Simple Old Songs Highly

Has American Ragtime concealed within its syncopated form the germ of the coming music of America — a deep, pulsated harmony that will some day be famed throughout the world as distinctive of this country, just as Wagner's harmonized discords are taken as symbolic of the spirit of the Teutons? Will the Bunny Hug of today be the epic of tomorrow?

So declares Alexander Stewart, president of the Alameda County Music Teachers' Association, and director of the great concert that will, on the evening of May 4, open the Municipal Auditorium's history as a music center.

Stewart has voiced an eloquent defense of ragtime — although none will be heard at the great concert he is going to direct. In fact, he does not play ragtime himself — nor does he like it — but in it, he declares, he can see the music of the future: a new school of melody built upon the foundation of the Tango strain.

HAS LATENT GERMS

"I do not," he declares, "share in the almost universal condemnation in which most musicians hold the popular ragtime music of the day. There is often so great an element of the cleverness in many of these melodies of the day and they seem so well to express the spirit of the American people that it is difficult to conscientiously and totally deprecate them. It would seem to the fair-minded musician that this so-called ragtime music has in it some latent germ of what is to be the true American music. Surely no musical form heretofore has seemed to so well express the exuberant vitality of the American nation. The fact also that other nations, especially the Germans and the French, have great difficulty in playing effectively our ragtime music is also an evidence that there is something characteristically American about it. Some day a great American composer will arise who will take the germ of real music which is hidden in this maze of musical eccentricity and will mold it into some really great music. In the meantime it is a pity that we have to stand for so much musical mediocrity and so much impure and brainless sentimentality in the words of these insipid songs.

"The difference between the popular music of today and the popular music of fifty or sixty years ago such as the melodies of Stephen Foster and other writers of the American folk songs, is that those latter songs have enduring merit in both music and the words while popular songs of today will hardly be remembered five years from now. These old songs, too, were pure in sentiment although simple in form. There was no ribald sentiment expressed in the words as in these later day melodies. Only the pure in musical art as in other lines of culture will endure and until our music of today is purged of its suggestiveness and brainless idiocy will it withstand the test of the years. Legislatures may adopt one of the popular songs of the day as an official state song but unless the song has enduring qualities of melody and of words it will not live in the hearts of the people. Great popular songs are not made to order. They grow out of some great expression of national feeling.

Ripe for Revival

"I believe that the time is ripe for a revival of the songs of other days. In the present rage for both ragtime music and for the ultra-modern music of the composers of the day, we have lost sight of the great wealth of material which lies almost forgotten among the folk songs of a half century or more ago. A dignified performance of some of these old melodies will do much to purge the musical atmosphere for a large part of the public who love really great music of the simpler type."

Stoke on Trent (Staffordshire, UK) Sentinel, May 25, 1915:

"All Change Here" The Latest Revue

Popular music, originality in humor, and gay stage effects are what the public want in a revue, particularly at holiday time, and on all these counts the most captious critic would have little reason to complain of the "All Change Here" revue, which is being presented at the Stoke Hippodrome this week.

The music, for the most part, consists of catchy American ragtime airs, but interspersed among these are one or two firm favorites which will very likely outlive the syncopated introductions from the States. The song "These Eyes" by Miss Kathy Temple and chorus, was one, and "The Parrot" by the same singer was another. As for the humor, there are one or two jokes that are real chestnuts, but audiences are forgiving when distinctly original quips are forthcoming and preponderate in number. Naturally there are a good many at the expense of the Kaiser, and those were received with particular heartiness.

The first scene of the revue is entitled "Yesterday," but it is a singularly long and introspective yesterday and includes the crinoline period. In the fashions' revue the crinoline dance is one of the principal attractions, the burlesque to the stateliness of the fashion models by "Pip and Melinda," the Lilliputians of the cast who appear similarly attired. There is a Yankee swing about this opening scene, the principal characters being Some New York (Mr. Percy F. Cooper) and Miss U.S.A. (Miss Donna Rita). The latter illustrates

Appendix

one or two of the latest ragtimes from across the herring pond, and throughout the revue proves the most versatile member of the cast.

The second scene is devoted to "Today," and is equally vivacious in movement, tunefulness, and color. The gaiety is preserved throughout, and judging by the reception it was given Monday night, there should be big houses during the week.

Newark (New Jersey) Daily Advocate, December 13, 1917:

JAZZ MUSIC FOE OF BLUES
Does not Consist, as Is Generally Believed, of Lot of Noise Without Rhyme or Reason

Various descriptions of jazz music have from time to time appeared, but none seem to hit the mark exactly, says a connoisseur of this art. The common impression is that it consists of a lot of peculiar and noisy sounds without rhyme or reason. This is not the case, however. It consists chiefly of syncopation, particularly accentuated variation of some of the instruments; improvisations by others, mingled with odd sound effects. Through all this the melody of the selections rendered must be distinguishable at all times — tin can noises, beating the life out of the drums, blasting by the brass instruments. It is entirely unnecessary. Contrasts between pianissimo and fortissimo passages should be shown just as much in jazz music as in the classics.

Another wrong impression is that jazz orchestras must consist of certain instrumentation. This also is not the case. The violin, cello, cornet, piano, or in fact any legitimate instrument, can be used. As jazz music is originally Ethiopian, the banjo and saxophone used merely to lend negro character to it.

The number of musicians that can jazz properly is said to be small, because it really requires good musicians, who must also be endowed with the swing or knock of performing it. Although many of the café and theater orchestras are composed of good musicians, those who can jazz are scarce. On the other hand, many of the self-styled jazz orchestras are misrepresentations, and cannot play the semi-classics or classics properly. Some cannot perform it properly, and to offset this, resort to noise and discord in imitation thereof. The percentage of musicians who can do justice to the classics and also play jazz is consequently even smaller. This kind of orchestra is exceedingly scarce.

Jazz music is rhythmic and inspiring. It is declared the best antidote for the blues.

Jefferson City (Missouri) Capital News & Post-Tribune, November 27, 1932:

Our American Music

About 40 or 50 years ago, jazz was neither born nor heard of. The popular hits of the day were such as "Little Annie Rooney." In 1925 a photo play by the same title was produced with Mary Pickford in the role of Annie Rooney.

Jazz of course is typically American. The cake walk is the parent of the jazz and originated from the fiery camp meetings of the Negroes of the South, where they sang spirituals and become so happy in their religion that they unconsciously dance what is known as the Cake Walk.

An old Negro once said, "White folks sing like da wish da had religion and us colored folks sings like da do sho-nuff have it."

An example of the Cake Walk is "Georgia Camp Meeting," which is probably the best known of any cake walk.

After the Cake Walk came what is known as rag-time music. Of this class, probably the most typical ever written is the "Maple Leaf Rag." Rag-time spasms too were popular, such as "You'll Have to Hurry" by Ralph Wood of Warrensburg, Ohio.

Then came the connecting link between the rag-time and the modern jazz of today. An example is "Alexander's Ragtime Band," by Irving Berlin.

Next we have the crooning songs, such as "Wall Street Blues," "Yellow Dog Blues," and even "St. Louis Blues." The originator of the Blues which are sometimes called indigo successes, is W.C. Handy.

Now in 1915 and '16 there came what was known as the Memphis Dixie bands from the South. These bands had no written music. They simply improvised and everything was by the ear. But gradually jazz began to be more respectable with good musicians and real written orchestration, which developed into a complicated jazz orchestration as Paul Whiteman with his Symphonic Jazz music such as "Rhapsody in Blue" and "Clap Your Hands" by Gershwin. His music is a mixture of reminiscences of Liszt and Chopin, and rhythms of the musical comedy sort. What will be derived from this music remains to be seen.

All these years since before the Civil War, America has had a music all its own in our Negro folklore. But it took the Checko-Slovakian, Dvorak, to make us realize this. He came over to visit America and was so taken with our Negro Spirituals, that he went home and wrote the classic symphony entitled the "New World Symphony," with the spiritual, "Goin' Home," for his theme.

A light opera, "The Show Boat," adapted from Edna Ferber's novel of the same name with lyrics by Oscar Hammerstein and music by Jerome Kern. This is a good imitation of Negro life and was one of the Muny Opera numbers for 1931. Two popular song hits of this opera were, "Why Do I Love You," and "Old Man River."

Toronto Star Weekly, November 21, 1959:

Mr. Ragtime Comes Home

After 50 years, ragtime's pioneer makes a Canadian comeback

Joseph F. Lamb, one of three great composers of that fabulous ragtime era that swept the country 50 years ago, recently made a Canadian comeback.

It began when pianist Bob Darch, an entertainer playing authentic ragtime at Toronto's Club 76, paradoxically Canada's newest old-fashioned saloon, told his audience of their claim to ragtime's only living pioneer. It was in Toronto that teenage Joe Lamb sold his first music for $5 while he was a student at St. Jerome's college, Kitchener (then Berlin) Ontario. In 1908 he met Scott Joplin, the Negro maestro, in New York. From there his music spread across three continents, and Joe moved to Brooklyn in 1911, though he continued to visit Canada. He settled quietly into business life, from which he has recently retired.

Toronto devotees decided he should return. The Joe Lamb fund poured into an antique whiskey bottle; Club 76 endorsed the project; and within days the long-forgotten composer of such old-time hits as "Sensation" and "American Beauty Rag" settled himself at the club's honky-tonk piano. His audience, most of them younger than the music they applauded, rose to cheer and sing as Joe accepted a gift from "The Ragtime Music Lovers of Toronto." His visit to Kitchener was just as heart-warming.

Jefferson City (Missouri) Post-Tribune, September 17, 1959:

Sedalia Stakes Claim to Ragtime Music Birth

SEDALIA, Mo. (AP)—When Alaska became the 49th state Texas lost a sure claim to fame. To regain the loss of face

Appendix

suffered by the addition of a bigger state, Texans are now claiming ragtime.

Missourians and all others that love the honky-tonk beat know that classic ragtime music was first heard in Sedalia, played in Sedalia, and published in Sedalia.

A Texan recently wrote in a Fort Worth newspaper that ragtime was a Texas product, living on in the home of a Burleson, Tex., couple who have spent considerable time and money tracing this bit of Americana to its origin.

Only a few weeks before the article appeared, the same couple spent several days in Sedalia interviewing old-timers and probing into the history of Scott Joplin, composer of the "Maple Leaf Rag."

The credit for the publication of the first classic ragtime number goes to John Stark of Sedalia.

More than a half century ago the hit-or-miss ragtime beat had been traveling all over the United States, weaving its way from one large city to the other, in and out of saloons and red light parlors. It was a Negro creation with no free outlet.

One day John Stark dropped by the old Maple Leaf Club in Sedalia. His ears drank in the intriguing music of the club's pianist. It was Scott Joplin, born in east Texas, playing compositions he devised and played in red light districts all over the nation. The Negro pianist was playing the numbers nightly at the Maple Leaf.

Stark was a music publisher. He invited Joplin to his music store and bought publishing rights to a creation they called the "Maple Leaf Rag." It made them big money and they moved to St. Louis, soon to become known as the center of ragtime.

Sedalia does not claim classic ragtime was created in Missouri. It was created in the heart and soul of Joplin, somewhere along the long line of honky-tonks he played from east Texas to Sedalia.

Sedalia does claim it gave classic ragtime to the world through the sheet music of John Stark.

Sedalia also claims the second greatest classic ragtime composer, James Scott. He was born in Neosho and worked 12 years in a music store at Carthage before moving to Sedalia.

One day this slender mulatto went to Scott Joplin with some of his compositions. Joplin sent him to Stark.

Stark was glad to publish the music, having had such a tremendous success with Joplin's "classic ragtime" — a label they devised in Sedalia.

An Alaskan, "Ragtime Bob" Darch, recently awakened Sedalia to its heritage in ragtime.

Darch appeared at a Chamber of Commerce breakfast. He brought an ancient upright piano, said to have been used in some of the toughest bistros of frontier Alaska. Along with the intimate knowledge of more than 6,000 tunes, he also brought a vivid verbal description of the origin and growth of ragtime.

Las Cruces (New Mexico) Sun-News, July 11, 1974:

Ragtime Making a Comeback
By Rich Seeley
Copley News Service

"It's the sort of music that would only be played in bawdy houses by black men," popular music fans said.

Mozart fans called it "inherently evil, the tool of the devil himself."

The musicians' union passed a resolution asking its members not to play it.

But that was 70 years ago and now with nostalgia this music is back and everyone thinks it's as wholesome as a pizza pie.

The music is ragtime. It's no longer played in bawdy houses — it's played in pizza joints and Disneyland.

It isn't low-life entertainment. It's family entertainment.

And it's being revived by young people. It attracts young musicians who are not turned on by rock, folk, jazz or classical.

Doug O'Brien of Hermosa Beach, Calif., is one of these musicians. He started out in the early '60s as a folk guitar player when that was the craze. When the coffeehouse closed after the fad passed, he became interested in the banjo and ragtime.

Now he makes his living as a traveling professional banjo player.

"I play ragtime and whatever else people want to hear," he says. "I'm not a ragtime purist. I'm an entertainer."

The purists, he explains, are mostly classical musicians who play ragtime for recreation. They follow very rigid rules that call for a slow, plodding tempo not popularly associated with ragtime.

These stuffy purists don't have to play at pizza parlors for a living and if they did they probably couldn't buy a small pepperoni pizza with what they'd earn.

"I tried playing classical ragtime," says Judy Carmichael, "but it was too slow and people wouldn't listen."

The particular brand of up-tempo ragtime Miss Carmichael plays is called "barrelhouse" but is popularly known as honky-tonk.

Scott Joplin is the black man who is the father of ragtime music. He was trained in classical music but the syncopated rhythm of his music sent Mozart fans running away with their fingers in their ears.

"Keep in mind how foreign the idea of syncopation was to all ears when this stuff was put down," says Greg Stevens of San Pedro, Calif. He plays ragtime piano and banjo as a hobby.

Ragtime, like jazz and even rock, is another contribution to music by black people, Stevens explains.

"Ragtime was created by black people putting their folk rhythms into a classical music framework," he says. "They brought in syncopation."

People called the syncopation "ragged time" and that eventually got shortened to ragtime and just plain rag.

Bibliography

Allen, Douglas. *Frederic Remington and the Spanish-American War*. New York: Crown, 1971.
Balio, Tino. *United Artists: The Company That Changed the Film Industry*. Madison: University of Wisconsin Press, 1987.
Bergreen, Lawrence. *As Thousands Cheer: The Life of Irving Berlin*. Cambridge: Da Capo, 1996.
Berlin, Edward A. *King of Ragtime: Scott Joplin and His Era*. Oxford: Oxford University Press, 1994.
_____. *Ragtime: A Musical & Cultural History*. Berkeley: University of California Press, 1980.
_____. *Reflections and Research on Ragtime*. New York: Institute for Studies in American Music, City University of New York, 1987.
Blesh, Rudi, with Kathleen Benson. *They All Played Ragtime*. New York: Alfred A. Knopf, 1950.
Broun, Heywood. *Anthony Comstock: Roundsman of the Lord*. New York: Wishart, 1928.
Campbell, W. Joseph. *Yellow Journalism: Puncturing the Myths, Defining the Legacies*. Westport: Praeger, 2001.
Castle, Vernon, and Irene Castle. *Modern Dancing*. New York: World Syndicate, 1914.
Chaplin, Charles. *My Life in Pictures*. New York: Grosset & Dunlap, 1975.
Conrad, Joseph. *The Secret Agent*. New York: Penguin, 1994 (orig. 1905).
Collier, Simon. *Tango!: The Dance, the Song, the Story*. London: Thames & Hudson, 1995.
Crawford, Richard. *America's Musical Life: A History*. New York: W.W. Norton, 2001.
Cromie, Robert. *A Short History of Chicago*. Nevada City: Lexikos, 1984.
Cronon, William. *Nature's Metropolis: Chicago and the Great West*. New York: W.W. Norton, 1992.
Curtis, Susan. *Dancing to a Black Man's Tune*. Columbia: University of Missouri Press, 1994.
De Jongh, Nicholas. *Politics, Prudery and Perversions: The Censoring of the English Stage, 1901–1968*. Toronto: Hushion House, 2000.
Doctorow, E.L. *Ragtime*. New York: Random House, 1975.
Douglas, George H. *The Golden Age of the Newspaper*. Westport: Greenwood, 1999.
Erdman, Andrew L. *Blue Vaudeville: Sex, Morals and the Mass Marketing of Amusement, 1895–1915*. Jefferson, NC: McFarland, 2004.

Bibliography

Evans, Mark. *Scott Joplin and the Ragtime Years*. New York: Dodd Mead, 1976.
Eyman, Scott. *Mary Pickford: America's Sweetheart*. New York: Donald I. Fine, 1990.
Forma, Warren. *They Were Ragtime*. New York: Grosset & Dunlap, 1976.
Gammond, Peter. *Scott Joplin and the Ragtime Era*. Grand Rapids: Abacus, 1975.
Gates, Henry Louis, Jr. *The African-American Century: How Black Americans Have Shaped Our Country*. New York: Simon and Schuster, 2002.
Giola, Ted. *The History of Jazz*. Oxford: Oxford University Press, 1998.
Goldberg, Isaac. *Tin Pan Alley: A Chronicle of the American Popular Music Racket*. Whitefish, MT: Kessinger, 2005.
Golden, Eve. *Vernon and Irene Castle's Ragtime Revolution*. Lexington: University Press of Kentucky, 2007.
Handy, W.C. *Father of the Blues*. New York: Macmillan, 1941.
Harding, Samuel Bannister. *Life of George R. Smith, Founder of Sedalia*. Whitefish, MT: Kessinger, 2007.
Harrison, Alferdeen. *Black Exodus: The Great Migration from the American South*. Toronto: Scholarly Book Services, 2002.
Hasse, John Edward. *Ragtime: Its History, Composers, and Music*. New York: Schirmer, 1985.
Hitchcock, Henry Russell, et al. *Rise of an American Architecture*. Westport: Praeger, 1970.
Hoskins, James. *Scott Joplin: The Man Who Made Ragtime*. New York: Doubleday, 1978.
Jacobs, Jane. *The Death and Life of Great American Cities*. New York: Vintage, 1992.
Jasen, David A. *Tin Pan Alley: The Composers, the Songs, the Performers*. New York: Donald I. Fine, 1989.
Johnson, Katie N. *Sisters in Sin: Brothel Drama in America 1900–1920*. Cambridge: Cambridge University Press, 2006.
Karolides, Nicholas J. *120 Banned Books: Censorship Histories of World Literature*. New York: Checkmark, 2005.
Keller, Allan. *The Spanish-American War: A Compact History*. New York: Hawthorn, 1969.
Leonard, Thomas C. *News for All: America's Coming-of-Age with the Press*. Oxford: Oxford University Press, 1995.
Levin, Floyd. *Classic Jazz: A Personal View of the Music and the Musicians*. Berkeley: University of California Press, 2002.
London, Jack. *People of the Abyss*. Sterling: Stylus, 1998 (orig. 1905).
_____. *The Road*. Whitefish, MT: Kessinger, 2004 (orig. 1907).
Lynch, Kevin. *The Image of the City*. MIT Press, 1960.
Marquis, Donald. *In Search of Buddy Bolden: First Man of Jazz*. London: Da Capo, 1978.
Mast, Gerald. *A Short History of the Movies*. London: Longman, 2005.
Medearis, Angela Shelf. *Treemonisha*. New York: Henry Holt, 1995.
Milton, Joyce. *Tramp: The Life of Charlie Chaplin*. New York: HarperCollins, 1996.
Miller, Donald L. *City of the Century: The Epic of Chicago and the Making of America*. New York: Simon and Schuster, 1997.
Mooney, Michael Macdonald. *Evelyn Nesbit and Stanford White: Love and Death in the Gilded Age*. New York: William Morrow, 1976.
Mott, Luther. *American Journalism: A History*. New York: Macmillan, 1962.

Bibliography

Nasaw, David. *The Chief: The Life of William Randolph Hearst*. Boston: Houghton Mifflin, 2000.
Otfinoski, Steven. *Scott Joplin: A Life in Ragtime*. New York: Scholastic Library, 1995.
Pickford, Mary. *Sunshine and Shadow*. New York: Doubleday, 1955.
Pinzer, Mamie, with Ruth Rosen and Sue Davidson. *The Maimie Papers*. New York: Feminist Press, 1979.
Preston, Katherine. *Scott Joplin: Composer*. New York: Chelsea House, 1988.
Rosenberg, Bernard, and David Manning White. *Mass Culture: The Popular Arts in America*. New York: Free Press, 1957.
Rydell, Robert W. *All the World's a Fair: Visions of Empire at American International Expositions, 1876–1916*. Chicago: University of Chicago Press, 1987.
Schafer, William J., and Johannes Riedel. *The Art of Ragtime: Form and Meaning of an Original Black American Art*. Baton Rouge: Louisiana State University Press, 1973.
Seldes, Gilbert. *The Seven Lively Arts*. New York: Harper, 1924.
Sinclair, Upton. *The Jungle*. New York: Doubleday, Page, 1906.
Smith, Willie, and George Hoefer. *Music on My Mind: The Memoirs of an American Pianist*. New York: Doubleday, 1964.
Southern, Eileen. *The Music of Black Americans: A History*. New York: W.W. Norton, 1997.
Spear, Allan H. *Black Chicago: The Making of a Negro Ghetto*. Chicago: University of Chicago Press, 1967.
Steffans, Lincoln. *The Shame of the Cities*. New York: McClure Phillips, 1905.
Stroff, Stephen M. *Discovering Great Jazz*. New York: Newmarket Press, 1955.
Tawa, Nicholas E. *The Way to Tin Pan Alley: American Popular Songs, 1866–1910*. New York: Schirmer, 1990.
Tichenor, Trebor Jay. *Ragtime Rediscoveries*. Mineola: Courier Dover, 1980.
Waldo, Terri. *This is Ragtime*. New York: Hawthorn Books, 1976.
Wells, H.G. *The Time Machine* and *The War of the Worlds*. New York: Ballantine, 1981 (orig. 1895 and 1988 respectively).
Wharton, Edith. *House of Mirth*. New York: Penguin, 1985 (orig. 1905).
Whitcomb, Ian. *After the Ball: Pop Music from Rag to Rock*. New York: Simon and Schuster, 1973.
_____. *Irving Berlin and Ragtime America*. London: Century, 1987.
Whitfield, Eileen. *Pickford: The Woman Who Made Hollywood*. Toronto: Macfarlane Walter & Ross, 1997.
Wright, John A. *African-Americans in Downtown St. Louis*. Mount Pleasant, SC: Arcadia Publishing, 2003.

Index

Alexander, Freddie (Lovie) 58
Alexander's Ragtime Band 84, 160
All Coons Look Alike to Me 36
Anheuser-Busch 182
Antoinette 60
Armory Show 147, 161
Armstrong, Louis "Satchmo" 171–172
Arpin, John 106
Augustan Club Waltz 42

Berlin, Edward 53, 86, 175
Berlin, Irving 1, 84–86, 99, 163
Bethena 60
Bill Bailey, Won't You Please Come Home 73
Binks' Waltz 60
The Black K.P.'s 39
Blais, Mimi 170, 179
Blake, Eubie 123
Blesh, Rudi 172
Block, Martin 174
Blondeau Tavern 149
Bly, Nellie 20
Bonds, Carrie Jacobs 73
Bradford, Harry 137
A Breeze from Alabama 53
Burns, Tommy 30
Busch, Adolphus 58

Campbell, Samuel Brunson 42, 80, 170
Carnegie, Andrew 23
Caruso, Enrico 73
Cascades 58
Castle, Irene 99, 101–103, 105–111
Castle, Vernon 99, 101–103, 105–111
Censorship 112–123
Chaplin, Charlie 150–158
Chauvin, Louis 18, 55
Chicago 16–19

Chicago *Defender* 19, 126
Chicago World's Fair 6–10
The Chrysanthemum 58
Clef Club Orchestra 81, 107
Cohen, James M. 38, 76
Colored Vaudeville Benevolent Association 70, 80
Combination March 33
Compton, Wm. Bingham (Bim) (also Lord Northhampton) 93–98
Comstock, Anthony 116–119
Conrad, Joseph 61, 63
Crosby, Bing 172
Crush Collision March 32
Cuney, Wm. Waring 30

Dancing, criticism of 104
Darch, Bob 177
Davison, Emily Wilding 160–161
DeMille, Cecil B. 149
Doctorow, E.L. 22–23
Dramatic Mirror 124

Easy Winners 53
Eckstein, Willie 150
Edison, Thomas 20, 73
The Entertainer 54
Epsom Derby 160
Ernst, Alfred 52
Eugenia 15, 60
Euphonic Sounds 81
Europe, James Reese 81, 106–108

Fairbanks, Douglas 154
Felicity Rag 105

Gardel, Carlos 83
Gibson, Charles Dana 90
Gladiolus Rag 69

Index

Golden, Eve 110
Goodman, Benny 171
Griffiths, David 153
Group of Seven 147
A Guest of Honor 56

Handy, W.C. 6, 159, 165
Harmony Club Waltz 33
Harney, Ben R. 12,-13, 66
Harris, Charles 3, 73, 75
Hayden, Scott 51
Hearst, William Randolph 44–45, 88, 110
Heliotrope Bouquet 18
Higdon, Robert A. 41
Hines, Ike 66
Hogan, Ernest 36
Horsley, David 149
Hutton, Jack 170

If 165
Immigration, U.S. and Canada 22
Indianapolis *Freeman* 56, 126, 137, 166
Irwin, May 115

Janis, Harriet 172
Jazz (jass) 78, 164, 171
Jeffries, James J. (Jim) 30
Johnson, Jack 30–31
Joplin, Belle (Jones) 51, 54, 82
Joplin, Lottie (Stokes) 1, 79–81, 168–169
Joplin, Monroe 32
Joplin, Myrtle (Johnny) 19
Joplin, Robert 81
Joplin, Scott 1, 24, 105, 112; and Cedar Rapids, Ia. 10–11; and Chicago 18; and Chicago World's Fair 6–10; and death 166; and health 60, 122–123, 165; and lost manuscripts 174; and *Maple Leaf Rag* 33–354, 41, 123; and New York 65–70; and parents Giles and Florence 26–30; and posthumous honors 175–176; and St. Louis 51–58; and St. Louis World's Fair 58–60; and Sedalia, Mo. 11–12, 28, 30, 33, 81; and *Scott Joplin* 176; and Texas Medley Quartette 3, 6, 27–29; and *Treemonisha* 67, 79, 86, 100, 105, 137–146

Krell, William H. 84

Lafrenière, Jean-Baptiste 14
Lamb, Joseph 55, 67–68

Leola 60
London, Jack 62–63
London *Standard* 132
London *Times* 15

Maple Leaf Club 33
Maple Leaf Rag 33–35, 40–41, 70, 160, 165, 170
Marbury, Elizabeth 108–109
March Majestic 53
Markham, Violet Anne (Daisy) 87, 93–98
Marshall, Arthur 18, 54, 58
McKinley, William 32, 55
Morath, Max 172
Musical News 133
Muybridge, Eadweard 155

Nesbit, Evelyn 87–93
Nethersole, Olga 115
New Orleans 77–78
New York *Age* 134–136, 142, 166–167
New York *Times* 126–127
New York *World* 20, 73
The Nonpareil 68

Olympic Games 60, 181
Original Dixieland Jass Band 164
Original Rag 33

Panic of 1907 70
Pankhurst, Emmeline 161
Paragon Rag 70
Paris Exposition 3
Pastor, Tony 66, 124
Peacherine Rag 53
Pickford, Mary 150–154, 156–158
Pineapple Rag 70
Pinzer, Mamie 121, 122
Please Say You Will 29
Plessy, Homer 29
Police Gazette 124–125
Prostitution 77, 119–122, 168
Pulitzer, Joseph 21, 88, 182
Pulitzer Prize 175

Ragtime: and approval 36–37, 130; and Canada 14–15; and criticism 112–113; and England 15, 132–133; and origins 12; and popularity 22, 127, 177; and technology 21
Ragtime Dance 42, 53
Remick, Jerome H. 73

220

Index

Remington, Frederic 39, 43–47
Roosevelt, Theodore 38, 46, 55–56
Rosenfield, Monroe 53, 71
Rossitor, Will 18

Le Sacre du Printemps 161
St. Louis 51–60, 181–183
St. Louis *Globe-Democrat* 133–136
St. Louis *Post-Dispatch* 126, 133
Sanger, Margaret 115
Sanger, William 116–117
Saunders, Otis 11
School of Ragtime 68
Schroeder, Theodore 118
Scott, James 55
Scott Joplin House 182
Scott Joplin Ragtime Festival 177
Scott Joplin Schottische 80
Searchlight Rag 69
Sedalia 11–12, 28, 30, 33, 81, 179–181
Seldes, Gilbert 22
Seminary Music Co. 70
Shaw, George Bernard 117–118
Sinclair, Upton 63
Snyder, Ted 70
Solace 70
Sousa, John Philip 21
Spanish-American War 38-
Stark, Elena 34
Stark, John 34, 53, 65–66, 70–71, 75, 105
Steffans, Lincoln 58
Stern, Joseph W. 69–70
The Sting 176
Stoptime Rag 71, 105
Strauss, Richard 82
Stravinsky, Igor 86, 161
The Strenuous Life 56
Sugar Cane 70
Sullivan, William 105–106
Sunflower Slow Drag 40
Sweatman, Barbara 175

Sweatman, Eva 175
Sweatman, Wilbur 165, 168–169, 174–175
Swipesy Cake Walk 53
Symphony No. 1 165
Syphilis 1, 55, 122–123, 166
Syracuse, N.Y., *Herald* 127, 131

Tango 83
Tanguay, Eva 114–115
Texas Medley Quartette 3, 6, 27–29, 81
Thaw, Harry 88, 90–93
There'll Be a Hot Time in the Old Town Tonight 38
Tilzer, Harry von 71, 75
Tin Pan Alley 60, 71–75, 84, 162, 168, 172–174
Treemonisha 2, 67, 79, 86, 100, 105, 136, 137–146, 174–175
A Trip to Coontown 38
Tucker, Sophie 164
Turpin, Thomas 9, 52, 58, 81
Twain, Mark 23, 60, 62

U.S. Postal Service 176

Victor Talking Machine Co. 73, 165

Wall Street Rag 70, 87
Walton, Lester A. 133–136, 167
Washington, Booker T. 55–56
Weiss, Julius 27
Wells, H.G. 61–63
Wharton, Edith 63
White, Stanford 90–91
Williams, Will and Walker 33
Wilson, Woodrow 168
World War I 168

Yankee Doodle Dandy 38

Ziegfeld, Florenz 76

www.ingramcontent.com/pod-product-compliance
Ingram Content Group UK Ltd.
Pitfield, Milton Keynes, MK11 3LW, UK
UKHW041951140426
5217IPUK00015B/751